Zev Vilnay

THE HOLY LAND

IN OLD PRINTS AND MAPS

Rendered from the Hebrew
by ESTHER VILNAY in collaboration with MAX NUROCK

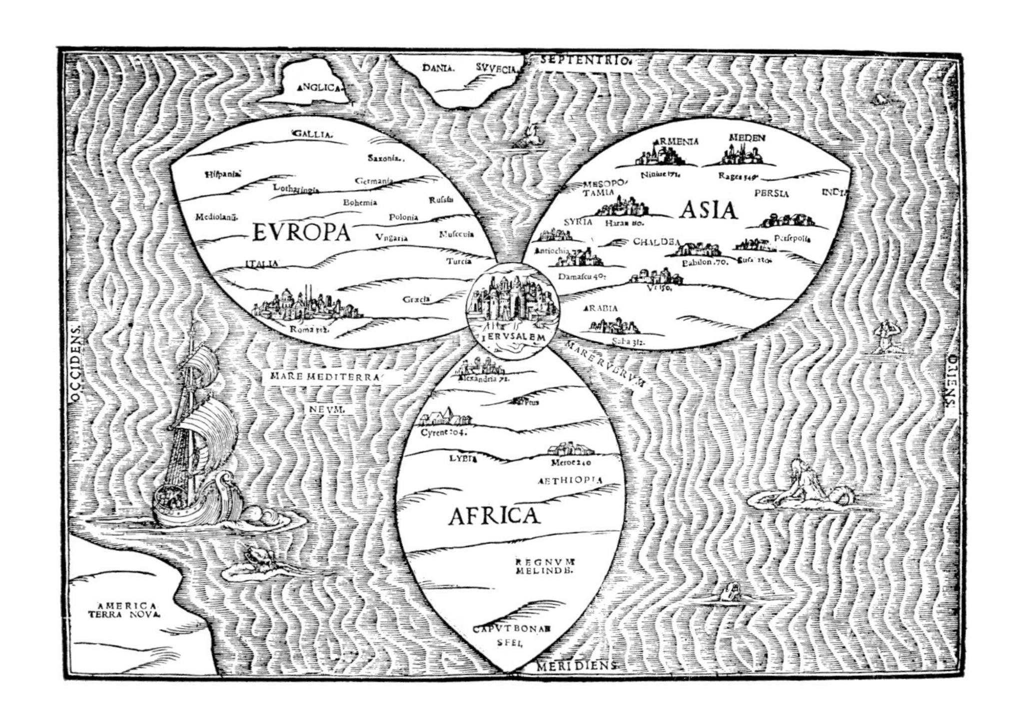

521 ILLUSTRATIONS

RUBIN MASS, PUBLISHER, JERUSALEM

Printed in Israel

The Illustrations, pp. 1—220 : Lychenheim & Son Ltd., Jerusalem

The General Survey, pp. VII—XL ; Achva Press, Jerusalem

The Blocks : M. Pikovsky Ltd., Jerusalem

FOREWORD

From the dawn of civilization the sites of the Holy Land have been the subject of a pictorial art which can be traced on the earliest monuments of human culture. This not unmitigated advantage was due to its strategic situation as a buffer-State between the two great powers which contended for supremacy over the ancient world, Egypt and Assyria.

The Pharaohs of the thirteenth and twelfth centuries B.C. adorned the walls of their palaces and temples with bas-reliefs describing their triumphs on foreign battlefields, of which not a few belong to the Palestinian terrain. These pictures, incised on the courses of stone, have remained to this day, among the beautiful ruins of Upper Egypt, a mute testimony of events that fashioned history.

The militant Assyrian kings of the eighth and seventh centuries B.C., no less, decorated their temples with pictures of the fortified towns they had overcome during their successful campaigns in the Land of Israel, where they enjoyed their most resounding victories. These bas-reliefs were brought to modern light by archaeological expeditions digging in the ancient mounds of Assyria — to-day Iraq, and were later transferred to the museums of Europe.

Under Byzantine rule, a new form of art, the mosaic, flourished in Palestine, reaching its peak in the fifth and sixth centuries A.D. The mosaic floors uncovered on Israel soil, this last hundred years, include pictures of the towns of the Holy Land that were famous in Byzantine times. Similar mosaics of the sacred sites have been found in Italy's old churches and basilicas.

Many of the Christian pilgrims who flocked to the Holy Land in the Middle Ages left the tale of their daring journeys, written in the language of their European homelands, and often embellished by pictures, mostly visionary, of the sacred sites they had come to worship at. Some of them also prepared pictorial maps of the Land and its main towns which give a fascinating insight into the first steps of the science of cartography.

Within the frame of Jewish popular art, more recent times have seen the proliferation of a great number of pictures, mostly fanciful, of the views and sites of the Holy Land hallowed by Jewish faith and lore. They have appeared in books and pamphlets describing the sacred sepulchres of Judaism and were also printed on objects of cult and scrolls of paper for the decoration of the Jewish home at special festivals.

Pictures of the Holy Land are to be found in many museums and in rare tomes and manuscripts preserved in great libraries. The kind assistance proferred by their staffs has been a considerable help to me in collecting the 521 pictures and prints from all sources which appear in these pages.

My warmest thanks are offered to all of them, in Israel and abroad: the Hebrew University and National Library, the Bezalel Museum, the Library of the Pontifical Institute — Jerusalem, the Maritime Museum — Haifa, the Bibliothèque

Nationale and the Louvre — Paris, the British Museum — London, the Bodleian Library — Oxford, the University Library — Cambridge, the Public Library of New York and the Vatican Library. I also wish to express my thankfulness to the owners of private libraries and collections who have allowed me to publish their treasures: H. Feuchtwanger and C. Hyman in Jerusalem, J. Halpert in Tel Aviv.

The work of my wife Esther and the collaboration of Max Nurock and his scholarly remarks were a tremendous asset in the 'anglicization' of this book.

My deepest appreciation and indebtedness go to Rubin Mass for his untiring efforts to publish the work in fitting form and also for his valuable comments and suggestions.

Jerusalem *Z. V.*

I. GENERAL SURVEY

II. THE ILLUSTRATIONS

I. TOWNS OF THE HOLY LAND ON EGYPTIAN AND ASSYRIAN MONUMENTS

The oldest-known pictures of the towns of Israel are carved upon the crumbling monuments of ancient Egypt and Assyria, those contentious empires of a by-gone world which, in unregenerate rivalry, bestrode the Fertile Crescent, overshadowing that earliest cradle of the culture of man. The Land of Israel was the bridge linking the twain and, conversely, their natural cockpit; across its territory they fought, each intent to establish dominion over its strategic places, and thus to secure its own frontiers. All the length of the Land ran the 'Way of the Sea', Via Maris of the Romans, a crowded artery for the traffic of the distant years, along which cavarans straggled in time of peace and armies marched in time of war. The towns built on its alignment and in its vicinity are among the most venerable in the world, and their annals mirror most of the events which shaped the history of the Middle East since the dawn of civilization. Back from successful forays on Palestinian soil, the conquerors eternalized their respective victories in engravings and texts upon the walls of their ornate palaces. The conquered sites are invariably represented as in season of war, with fortifications, battlements and towers, and the 'captions' are inscriptions which give their names, in Egypt — in hieroglyphic characters, in Assyria — in cuneiform, names that are often emblazoned, too, in biblical record. The inhabitants are shown fully armed and in combat, or in abject surrender to the enemy forces of assault. Some of the pictures are enlivened by illustrations of the urban precincts and of the local flora.

The Egyptian specimens are undisturbed still where they were originally graven upon stone, mostly in Upper Egypt, among the magnificent ruins of Karnak; the Assyrian counterparts have been taken away to European museums, and principally to the British Museum and the Louvre.

The most aged were found in Egypt of the thirteenth century B.C., from the heyday of the nineteenth dynasty which gave Egypt its greatest rulers and warriors. One of the most highly renowned in their number was Seti I, who reigned in the years 1313—1292 B.C. About 1310 B.C., half a century before its conquest by the Israelites, he waged a torrential campaign in Canaan, overran Beit-Shean, an important staging-post on the 'Way of the Sea', and, in triumph, set up a beautiful monument which was brought to light in the course of modern excavations of the ancient mound in 1928. The Pharaoh pursued his victorious path as far as Kedesh in Upper Galilee, the same which was to be vanquished by the tribe of Naphtali and become a 'city of refuge'. To-day nothing of its grandeur is left but a bare mound upon a height near the new village of Ramot-Naphtali. In Upper Egypt, on the walls of the wondrous palace of Seti, at a place now known by the Arab name of Medinet-Habu, is a large bas-relief of Kedesh besieged, resisting the Egyptian host (figure 455).

The famous Hall of Columns in the Temple of Karnak, another monument of Seti I, marks a second memory of the expedition. On one wall the theme of a gigantic carving is his return in glory through the Desert of Sinai, riding in a splendid chariot drawn by two curvetting white coursers with tossing plumes, while manacled prisoners trudge in serried ranks in front and behind. Here and there, in the background, are incised cities and garrisons that punctuated the highway southwards to Egypt. In the top left-hand corner, a bastioned city is presented as a stylised fortress, and next to it are earthen jars, rolled papyri and a tray of lotus blooms; below, the citizens are shown lifting up

Seti I, King of Egypt, riding in triumph

their hands in submission. Vestiges of the hieroglyphs above the fortress can be deciphered as 'the town . . . '. The name is utterly erased and can only be surmised. From its position in the carving it is usually identified as Rafiah on the southern Palestinian coast, on the edge of the Sinai wilderness: to-day its place is taken by the Arab village of Rafah in the Gaza Strip, still on the arterial highway and railroad to Egypt. On the sea-shore close by, a desolate tel shrouds the site of the former greatness of what had been a vital point on the 'Way of the Sea', one of the chain of strongholds built up and down the fringe of the Mediterranean for all the length of this busy life-line of antiquity. The bas-relief even marks the wells that served travellers, civilian or soldier, in the sandy wastes ; to the right is a canal within parallel lines, and fish and crocodiles swim in its waters. This conduit traverses the Suez Canal zone, betwen the delta of Lower Egypt and the Mediterranean Sea (see figures 483—484).

Rameses II, son and heir of Seti I, was king over Egypt in the years 1292-1225 B.C. He would be the Pharaoh of Exodus, and it is believed that it was at the end of his reign that the Children of Israel began their long trek through Sinai. Following the precept of his father and predecessor, this Rameses also conducted military operations in the north, and the fretted walls of his palaces, as well, exhibit bas-reliefs of the towns subdued by his armies. Ashkelon, on the Mediterranean, had been an eager Egyptian target from time immemorial. The Pharaohs constantly strove to gain control over it and use it as a forward maritime base conveniently close to their own lands. Rameses II took it in 1280 B.C., and bade his masons perpetuate the much prized victory on the walls of his Karnak palace (figure 245). Before this exploit, in 1285 B.C., he had mastered other Palestinian habitations and portrayals of certain Galilean towns among them still hold the eye. One shows Merom taken and its people carried off into captivity (figure 453); apparently this is the Merom which afterwards earned distinction as a decisive battlefield of Joshua, son of Nun, and according to one opinion it stood where now stands the village of Meiron, next to Zefat (Safad). Other scholars assign it to a ruin north-east of Zefat, adjoining the Arab village of Marun er-Rass which is now within the territory of Lebanon.

Beit-Anat, mentioned in the Bible as belonging to the tribe of Naphtali, was another strong town of Galilee. A bas-relief chronicling its capture by the Egyptians was also found in Upper Egypt (figure 454) ; its site cannot be determined with exactitude, but one hypothesis sets it at a tel near Bueina, an Arab hamlet by the side of the Zefat—Acco highway, in the mountains of Galilee.

Of a subsequent period are pictures of Palestinian towns which were uncovered by archaeologists digging among the ruins of Assyria, the Northern Iraq of our times, of towns that fell into the hands of Assyria's warrior kings. About 889 B.C., Shalmaneser III, outstanding among them, invaded the Land of Israel from the north, sweeping first down the coast of Lebanon and seizing Tyre and other places. Several inscriptions recounting incidents of this campaign were brought to light in the excavations, and the name of Ahab, King of Israel, is upon a list of monarchs overthrown by Shalmaneser and become tributary to him. In Northern Iraq, too, at a site now named Tel Balawat, near the River Euphrates, a chance turn of the spade threw up panels of beaten brass that plated the portals of Shalmaneser's palace; one scene depicts Tyre set on an island and the townspeople yielding to the Assyrians, who carry away the booty in small craft. The panels are now in the British Museum (figure 393).

Tiglath-Pileser III, King of Assyria

In 732 B.C., in his turn, Tiglath-Pileser III, another formidable Assyrian fighter, invaded the country, again from the north. The Bible echoes the episode : "In the days of Pekah king of Israel came Tiglath-Pileser king of Assyria, and took . . . Galilee, all the land of Naphtali; and he carried them captive to Assyria" [1]. Further testimony was forthcoming in the excavations of Tiglath-Pileser's palace, a stone plaque with a carving of a fortified town, its inhabitants capitulating to the Assyrian soldiery ; the carving is captioned by a cuneiform inscription which identifies the town as Gazru, that is Gezer, famed in biblical history, on the highway from Jerusalem to Jaffa. Tiglath-Pileser went on to cross into Transjordan, reducing important centres on his way. A second scene shows the storming of a town, its defenders, too, carried into captivity, its cattle driven over to the enemy; here the inscription gives the name Astartu, that is, Ashtarot-Karnaim, a town known to us from the life of the Patriarch Abraham, and afterwards, during the conquest of Transjordan by Moses and the Hebrew tribes, a stronghold of Og, King of Bashan. Ashtarot-Karnaim was on the verge of the Syrian desert, and its site to-day is occupied by a lonely hillock in southern Syria which keeps the ancient name in slightly altered form, Ashtara (figure 470). This relief, likewise, is in the British Museum.

Sargon, King of Assyria

Sennacherib, King of Assyria

Hard on the heels of Tiglath-Pileser III came Sargon, who thrust into the Land in 711 B.C., and, taking the 'Way of the Sea' southwards, reached the Kingdom of Judah. The carvings on the walls of the palace in his capital, Dur-sharruken, to the Arabs of to-day Khorsabad, an insignificant mound, describe his taking of Ekron, an important biblical town, and Gibton, which may be the 'Gibton of the Philistines' mentioned in the Holy Scriptures, and possibly stood on the coast, where ultimately was the Arab village of Kubeiba neighbouring Rehovot; the biblical name has now been evocatively given to a new settlement in the vicinity.

Another, and large, relief from Sargon's palace shows a fortified town built on an island; from it float away rafts made of trunks of the cedars of Lebanon. Most probably it is Tyre, which traded in timber with its neighbours; once upon a time Hiram, its famous king, purveyed cedar-logs to King Solomon for the building of the Great Temple of Jerusalem, and they were ferried down in rafts to the roadstead of Jaffa.

The next Assyrian ruler to harass Judah was Sennacherib, in 700 B.C., in the reign of Hezekiah, when he invaded Lachish, in the south, and established it as the headquarters of his troops: "He was before Lachish, and all his power with him . . ." [2] The control of Lacish, a site crucial in the strategy of the region, was highly esteemed by Sennacherib and the event is told upon the palace walls at Nineveh, his capital. In that record of stone, Lachish is besieged by the Assyrians, its inhabitants resist but are overcome; this, now in the British Museum, is one of the largest reliefs found in ageless Nineveh and it brilliantly lights up the Bible text. There appear on it, also, the Assyrian camp, the conquering king enthroned, while roundabout the craftsman has meticulously carved the shapes of trees and plants characteristic of Lachish's area; vines, fig-trees and date-palms (figures 251-260).

In the palace in Nineveh is another relief, of a beleaguered town on a mountain-top and around it a wall of which one gate is visible. A fragment of the Assyrian inscription above the highest tower reads : '. . . alammu', seemingly the last syllables of the name 'Urusalammu', which is the Assyrian form of Jerusalem. This relief, too, is in the British Museum (figure 1).

[1] II Kings, 15, 29.
[2] II Chronicles, 32, 9.

II. DESIGNS OF TOWNS UPON ANCIENT MOSAICS

Most of the mosaics in Palestine are of Byzantine dating, predominantly of the fifth and sixth centuries A.D. The Greek craftsmen who put them together liked to set pictures of towns they knew among their patterned motifs. One spectacularly conspicuous work which has survived is a map of Palestine in multi-coloured tesserae, diversified with many pictures of towns and places of contemporary renown ; it is still *in situ*, where it was discovered, in a church of the townlet of Madaba in Transjordan, and is named, accordingly, the Madaba Map. It was made in the sixth century and sets forth a variety of locations of that epoch, each designated by its Greek name. In the centre is a beautiful image of Jerusalem with its ramparts, towers and gates, its major buildings, the Church of the Holy Sepulchre and the several shrines (figures 2-4, 121). East of Jerusalem are to be seen Jericho and its storied palm-trees (figure 205), and the Dead Sea close by, with two barques sailing on its silent waters. The River Jordan, in which fish are shown swimming, falls into the Sea ; one fish, which has reached that outlet, and apparently savoured the bitterness of the briny waters, is turning back in flight, and swims against the current (figures 215-217). On the shores of the Sea are marked the Hot Springs of Callirhoe and the town of Zoar (figure 230). North of Jerusalem is Shekhem, registered by its Roman-Byzantine name of Neapolis — New Town, which the Arabs eventually corrupted into Nablus (figure 310). On the coastal plain stand Lod and its church, and, more to the south, Ashkelon (figure 247), and Gaza (figure 238). The high expanses of the Desert of Sinai are represented and the settlements on the adjacent coast (figures 485—487).

Other mosaic floors of the sixth century were cleared west of Madaba, on the heights of Mount Nebo ; one preserves a view of the Great Temple of Jerusalem (figure 56). In a coeval mosaic from the Arab village of Ma'an in Transjordan, on the site of ancient Baal-Maon, there is, among many, a view of Ashkelon (figure 246). Jerash—Roman Gerasa—in Transjordan also, in the heart of the Mountains of Gilead, is notable for beautifully decorated mosaics, and Egyptian Alexandria is in their catalogue of illustrations.

Urban Palestine also appears on the mosaics of famous churches, especially from Rome and Ravenna. The cities of Jerusalem and Bethlehem are usually set one opposite the other. There is a splendid picture of Jerusalem and its historical sites in a fourth century mosaic of the Church of Santa Pudenzianna in Rome (figure 5). The Cathedral of San Giovanni in Laterano, too, displays a mosaic with colourful designs of Jerusalem and Bethlehem (figures 6-7, 176). The church of Santa Maria Maggiore, likewise in Rome, has a fifth century mosaic with a Jerusalem fashioned in it (figure 8), as well as another of the fall of Jericho to the Israelites (figure 204). Jerusalem and Bethlehem are depicted, too, in a sixth century mosaic in the Basilica of San Lorenzo fuori le Mura — 'Outside the Walls', of Rome (figure 9). A similar mosaic decorated the St. Peter of Rome of the fourth century, which was demolished in the fifteenth century to make place for the new basilica (figure 11). Jerusalem and Bethlehem are again in evidence on ancient mosaics in St. Vital of Ravenna (figure 10).

III. VIEWS OF THE HOLY LAND IN THE WRITINGS OF CHRISTIAN PILGRIMS

Christian voyagers who visited the Holy Places all down the ages penned numerous testimonies of their pilgrimages and the tales burgeon into drawings of local landscapes, which often are nothing other than figments of pious imagination. Jerusalem and its sacred sites make up the major part of these drawings. The city is commonly shown in its eastern aspect, as it appears from the heights of the Mount of Olives, a 'belvedere' that affords a magnificent panorama of the fortified wall, the gates and, more especially, Mount Moriah and the Temple area. In the centre of the Temple court rises the Mosque of Omar (the Dome of the Rock) and its large cupola, which symbolised, for both Christian and Jewish pilgrim, the Solomonic Temple of antiquity. The Church of the Holy Sepulchre, and the Tomb of St. Mary in the Valley of Kidron, are portrayed in varying fashions. The pilgrims frequently limned a general prospect of the Mount of Olives, site of Jesus' ascent to Heaven, and another favoured subject is the building where Jewish tradition places the Tomb of King David and Christian folklore the Hall of the Last Supper — the Coenaculum. Many books present pictures of the Church of the Nativity in Bethlehem, the Tomb of Rachel at the entrance to that town, and the village of Ein-Karem, birth-place, according to popular belief, of St. John the Baptist.

Jaffa and its port, where most of the pilgrims disembarked, is also variously depicted. The travellers sketched as well the sites they passed on the highway from Jaffa to Jerusalem : Ramla, which they confused with Rama, birth-place of that Joseph of Arimathea who took Jesus down from the cross ; Lod or Lydda, the twin town of Ramla, where St. George was born and is buried, and over his tomb a Greek Orthodox church stands to this day ; Latrun, known by the Latin name — Castellum boni latronis — the Castle of the Good Thief, because, so legend has it, it was the native village of Dimas, the Good Thief, who was crucified at Jesus' side ; the Latin 'latronis' explains the modern usage of Latrun. The tombs of the Maccabees were shown near by, and figure frequently in illustrations of the village.

Some books delineate the Arab village of Abu-Ghosh, which the pilgrims named St. Jeremie ; according to a misguided tradition this was held to be the site of Anatoth, where the Prophet Jeremiah was born. The Arab village of Kolonia, now derelict, next to the settlement of Motza, is also featured, for among Christian pilgrims of the Middle Ages an erroneous conviction was current that the little rocky vale that stretches below it is the biblical Valley of Elah, where David the Shepherd fought Goliath the Philistine. The true Valey of Elah is much further to the south-west, in a lonely part of the Mountains of Judah. For the benefit of the pilgrims, to satisfy their longings without endangering their lives, the mediaeval guides conveniently located the valley in the approaches of Jerusalem, on the main thoroughfare to the city ; many devout travellers recorded how intense was their emotion on visiting the famous duelling-ground, where they would gather small smooth pebbles — fondly conceived as replicas of David's slingshot — from the river bed that deeply bisects the little vale, as souvenirs and amulets possessing mysterious healing virtues.

In Galilee, the pilgrim-artist for the most part took as his subject Nazareth and its churches, Mount Tabor — the site of the Transfiguration on the border of the Valley of Jezreel (Esdraelon), and Tiberias on the shores of the Sea of Galilee. Haifa is chosen, too, because of its proximity to Mount Carmel and the Cave of Elijah, which both Jews and Christians were wont to include in their itineraries. The town of Acco, or Acre, only starts to appear in the later period, after it won notoriety as the scene of Napoleon Bonaparte's defeat in 1799.

Few pilgrims undertook the hazardous journey to Sinai, the Desert of the Wanderings, to enjoy the felicity of standing at the spot where the Law was given to Moses. Some, who did, left strange drawings of Mount Sinai, Mount Horeb and the still extant sixth-century Monastery of St. Catherine. It was not until the end of the nineteenth century that travellers ventured to penetrate into Transjordan as well and inspect its famous ruins : Jerash — Roman Gerasa, Amman — biblical Rabath-Ammon or Amman — Roman Philadelphia, and renowned Petra — ancient Sela of the Bible.

The landscapes in pilgrim literature of the end of the Middle Ages are childishly primitive and in the main imaginary. Not many pilgrims were accomplished draftsmen. Once back in their homes, they would describe to a local artist the terrain they had seen, and he then would draw it accordingly, but with no first-hand knowledge of the real vision. Often he introduced characteristic motifs of his own surroundings : the kind of houses to be found in his native town, the fortresses and towers familiar to his environs, the plants and trees growing in his countryside, the outline of the mountains rising on his everyday horizon — all completely foreign to the Palestinian scene.

In many cases, the inhabitants of the Land are faithfully shown attired in the picturesque costumes of their times. There were, too, pilgrims who observed the plants and animals of the Holy Land, although their recorded notions of the flora and fauna were largely fanciful, and put exceptional emphasis on the species mentioned in the Bible.

An idealized presentation of Jerusalem, and its towers and portals, adorns a Latin manuscript describing the travels of the French monk Arculfus, who visited Palestine in 679 A.D., a short time after the Arab conquest (figure 12). This manuscript also displays plans of the Holy Sepulchre, the Church of the

Ascension on the Mount of Olives, venerated shrines on Mount Zion, and Jacob's Well in the Mountains of Samaria. [1] An ancient Greek manuscript, also of about the seventh century, named 'The Scroll of Joshua', is preserved in the Vatican Library; [2] it illustrates the battles fought by the son of Nun, and the Israelitish subjugation of Canaan in the Valley of Aijalon, and among other things one sees the Israelites breaching the walls of Jericho (figure 206) and Joshua's encounter with the Angel of God (figure 207).

The period of the Crusades, in the twelfth and thirteenth centuries, enriched Palestinian literature with pictorial maps of Jerusalem, Acco, and their vicinities (see next chapter). From the same period, also, are dated many reproductions of seals of important cities, each bearing on its obverse the likeness of the governor and on the reverse a relief of the citadel. Pictures of all these seals were collected by the Italian writer S. Paoli and published, in 1735, in his book on the Crusader era in Palestine. [3] Some are included in these pages: the seals of Jerusalem (figure 133), of Jaffa (figure 261), of Ramla (figure 296), of Caesarea (figures 319-320) and of Haifa (figure 330).

In the fourteenth century the Englishman Sir John Maundeville, professing to be a pilgrim who had allegedly visited the countries of the Middle East in the year 1336, published an interesting description of them, of which several versions have remained, some in the original and others in translation. [4] One version made in the year 1482 shows a picture of Sir John himself (figure 284), and another of the tree of the Patriarch Abraham at Hebron (figure 200).[5] Another manuscript, preserved in the Library of the British Museum, conjures up a picture of Jerusalem which is now published for the first time (figure 23). [6] The same library possesses a collection of pictures, attributed to the travels of Maundeville, of which one shows pilgrims disembarking at a port. [7] The port and its town, probably Jaffa, are portrayed with a wealth of circumstantial detail; the Christian pilgrims entering the town pay toll to the Moslem guards at the gate (figure 266).

An authentic pilgrim of the fourteenth century was the Italian Jacobus of Verona, known after his birthplace in Northern Italy. He was in the Holy Land about the year 1336 and collected his impressions in his 'Book of Travels' — Liber peregrinationis. [8] He reached as far as Sinai and left a naive drawing of the mountains, marking the buildings which stood at the time (figure 501).

In the fifteenth century, the better security provided by the Moslem Mameluke governors attracted a great number of pilgrims to the Holy Land. The most renowned is the German Bernhard von Breidenbach, who visited it in 1483. The record of his travels, accompanied by excellent illustrations, the work of E. Reuwich (Rewich), saw the light in 1486, as one of the first books ever printed about Palestine. [9] A large pictorial map annexed to it gives a view of the Land with walled Jerusalem and its main buildings in the centre (figure 25), Jaffa and a pilgrim vessel at anchor in its port (figures 262, 282), Ramla (figure 297), next to Lydda or Lod (figure 304), Haifa and Mount Carmel (figure 333), and Mount Sinai (figure 502). The frontispiece carries a design of the Holy Sepulchre (figure 124).

Conrad von Grünemberg, another German pilgrim, who came out in 1486, also supplemented his words with drawings, among them one of Jerusalem as from the crest of the Mount of Olives. [10]

In 1475, a Latin book appeared in the town of Lübeck, Germany, among the first to be decked out with printed pictures. [11] One of them represents the whole area of Jaffa and Jerusalem with their settlements: Ramla, indicated as Rama, and Emmaus holy to the Christian world. The other maps furnished in the book are: one of the Holy Land and one of the entire world, showing Jerusalem at its navel.

The anonymous historian known as the Citizen of Nürnberg published in that town, in 1493, a Latin work on world history entitled 'Liber chronicarum', with many illustrations [12] — one, purely invented, of Jerusalem in ruins, which is the work of an artist who was the teacher of Albert Dürer.

In 1496, Arnold von Harff, a third German pilgrim, toured the Holy Land. He left a book of travels complete with sketches of Palestinian types, [13] a Christian pilgrim making his way up from Egypt, an Arab warrior on a galloping steed and brandishing a lance, and a portrait of the author himself.

The Bibliothèque Nationale of Paris has in its possession an interesting fifteenth century picture of Jerusalem and its surroundings (figure 24). [14]

Jean Fouquet was a fifteenth-century French artist, well-known in his time; among his main works is a series of illustrations for Josephus Flavius' 'History of the Jews', of which the originals are kept at the Bibliothèque Nationale of Paris. [15] One is of the Israelites marching around the tottering walls of Jericho; the houses are drawn in the style of French buildings of the end of the Middle Ages, with gabled roofs from which chimneys protrude. Another represents the Temple as an impressive mediaeval cathedral.

In the sixteenth century several tales of Palestine were written by Christian pilgrims who first saw it under Turkish rule, and in some of them landscapes are included. In 1520, Heinrich Wölfli (Lupulus) wrote an account of his journey to Jerusalem in Latin, of which the German edition only has survived, with graphic renderings of pilgrims landing, of their attempts to rid themselves of the lice that infested them on board ship, and of a long caravan of them starting out for Jerusalem. [16]

In 1547, the French traveller Pierre Belon wrote an intriguing narrative of his journeys in the East. [17] He was the first pilgrim to mention local flora and fauna, but his book, nevertheless, contains only fictional representations of the plants and animals he purports to have seen; his pictures of natives in indigenous dress and carrying the arms of the period are more factual (figure 469).

About 1560, the Italian Bianco Noé published in Italian a pamphlet which went into many editions, describing a 'Voyage from Venice to Holy Jerusalem and Mount Sinai'. [18] In fact, it was plagiarised from the work of another Italian named Cola, published in about 1500. Noé's edition is furnished with primitive pictures of places in the Holy Land.

Sebastian Münster, a German Franciscan of the sixteenth century, was a learned scholar of Judaica and the Hebrew language, and instituted the study of these subjects in the universities of Germany and Switzerland. Among his publications was 'Cosmografey', a kind of historical-geographical encyclopaedia, which appeared in German in 1544, [19] and in Latin in 1552. It includes a general conspectus of Jerusalem seen from the east (figure 26), a curious view of Acco and a pictorial map of the Holy Land.

Some pilgrims of the sixteenth century also left drawings of Mount Sinai. The three who deserve to be cited are the German J. Helfferich, who was a visitor in 1565 [20] (figures 504, 509), Christophori von Haimendorf in 1566 (figure 505) [21] and Bernhard Walter von Walterswyl in 1587 (figure 503). [22]

Three more of Hellferich's drawings appear in these pages : a turbaned young Jew in flowing cape (figure 106), the Governor of Jerusalem mounted on a horse (figure 115), and a tourist on camel-back, under a canopy (figure 289).

In a book which appeared in 1581, Salomon Schweigger, another German pilgrim, printed many attractive pictures : the ship which brought him to the shores of the Holy Land (figure 283), the caravan making its way from Jaffa to Jerusalem (figure 288), a comprehensive sight of Jerusalem from the Mount of Olives (figure 27), and a reproduction of the Turkish passport that was delivered to him at the start of his journey, carrying the seal of the Sultan in Constantinople (figure 295). [23]

J. Zuallart, a Flemish Belgian, was in the country in 1586, and in the following year published an important work in Italian, copiously illustrated, which was rendered into many languages. [24] The chapter recounting his arrival in the Holy Land displays a picture of the few houses of Jaffa, the small port, and the caravan setting forth from the seashore to Jerusalem. On the way thither, the author provides views of Ramla, or, as he calls it, Rama (figure 298), of Latrun or Domus boni latronis (figure 307), of the Arab village of Abu-Ghosh which, again accepting an early blunder, he claims as the birthplace of the Prophet Jeremiah and so designates it (figure 156), and of the village of Kolonia where the little glen is once more magnified into the Valley of Elah of biblical memory (figure 154). Of Jerusalem itself there is a broad semblance taken from the west, with fortified wall, Jaffa Gate and Tower of David (figure 146), and another showing it with its Holy Places. There are separate pictures of the Holy Sepulchre and the Tomb of Mary, Mount Zion and the building of the Tomb of David with the Coenaculum in the upper storey (figure 137), the Mount of Olives (figure 148), the 'Hand' of Absalom, the Golden Gate, a panorama of the area extending from Jerusalem to Bethlehem (figure 159), the Monastery of Mar Elias (figure 160), the Tomb of Rachel (figure 164), a plan of the Church of the Nativity in Bethlehem, and the steep, rocky descent from Jerusalem to Jericho, the Jordan and the Dead Sea (figure 202).

The drawings of Zuallart were copied in their chronicles by other pilgrims, notably the Flamand Johan van Kootwyck (Cotovicus), who visited Palestine in 1596, [25] the Englishman George Sandy in 1610, [26] and the Spaniard Antonio de Castillo in 1627. [26*]

The Englishman Edward Webbe performed his pilgrimage in the year 1590, and in the very same year published a short account of it, with a picture of himself setting out from his home on his venturesome journey (figure 285). [27]

The Italian monk Bernardo Amico came to Palestine in 1593, and was for a few years Father Superior of the Church of the Holy Sepulchre. He wrote an informed book on the shrines of the Holy Land [28], lavishly illustrated with plans and pictures, among them one of Jerusalem and its near vicinity which is the first to mention the Jewish Quarter in the Old City (figure 29).

In the seventeenth century a further batch of works, usually illustrated, made its appearance. The Italian monk Francesco Quaresmus was in the country in 1618, officiating, as did his precursor Amico, for a few years as Head of the Church of the Holy Sepulchre. Meanwhile he compiled, in Latin, a large and detailed work on his studies and observations ; [29] in it is a large picture of Jerusalem and its important shrines as seen from the Mount of Olives, with small supplementary sketches of the historical events which took place at each site (figure 34).

The French Franciscan Eugène Roger came in 1631. His visit lasted some years and the yield was a historical tome containing pictures of Nazareth, the first such occurrence in pilgrim literature (figure 406), the Tomb of Rachel (figure 165), the Monastery of Mar-Saba in the Wilderness of Judah (figure 181), a Jew in the Holy Land (figure 100), the Heads of the Christian Churches in Jerusalem (figures 116-118) and a portrait of the Druze Governor of Galilee and Lebanon, Fakhr ed-Din (figure 468). [30]

At the beginning of the seventeenth century there lived in the Carmelite Monastery on Mount Carmel a Spanish monk, Prospero dello Spirito Santo, who left, as of the year 1632, an over-all view of the Bay of Haifa, Mount Carmel and Acco, the first drawing of this area to appear in print [31] (figure 335). Father Prosper died in the monastery in 1653 ; a plaque in his memory is set in the floor of the Carmelite Church on the mount.

A French traveller of the year 1652, Jean Doubdan, committed to writing a narrative of his journey with a view of the Valley of Jezreel, Mount Tabor rising by its side and Jesus undergoing the 'Transfiguration' on its crest (figure 398). On other pages appear Haifa, then an insignificant village on its circular bay, and Mount Carmel (figure 337), a vista of the Mount of Olives in Jerusalem, and a view of the Mount of the Temptation, next to Jericho, sanctified by the Christian creed. [32]

The German pilgrim, Electus Zwinner, was in Palestine in 1658. His composition, entitled 'Blumen-Buch'—Book of Flowers, has a few illustrations, of which the most interesting is of Jaffa and its haven seen from the sea (figure 265). [33]

In 1660, Laurence d'Arvieux came and wrote an informative book of travel, to which is appended a view of Haifa and of Mount Carmel, its slope occupied by a Beduin encampment of tents in strictly European style (figure 336). [34]

The Dutch pilgrim Antonius Gonsales, obviously of Spanish descent, has recorded, in a manuscript entitled 'Hierusalemsche Reyse', the impressions of his visit in 1661 [35]. The book contains views of his points of pilgrimage in the order of his itinerary : first, Jaffa where he set foot in the Holy Land, then Ramla (figure 299), Latrun, Abu-Ghosh (figure 157), the supposed Valley of Elah at the entrance to Jerusalem, a view of Jerusalem, the Holy Sepulchre, the Mount of Olives, the way from Jerusalem to Bethlehem and the shrines along that way, the area of Jerusalem and Bethlehem, Nazareth and its sacred spots and finally maps of Galilee and, the first such in the literature, of Mount Carmel (figure 353).

In his 'Histoire et Voyage de la Terre Sainte', the Frenchman J. F. Goujon, after a visit in 1668, published charming illustrations of Mount Tabor and the Valley of Jezreel girt by mountains (figure 399) and of the Mountains of Sinai with their holy sites (figure 507). [36]

The German Otto Friedrich von der Gröben did his pilgrimage in 1675, and his resultant 'Orientalische Reise-Beschreibung' appeared in 1694. [37] The text is brightened by a few untutored drawings : pilgrims' vessels approaching the coast of the Holy Land, a caravan proceeding from Egypt (figure 490), and a view of Mount Sinai (figure 506).

The Nederlander Olf Dapper never was in Palestine, but made a detailed study of all the published literature, and then wrote a massive book on the history of the country, which appeared in Dutch in 1677 and afterwards in a German version, with a wealth of illustration, all contrived and with no affinity to the local truth. [38] The artist did, however, endeavour to convey the usages and customs of the Holy Land. At the 'Hand' of Absalom in the Valley of the Brook of Kidron, east of Jerusalem, wrathful pilgrims hurl stones at this monument to an unruly son who dared rebel against a righteous father . . . The book illustrates Ein-Karem (figure 152), the counterfeit Valley of Elah (figure 155), the Tomb of Rachel (figure 166), Latrun (figure 308), Ramla — Ramma (figure 300), Jaffa (figure 267), and includes pictorial maps of the Sea of Galilee (figure 439) and of Lake Hula and its shores (figure 459).

The Dutch artist Cornelius de Bruyn arrived in 1681, with the express purpose of drawing the famous sites. He tells of the risks he ran in accomplishing it, for the fanatical Arabs regarded his doings with explosive suspicion. Once, wishing to sketch Jerusalem from the top of the Mount of Olives, he set out with a basket of provisions, as if it were only in his mind to picnic on that holy hill. Whenever an Arab drew near, he would hide his paper and crayons, take out his food and begin to munch with great gusto . . . The numerous drawings which appeared in his memoirs, in 1688, opened a new chapter in the development of illustrative art in the narratives of pilgrims to the Holy Land [39] ; here for the first time were the products of direct observation without flight of imagination or foreign influence. His most interesting efforts depict Jaffa and its port, nearby Rama (figure 301) and its ancient water cistern named after St. Helena (figure 303), an interior view of the Holy Sepulchre (figure 126), Haifa and Mount Carmel (figure 339), the Crusader Church of St. Andrew in Acco (figure 365) and Tiberias on the Sea of Galilee (figure 417).

In 1650, a short pamphlet printed in English, entitled 'Two Journeys to Jerusalem', had for frontispiece a pilgrim on camel-back, with the following inscription below : 'The manner of Travelling upon Dromedarys' (figure 290) ; there is also a rudimentary picture of Jerusalem 'as it now is' (figure 31). [40]

In 1697, Henry Maundrell, a chaplain at the English Consulate in Aleppo, Northern Syria, set out on a journey to the Holy Land, and a book entitled 'Journey from Aleppo to Jerusalem' [41] which appeared in the same year, was the product ; among its few pictures are views of Haifa, Mount Carmel and the bay seen from the sea (figure 338), patently copied from the illustration by J. Doubdan (figure 337).

With the advance of typography and progress in the making of clichés, the eighteenth century saw a much ampler use of illustration in pilgrim writings, although the Italian voyager Pietro Antonio in his 'Guida fedele alla Santa Città di Gierusalemme', published in 1703 [42], is still amateurish in his artistry especially of the Holy Places: Bethlehem (figure 177), the building over the Cave of Machpelah in Hebron (figure 191), and Tiberias (figure 418), for example.

Many pictures of the Holy Land intersperse the formidable 'Dictionarium historicum chronologicum, geographicum et litterarium Bibliorum' of Augustus Calmet (1722), which was put into several European languages. [43] The frontispiece of the book 'Peregrinus in Jerusalem' of P. Angelicus Myller, a traveller of the year 1726, which was printed in 1729, [44] gives a view from the sea of Jaffa and its port, the gateway to Jerusalem (figure 268).

The Frenchman L. F. Cassas, architect by profession and painter by choice, visited Palestine in 1772. In contrast to his predecessors, he paid special heed to the ruins he observed along the way and was at great pains to reconstruct their appearance as they may have looked, intact, centuries before. His book 'Voyage pittoresque de la Syrie'. [45] which appeared in serial form, provides pictures of the Holy Places as they were in his time and their reconstruction as his imagination, allied to professional knowledge, envisaged them in the past: his reconstructions of the Tombs of the Kings, the 'Hand' of Absalom and the Tomb of the Prophet Zechariah in Jerusalem are noteworthy.

In 1799, Napoleon Bonaparte invaded Palestine from Egypt, engaged the Turkish forces and laid siege to Acco. The stubborn defence put up by the Turks, under the town's famous governor, Jazzar Pasha, compelled him to abandon the venture after a few months and forget his dream of expansion in the East. But it enriched the literature of the Holy Land with a plethora of pictures, mainly of Acco (figures 367-372), a plan of the battle for the town (figure 373), [46] a drawing of Frenchmen in combat there (figure 374), a portrait of Jazzar Pasha on the ramparts (figure 368), [45] and a picture of French soldiers crossing the Desert of Sinai on camel-back (figure 492). [47]

In the nineteenth century, in the aftermath of Napoleon's abortive invasion, several illustrated books appeared, some written by officers belonging to the naval forces led by the English Admiral Sir Sidney Smith, who had helped the Turks to drive the French back. One is by J. B. Spilsbury, surgeon of the 'Tiger', a battleship of the English fleet. Spilsbury, a landscape painter by hobby, travelled through Palestine after Napoleon's withdrawal, painting, as he went, both the scenery and the modes of life of the inhabitants, and published the results in 'Picturesque Scenery in the Holy Land' — 1803. [48] Very striking are the man-of-war 'Tiger' itself at sea, Jazzar Pasha dispensing justice as he sits cross-legged on a carpet, rod of flagellation in his hand, lethal axe by his side (figure 369). Here one sees the market of Acco with buyers and sellers in strange oriental garments, there an English soldier attending the burial of one of Napoleon's generals fallen in battle, while French soldiers peer out of a nearby trench, or the French camp in the Valley of Jezreel, at the foot of Mount Tabor (figure 396), the caravanserai of Jub Yusef in the Mountains of Upper Galilee, once a halt of consequence on the trail between Syria and Egypt, now an empty ruin not far from Rosh-Pinna, the Bridge of the Daughters of Jacob spanning the upper Jordan, and on the Mediterranean littoral the relics of Caesarea and Athlit. Spilsbury adds an account of his journey to Jerusalem in the Admiral's retinue. While the 'Tiger' was anchored off Jaffa, Sir Sidney received a special permit from the Grand Vizier to visit Jerusalem, and on the frontispiece of his book Spilsbury draws the Vizier surrounded by his guards, ceremoniously seated in his tent as he hands the permit to Sir Sidney, while in a self-portrait the painter-physician looks on. In the National Gallery of Portraits, London, there is a painting of Sidney Smith in Acco by John Eckstein (figure 371).

Cooper Willyams was a chaplain in the fleet, and he, too, surveyed Palestine and the surrounding lands and painted much; his 'A Selection of Views in Egypt, Palestine', published in 1822,[49] assembles original drawings made on the spot, with historical and geographical commentary in English and French. There are two excellent pictures of Haifa and its waterfront ; one, of the crescent bay fringed by mountains, as seen from the heights of Mount Carmel, and the second of nascent Haifa enclosed within its walls and protected by a small fortress that is seen above it (figures 340-341).

The artist tourists of the nineteenth century were interested not in the Holy Places alone but also in the divergent landscapes of Palestine and the appearance and customs of its peoples ; they drew realistically and exemplify the period with precision. Their canvases of far-away sites were done at peril of life, for the Arabs evinced over hatred, especially of unbelievers who fixed in pen or paint the likeness of their religious landmarks : such irreverences were revolting to Moslems, and they looked indignantly upon the 'infidels' who came to desecrate a heritage of faith.

In 1804, a large collection of pictures appeared in a book by one L. Mayer, 'Views in the Levant', which went into many editions and translations.[50]

The spirited and distinguished traveller J. L. Burckhardt, of Swiss origin, explored Palestine and Transjordan in 1812 ; ten years later he published his findings, in English and German,[51] in a volume which contains a plan of Tiberias with its outer rampart and the smaller inner wall protecting the Jewish Quarter (figure 434), a map of the ruins of Gerasa, and a drawing of the splendid ruins of Petra which he was the first European to rediscover.

The Englishman J. S. Buckingham was equally intrepid. The year 1816 saw him in Palestine, and his chronicle, printed in 1821,[52] illustrates with special interest an unpretentious Haifa in the shadow of the 'Head' of Carmel (figure 342), and the Roman gateway of Gerasa (figure 472).

In 1818, there was a distinguished visitor from France, Count Auguste de Forbin, who combined the talents of painter, poet and historian of art ; after discharge from Napoleon's army, he held the post of Director of National Museums in France and founded the Museum of Luxembourg in Paris. He probed the remotest places too, and painted sites and scenes previously unrecorded : his paintings appeared in a beautifully illustrated text under the title 'Voyage dans le Levant' in 1819 and in a seperate album ; the finest among them is one of ruined Ashkelon (figure 249).[53]

J. L. Burckhardt

William Rae Wilson, a Scot, inherited a large fortune in his youth, and spent it in travelling widely ; the many books he wrote about his journeyings enjoyed immense popularity. At first he set his face towards the Orient, and in the summer of 1818 visited Egypt, whence he sailed for Palestine and went ashore at Jaffa at the beginning of 1819, to observe and afterwards describe the havoc wrought in the land by Bonaparte's invasion twenty years earlier. On his way to Jerusalem he lodged at the self-same monastery in Ramla that had given shelter to Bonaparte, and at Abu-Ghosh paid customary toll to the ruling Arab family as insurance against less legitimate exactions by highwaymen. The Holy City itself took up much of his time and study, but he found leisure to descend to Jericho through the Wilderness of Judah, to the River Jordan and the Dead Sea. From Jerusalem he went north into the Mountains of Samaria and Nablus, ancient Shekhem, then swung to the Valley of Esdraelon and so to Nazareth, which he scrutinized most conscientiously. From Nazareth he explored Galilee, whereafter Tiberias and Mount Tabor, and then Acco, Haifa and Mount Carmel were final stages on his path of departure along the beaches to Lebanon and Syrian Damascus. His experiences were published in 1822 ;[54] some of the views of Palestine he reproduced were drawn by A. P. Harrison, who followed sketches made on the spot by the author ; among those which call for special mention are Jerusalem and its Holy Places (figure 36), the Mount of Olives (figure 149), and a caravan coming down the steep slopes of the Mountains of Judah into the depression of the Wilderness of Jericho, while afar the Jordan winds its way to the Dead Sea beneath the easterly hills of Gilead and Moab (figure 203).

In 1828, a second French nobleman arrived, Léon, Comte de Laborde, who reached as far as Edom and rose-red Petra. His 'Voyage de l'Arabie Pétrée' (1830),[55] with an abridged version in English, is rendered particularly attractive by numerous pictures he drew himself, engraving the blocks with his own hands; as most striking instances: the town of Tiberias and the Sea of Galilee (figure 420), Tiberias shattered by earthquake (figure 421), a bridge over the Jordan (figure 466), a caravan of Moslem pilgrims entering Aqaba on the Red Sea, on its way to Mecca and Medina (figure 476), and breath-taking Petra (figures 477-480).

Léon, Comte de Laborde

Adrien Dauzats, a well-known French painter, travelled extensively in the East in 1830. Collaborating with Alexander Dumas, he wrote 'Quinze jours au Sinai' (1839) [56], unillustrated save for two small sketches: of the Monastery of St. Catherine and the Rock of Moses on Mount Sinai. On the other hand, many of his pictures appear in a work by Baron Isidore Taylor, a Belgian of English parentage, who, with Louis Reybaud, wrote 'La Syrie, l'Egypte, la Palestine et la Judée,' published in France in 1839," [57] and profusely illustrated by Dauzats: Acco and its market and mosque (figures 382-383); Jaffa, from the sea, modernistically drawn (figure 272); Jerusalem: the Jewish and Christian Quarters, the Holy Sepulchre, the Tower of David, the Damascus Gate, the Pool of Siloam, the entrance to the Tombs of the Kings; Christians of Bethlehem (figure 179); a building in Gaza (figure 244); the interior of the Church of the Annunciation in Nazareth; the Upper Galilean caravanserai Jub Yusef (figure 442); a strange picture of Zefat (Safad) in the hills; the Bridge of the Daughters of Jacob across the Jordan (figure 467); remains of a Roman temple in Gerasa (figure 473); the amphitheatre in Amman, the Roman Philadelphia (figure 474); and the Beduin guards of a caravan in Sinai. Taylor also prints pictures by Mayer of: Jerusalem, the Temple court and the Tombs of the Sanhedrin, Jericho, Caesarea, a caravan in the oasis of Firan in the Desert of Sinai and the interior view of the Monastery of St. Catherine (figure 511). A lovely view of the monastery appears in a small pamphlet published by the British Museum (figure 514). [58] There is also an interesting view of it in the book 'Wanderungen' by the German Christian Döbel, who traversed the Near East in 1834; it is shown entirely encompassed by a high wall (figure 512). [59]

The book of the Englishman T. H. Horne (1836) is entitled without reticence: 'The Biblical Keepsake, or Landscape Illustrations of the most remarkable places mentioned in the Holy Scriptures... made from Original Sketches taken on the spot and engraved by W. and E. Finden'; [60] one such illustration is of Mount Carmel and Haifa (figure 344).

Baron J. Taylor

In 1837, J. M. Bernatz, a German painer, visited Palestine; the consequence was a book written in German (1839) with a composite frontispiece of a caravan on its way to the Holy Land, of Hebron and the Cave of Machpelah, Bethlehem, Mount Tabor, the Tower of David, Jerusalem and the Temple court. He also published 'Palästina, Neues Album des Heiligen Landes' in 1855, with a further series of pictures, many in colour, and captions in English, German and French; [61] the Temple area and the Wailing Wall, worshippers at the Wall, the village of Ein-Karem, Shekhem which is Nablus, Kefar-Kanna (Canna) in Lower Galilee, Zefat (figure 443) and the Bridge of the Daughters of Jacob are of especial merit.

David Roberts, a second Scot, started his artistic career as a stage decorator in London and then went over to landscape painting. In 1838, he embarked on a devious and dangerous journey through the Near East, palette in hand, first a painstaking survey of Pharaonic Egypt's great monuments along the banks of the Nile, then into the Desert of Sinai, in nomad dress. He climbed the historic peaks of the Wilderness of the Wanderings, made the Gulf of Eilat, and after a halt at the village of Aqaba there continued to the Mountains of Edom, to linger awhile in the fabulous beauty of Petra; he was one of the first travellers to reach that long forsaken wreck again, and carefully drew all he saw. Jerusalem, then stricken by plague, he avoided, and instead, from Hebron went down to Gaza, Ashkelon and Jaffa on the coast; but in the end he could visit the Holy City, and thus outwards to Jericho and the Dead Sea, Samaria and Galilee, returning home through Lebanon. He published his paintings and drawings in 1842 in three imposing volumes 'The Holy Land, from Drawings made on the Spot'; this artistic contribution to knowledge of Palestine impressed his contemporaries profoundly, and earned him considerable fame: [62] the ruins of Ashkelon (figure 250), Acco and its surroundings (figure 378), and Tiberias on the lake shore of Galilee, reprinted in the book of the Abbé Georges Darboy in 1852 (figure 427), are perhaps the most remarkable of Roberts' works.

In 1840, a party of Royal Engineers undertook a survey in Palestine for the British War Office. Its report, 'Papers of the Corps of Royal Engineers' [63], includes numerous pictures and drawings, such as a plan of Haifa, unprecedented in literature (figure 352), a general view of el-Arish, the sole town of Sinai (figure 495), and a map of Acco at the time of Napoleon's siege, which is an English version of the French production (figure 373).

In 1840, Frances Egerton, a member of the English aristocracy, published the impressions of her trip in the previous year ; the title was 'Journal of a Tour in the Holy Land', [64] and the illustrations include a panorama of the Valley of Jezreel (Esdraelon) as she perceived it (figure 402), and a view of Tiberias and its lake (figure 422).

An important item in pictorial description of Palestine must be credited to William H. Bartlett, who came twice to the Holy Land, in 1842 and 1853. He travelled with ample equipment of colours and pencils and in his heart was a great reverence for the Holy Places and historical sites, so that he laboured to render truthfully the reality he saw, holding imagination sternly in check. He published 'Walks in and about the city and environs of Jerusalem' (1884), a very popular book, 'Forty days in the desert on the track of the Israelites' (1848), a narrative of his Sinai journey, and 'Footsteps of our Lord' (1851). A fourth volume, 'Jerusalem revisited', appeared posthumously after his second trip, for he died on the way home and was buried at sea. [65] Many of Bartlett's pictures may also be found in John Carne's 'Syria, the Holy Land' (1845), [66] and in Henry Stebbing's 'The Christian in Palestine' (1847) ;[67] they feature Jews praying at the Wailing Wall (figure 88), a Christian family in Jerusalem (figure 119), the Church of the Holy Sepulchre (figure 125), the Golden Gate (figure 127), the Jaffa Gate and the Tower of David (figure 130), the buildings over the tomb attributed to King David (figure 143), Hebron (figure 184), Jaffa from the mainland (figure 269), the army of Ibrahim Pasha, the Egyptian viceroy, encamped on the dunes facing Jaffa (figure 270) ; a Turkish guard on Jaffa's harbour (figure 273), Samaria (figure 316), the port of Caesarea (figure 322), Haifa and Mount Carmel from the east (figure 343) and from the west (figure 345), the caravanserai Khan et-Tujjar — the Inn of the Merchants — in Galilee, at the foot of Mount Tabor (figure 401), Tiberias and the lake (figures 423, 426), Zefat in Galilee (figure 444), and the Spring of Moses in Sinai (figure 496).

Otto Georgi waited for ten years after a visit in 1845 to publish 'Die Heiligen Statten nach Originalzeichnungen nach der Natur', with particularly good pictures of Bethlehem (figure 175), and Nazareth with Mary's Well (figure 409). [68]

In 1847, John Gadsby, a talented traveller, entered Palestine from Egypt through the Desert of Sinai, to add to the gallery of the Holy Land, in his 'Wanderings' (1855), an admirable picture of an Englishman mounted on a camel, while a native guide on foot in front points out the way (figure 493)[69].

In 1848, an American expedition under Captain W. F. Lynch, sponsored by the United States Navy, surveyed the River Jordan and the Dead Sea, and its report illustrates various sites of the itinerary (figure 233), the outflow of the Jordan from the Lake of Tiberias (figure 440), Ein-Gedi on the shore of the Dead Sea, the Beduin guard of the expedition (figure 234), and the Well of Mary in Nazareth (figure 416). [70]

In mid-century, the Englishman W. Tipping, venturesome and erudite, broke new ground. He was the first stranger to climb the steep peak of Mount Mezada (Massada) in the far Judean Wilderness, last stronghold of the ultimate Jewish rebellion against Rome. A number of Tipping's drawings were used in a new edition of the works of Josephus Flavius, printed in London [71] : Damascus Gate in Jerusalem (figure 128), Mezada (figure 232), Gaza (figure 243), Caesarea (figure 323), and the Hot Baths of Tiberias (figure 432).

In 1848, two French writers, J. Yancski and J. David, published a book entitled 'Syrie ancienne—Syrie moderne' with good illustrations of Palestine, among them the caravanserai in Acco called the 'Inn of the Columns' (figure 366). [72]

The Englishman J. A. Spencer was in the region in 1849 and wrote 'The East, Sketches of Travels in Egypt and the Holy Land' (1850) [73] ; a fine view of Tiberias (figure 424) is among his sketches.

C. W. M. van de Velde, of the Low Country, was a very thorough young observer. After his first visit — he was in Palestine on two occasions, spaced by a a decade — he published : 'Reis door Syrie en Palestine', first in Dutch in 1854, then in English and German translations ;[74] one of the best illustrations in it is of Haifa and its bay (figure 346). He also published in French 'Le pays d'Israel', richly illustrated. [75]

The Germans E. W. Schulz (1851) published his impressions under the title 'Reise in das Gelobte Land', [76] distinguished especially for its pictures of Nazareth (figures 411-412), Tiberias (figure 425), and Zefat (figure 445), which few before him had attempted.

In 1860, 'La Terre Sainte' appeared in Paris ; the author was J. J. Bourassé, who had been in the Holy Land nine years previously, and now presented a novel crop of illustrations : [77] a street in the Old City of Jerusalem (figure 110), the Church of the Nativity in Bethlehem (figure 178), the Monastery of Mar Saba in the Wilderness of Judah (figure 182), ruins of Samaria (figure 317), Nazareth (figure 410), and the Monastery of St. Catherine in the Mountains of Sinai (figure 513).

In 1852, there came out in France a book entitled 'Jérusalem et la Terre Sainte', unassumingly over the initials G. D., which hid the identity of the Abbé Darboy ; [78] some of the pictures in it are copied from the work of David Roberts : the Temple Mount in Jerusalem (figure 68), and Jaffa (figure 275).

The year 1856 was epochal, as seeing the first published photographs of Palestine: these were in 'Jérusalem' by Auguste Salzmann, which was issued in France. [79]

In his story, 'Terra Santa, aspirazione religiose', Igino Martorelli of Milano (1854) offers a few illustrations [80], notably of Jerusalem, Mount Tabor and Nazareth (figure 413).

In 1862, a gorgeous album, 'Souvenirs de Jérusalem', was printed in Paris, testifying to a visit to Palestine by a group of French naval officers ; [81] the large caravan setting out from Jaffa for Jerusalem (figure 281), and the group inspecting the fabled sights of the Holy City, are well portrayed.

Ermete Pierotti was an Italian engineer employed by the Turkish administration in Jerusalem in 1854-1866. He prepared a map of the city, and in 1864 published 'Jerusalem explored', with an abundance of illustrations. [82]

In 1858, an American traveller, Henry Stafford Osborn, wrote 'Palestine, past and present', [83] stressing, among other hazards, the trials of pilgrims arriving on a stormy day (figure 286).

William Thompson, an American too, was a missionary who spent twenty years of his life in Syria and Palestine in the middle of the nineteenth century. His work, 'The Land and the Book'', [84] has good views of Beersheba (figure 235), Lod or Lydda (figure 306), and of Haifa and Mount Carmel (figure 347).

The English scholar H. B. Tristram was often in Palestine, making his bold way into places until then unapproachable by Europeans. His 'The Land of Israel' [85] shows him in bivouac next to an ancient well in bleak Beersheba (figure 236), and also the ruins of Rabath-Ammon, to-day Amman, capital of the Hashemite Kingdom of Jordan (figure 475). A second book by him, 'Scenes in the East' (1870), has a coloured picture by A. A. Isaac: Jaffa and the area of sand dunes extending north of the town, where Tel Aviv now rises (figure 278). [86]

The German Count A. Wartensleben's 'Jerusalem Gegenwärtiges und Vergangenes' (1868) gives a vista of Jerusalem within its wall, drawn a short time after the first building of the New Town arose to the west (figure 38). [87]

In 1868, John MacGregor, being young and bold, explored the unknown region of the Hula Valley and its marshes in a flimsy canoe. His account is variegated by entertaining pictures of Beduin attacking him there (figures 461-464) and a map of the 'Hooleh Morass' (figure 465), which today have great contrasting historical significance, for the pestilential swamps have been drained by Jewish settlers and the valley is transformed into blossoming acres. [88]

Sir Charles William Wilson, a senior officer in the British Army, was among the first modern explorers of the Holy Land, in 1864-1865, and, on behalf of the War Office, prepared maps of Jerusalem; this was the first step towards the founding of the British 'Palestine Exploration Fund', which was to do such fine work in that field. Wilson also contributed to the preparation of a survey and detailed map of the Sinai Peninsula in 1868-1869. In 1880, publication began, in London, of his superb 'Picturesque Palestine', [89] which the German scholars Guthe and Ebers afterwards published in German with all its illustrations; [90] many of them also appear in V. Guérin's 'La Terre Sainte'. [91] Wilson's draftsmanship was excellent. Among his views of Palestine, Sinai and Syria, the following are of particular interest: the Holy Cave in the Dome of the Rock (figure 72), Jaffa Gate in Jerusalem (figure 129), the Cave of King Zedekiah adjoining the Damascus Gate, the Valley of the Brook Kidron and the Spring of Rogel, the Pools of King Solomon south of Bethlehem, a water-place (sebil in Arabic) at the entrance to Jaffa (figure 280), the square tower of Ramla (figure 302), the holy Tombs of the High Priests Eleazar and Pinhas beside Shekhem (Nablus), the ruins of Atlit, Castrum Peregrinorum of the Crusaders (figures 328-329), Rosh-Hanikra — Head of the Grotto (figure 392), the remains of a caravanserai near the Arab village of Lajjun (the Legion), next to Megiddo which is Armageddon, and, at Meiron, the Tombs of Shimon son of Yohai and Yohanan ha-Sandler (the cobbler) (figure 45). The last picture was subsequently copied by a devout Jew and printed on a separate folio with a Hebrew poem eulogising the holy men buried in Meiron. Other pictures from the same book which appear in this volume are the valley in Sinai named in Arabic Gharandal, probably Elim of the Wanderings (figure 497), the oasis named in Arabic Firan — Rephidim of the Holy Scriptures (figure 498), and the Mountains of Sinai (figures 515-516).

H. B. Tristram

Ch. W. Wilson

'La Syrie d'aujourd'hui', also of considerable proportions, was produced by the Frenchman P. Lortet, in 1884, [92] with numerous pictures drawn in the course of voyages to the Levant in 1875 and 1880. Among its hundreds of illustrations there are beautifully executed pictures of : two Jews in prayer at the Wailing Wall (figure 90), a learned argument in Jerusalem (figure 101), vendors of women's trinkets and kerosene lamps in Jaffa (figures 276-277), Ein-Karem, birthplace of St. John the Baptist (figure 153), the Monastery of Mar-Saba (figure 183), an ancient well of Beersheba (figure 237), the townlet of Lod or Lydda (figure 305), Acco under Turkish rule, with a battery of cannons on its battlements (figure 376), a private house in Acco (figure 388), a Moslem couple of Acco (figure 389), Tyre from the mainland (figure 394), the Arab village of Zarin on the site of ancient Jezreel (figure 403), Arab women filling pitchers at Mary's Well in Nazareth (figure 415), Jews of Tiberias (figure 430), the village of Majdal which was Magdala of Mary the Magdalene (figure 441), and the Valley of Hula seen from the village of Hunin (figure 456).

The Swiss couple, F. et E. Thévoz, were in the Holy Land in 1887, and published their collection of photographs, 'La Palestine illustrée', in 1888-1891 in Lausanne ; among them are the ancient harbour of Caesarea (figure 324), ruins of an ancient building in Caesarea (figure 325), the village of Tantura (figure 326), and the village of Achziv on the Mediterranean shore (figure 390). [93]

In 1894, the Paris publishing house, 'La Maison de la Bonne Presse', issued an 'Album de Terre Sainte' with almost five hundred photographs, with titles in French and Spanish, which had been taken by anonymous artists in Palestine in 1893 ; [94] among thtem are the town of Beit-Shean (figure 405) and the Gate of Tiberias which was demolished about fifty years ago (figure 431).

To study and scrutinize how bygone generations of draftsmen, painters and photographers saw — and sought in their pictorial arts to make immortal — the Holy Land and its historical sites is an instructive and enlightening pursuit, especially where great changes have recently occurred. Then do these illustrations bear visual witness to the majestic unfolding of the Land since the Children of Israel came back to their ancestral home.

1 Arculfus, Relatio de locis sanctis. T. Tobler, Planography of Jerusalem, 1858, pl. 1. J. Fergusson, Temples of the Jews, 1858, p. 240. P. Geyer, Itinera Hierosolymitana, 1898, pp. 231, 244, 250, 271.
2 Roma, Bibl., Vatican: Palat Graec, 431. Dictionnaire d'Archéologie Chrétienne, VII, 1927, p. 2677.
3 S. Paoli, Diplomatico del Sacro Militare Ordine Gerosolimitano, 1735. G. Schlumberger—F. Chalandon. Sigillographie de l'Orient Latin, 1943.
4 'Here begyneth a lytel treatyse of the Holy lande towarde Jherusalem', 1499.
5 M. Letts, Sir John Maundeville, 1949. Spencer Collection — M. Velser, 1482.
6 London, British Museum, Add. 37049.
7 British Museum, Add. 24189. G. F. Warner, The Buke of John Maundevill, 1889.
8 Jacobus de Verona, Liber peregrinationis, 1950. H.F.M. Prescott, Once to Sinai, 1948, p. 88.
9 Bernhard von Breidenbach, Peregrinationes, 1486. Erhard Reuwich (Rewich).
10 Conrad von Grünemberg: Das Heilige Land in Vergangenheit und Gegenwart, 1941, 1952. General-Landesarchiv Karlsruhe.
11 Rudimentum Noviciorum, 1475, Lübeck. A. E. Nordenskiöld, Facsimile Atlas, 1889.
12 H. Schedel, Liber chronicarum, 1493, Nürnberg.
13 Die Pilgerfahrt des Ritters Arnold von Harff, 1860.
14 Paris, Bibliothèque Nationale, Ms. français 9087, fol. 85v. J. Ebersolt, Orient et Occident, 1929, Pl. XI. Livre d'Heures de René d'Anjou. M. Join-Lambert, Jérusalem, 1956, p. 112-3.
15 Bibliothèque Nationale, Paris : Ms. français 247. P. Durrieu, Les Antiquités Judaiques et le Peintre Jean Fouquet, 1908.
16 Heinrich Wölfli (Lupulus), Mea Syriaca profectio. Syrische Reiss oder faart gan Hierusalem... 1582. (R. Röhricht, Bibliotheca Geographica, Palaestinae, 1890, p. 176). H. Bloesch, Heinrich Wölflis Reise nach Jerusalem, 1929. — Bürgerbibliothek.
17 Pierre Belon, Les observations de plusieurs singularitéz et choses mémorables trouvées en ... Judée..., 1553.
18 Bianco Noé, Viazo da Venecia al sancto Jherusalem et al monte Sinai, 1560 (?).
19 Sebastian Münster, Cosmografey, 1541.
20 J. Helfferich, Kurtzer und Wahrhaftiger Bericht von der Reise aus Venedig nach Hierusalem... auff den Berg Sinai... 1577.
21 Christophori Füreri ab Haimendorf... Itinerarium Aegypti, Arabiae, Palestinae... 1570.
22 Bernhard Walter von Walterswyl, Beschreibung Einer Reisz ausz Teutschland bisz in das gelobte Landt Palaestina unnd gen Jerusalem, auch auff den Berg Synai, 1609.
23 Salomon Schweigger, Reyssbeschreibung aus Teutschland nach Constantinopel und Jerusalem, 1581. J. H. Mordtmann: Mitteilungen zur Osmanischen Geschichte, I, 1921-2.
24 J. Zuallart, Il devotissimo Viaggio di Gierusalemme... 1587.
25 Johann van Kootwyck, (Joanne Cotovicus), Itinerarium Hierosolymitanum et Syriacum, 1619.
26 George Sandy, Travailes containing a History of the Turkish Empire... a Description of the Holy Land, of Jerusalem... 1615.
26* Antonio del Castillo, El devoto Peregrino y Viage de Tierra Santa, 1656.
27 "The rare and most wonderfull thinges which E. Webbe... hath seene... in his travailes in the cities of Jerusalem, Dammasko, Bethlehem and Galely and in the Landes of Jewrie..., 1590.
28 Barnardino Amico, Trattato delle piante et Imaginj de sacri edifizi di Terra Santa..., 1609.
29 Francesco Quaresmus, Elucidatio Terrae Sanctae historica, theologica, moralis, 1639.
30 Eugène Roger, La Terre Saincte, 1646.
31 Marie-Bernard du Sacré Coeur, Le Mont Carmel, 1911, p. 36.
32 Jean Doubdan, Le Voyage de la Terre Sainte, 1657.
33 Electus Zwinner, Blumen-Buch, Dess Heiligen Landes Palestinae, 1661.
34 Laurence d'Arvieux, Voyage... dans la Palestine, 1717.
35 Antonius Gonsales, Hierusalemsche Reyse, 1673.
36 Jacques Florent Goujon, Histoire et Voyage de la Terre Sainte, 1670.
37 Otto Friedrich von der Gröben, Orientalische Reise-Bescreibung, 1694.
38 Olf Dapper, Bescryving van gantsch Syrie en Palestyn of Heilige Landt, 1677. Asia oder genaue und gründliche Beschreibung des gantzen Syrien und Palestinas..., 1681.
39 Reyzen van Cornelius de Bruyn door de... van Aegypten, Syrien en Palestina, 1688.
40 Two Journeys to Jerusalem, 1650.
41 Henri Maundrell, Journey from Aleppo to Jerusalem at Easter 1697.
42 P. Antonio, Guida fedele alla Santa Città di Gierusalemme e descrittione di tutta Terra Santa, 1703.
43 A. Calmet, Dictionarium historicum, chronologicum, geographicum et litterarium Bibliorum, 1722.
44 P. Angelicus Myller, Peregrinus in Jerusalem, Fremdling in Jerusalem, 1729.
45 L. F. Cassas, Voyage pittoresque de la Syrie... 1886.
46 J. Praver, Historical Maps of Acco (Acre): Erez-Israel, II, 1953 (Hebrew).

[47] Barthelemy et Méry, Napoléon en Egypte, 1824.
[48] J. B. Spilsbury, Picturesque Scenery in the Holy Land and Syria delineated during the campaigns of 1799 and 1800, 1803.
[49] A Selection of Views in Egypt, Palestine ... from the original drawings by Rev. C. Willyams, 1822.
[50] L. Mayer, Views in the Levant, 1801. Views in Palestine (1804). Ansichten von Palästina, 1810-4.
[51] J. Ludwig Burckhardt, Travels in Syria and the Holy Land, 1822.
[52] James Silk Buckingham, Travels in Palestine through the countries of Bashan and Gilead, 1821.
[53] Louis N. Comte de Forbin, Voyage dans le Levant, 1819.
[54] William Rae Wilson, Travels in the Holy Land...., 1822.
[55] Comte Léon E. S. J. de Laborde, Voyage de l'Arabie Petrée, 1830-3.
[56] A. Dumas—A. Dauzats, Quinze jours au Sinai, 1839.
[57] Baron Taylor—Louis Reybaud, La Syrie, l'Egypte, la Palestine et la Judée..., 1839.
[58] British Museum : The Mount Sinai Manuscript of the Bible, 1934.
[59] E. Ch. Döbel, Wanderungen ... 1837-40.
[60] T. H. Horne, The biblical Keepsake, or Landscape Illustrations of the most remarkable places mentioned in the Holy Scriptures ... made from Original Sketches taken on the spot and engraved by W. and E. Finden, 1936. Landscape Illustrations of the Bible, 1836.
G. Gr(and)—A. Egron, La Terre Sainte ... Gravures ... de Rouargue, Aubert et autres artistes, 1837.
[61] J. M. Bernatz, Bilder aus dem Heiligen Lande ... Original-Ansichten ... 1839. Palästina, Neues Album des Heiligen Landes, 1855.
[62] David Roberts, The Holy Land from Drawings made on the Spot, 1842-9.
[63] Papers of the Corps of Royal Engineers, VI, 1843.
[64] Frances Egerton, Journal of a tour in the Holy Land, 1841.
[65] William Henry Bartlett, Walks in and about the city and environs of Jerusalem, 1844.
Forty days in the desert on the track of the Israelites, 1848. Footsteps of our Lord, 1851.
Jerusalem revisited, 1855.
[66] John Carne, Syria, The Holy Land (1845). [67] Henry Stebbing, The Christian in Palestine (1847).
[68] Otto Georgi, Die Heiligen Stätten nach Orginalzeichnungen nach der Natur, 1854.
[69] John Gadsby, Wanderings, 1855.
[70] W. F. Lynch, Narrative of the United States Expedition to the River Jordan and the Dead Sea, 1849.
[71] W. Tipping: Jewish Wars, ed. R. Traill, 1847-1851.
[72] J. Yanoski—J. David, Syrie ancienne et moderne, 1848.
[73] J. A. Spencer, The East, sketches of Travels in Egypt and the Holy Land, 1850.
[74] C.W.M. van de Velde, Reis door Syrie en Palestine, 1854. [75] Le pays d'Israel, 1857-8.
[76] E. W. Schulz, Reise in das Gelobte Land, 1852.
[77] J. J. Bourassé, La Terre Sainte, 1860.
[78] Jérusalem et la Terre Sainte, Notes de voyage, receuillies et mises en ordre par l'abbé G(eorges) D(arboy); Illustrations de M. Rouargue, 1852.
[79] A. Salzmann, Jérusalem—études et reproductions photographiques des monuments de la Ville Sainte, 1856.
[80] Igino Martorelli, Terra Santa, aspirazione religiose, 1854.
[81] Souvenirs de Jérusalem, Album dessiné par M. le contreamiral Francois Edmond Paris, lithogr. par M. M. Clerget, Bachelier, J. Gaildrau et Fichot, 1862.
[82] Ermete Pierotti, Jerusalem explored, being a description of the ancient and modern city, 1864.
[83] Henry Stafford Osborn, Palestine, past and present, 1858.
[84] W. M. Thompson, The Land and the Book, or biblical illustrations drawn from the manners and customs, the scenes and the scenery of the Holy Land, 1881.
[85] H. B. Tristram, The Land of Israel, a journal of travels in Palestine, 1865. [86] Scenes in the East, 1870.
[87] A. Graf Wartensleben, Jerusalem—Gegenwärtiges und Vergangenes, 1868.
[88] John MacGregor, Rob Roy on the Jordan, 1869.
[89] Ch. W. Wilson, Picturesque Palestine, Sinai and Egypt, 1880.
[90] G. Ebers—H. Guthe, Palästina in Bild und Wort, 1884. [91] V. Guérin, La Terre Sainte, 1882.
[92] P. Lortet, La Syrie d'aujourd'hui, Voyages dans la Phénicie, le Liban et la Judée, 1884.
[93] F. et E. Thévoz, La Palestine illustrée. Texte explicatif par Ph. Bridel (1888-1891).
[94] Album de Terre Sainte, ed. Maison de la Bonne Presse, (1894).

IV. THE HOLY LAND IN ANCIENT CHRISTIAN MAPS

The oldest views of Palestinian places are embodied in early maps of the Holy Land. The Madaba Map, on a Byzantine tessellated pavement of the sixth century, portrays a number of them with their Hebrew names rendered in Greek characters (see Chapter II).

Ancient maps always represent Jerusalem at the world's centre, obedient to the belief expounded by the Talmudic rabbis : 'The Land of Israel is in the centre of the world, Jerusalem is in the centre of the Land of Israel, and the Temple is in the centre of Jerusalem . . . '[1] A fascinating map of about 1250, attached to a Latin manuscript of the Psalms, now in the British Museum, shows Jerusalem at the mid-point of the world and all the continents clustered round it (figure 17).

A similar map, drawn about 1283, is preserved in Hereford, a country town of England (figure 18).[2] An earlier one, from the year 1224, is in Germany, in the monastery of Ebstorf, by which name it is known ; Haifa and its neighbour Acco appear on it (figure 331).[3]

A fantastic map of the world in the shape of a three-leaved clover, with Jerusalem set in the heart and the three old continents radiating outward, was published in 1585 in 'Itinerarium Sacrae Scripturae' by H. Büntig. In the bottom left-hand corner of it, the outline is marked of a section of a new territory, America—Terra Nova (figure 30).

Because of its sanctity to Christendom, no map of the Land of Israel, however ancient, failed to mention Jerusalem, and in the twelfth and thirteenth centuries, during the Crusader period, several such maps of the Holy City were produced. Dispersed now among several European libraries, they were catalogued and published, in modern times, by the German scholar R. Röhricht, in the German periodical dedicated to Palestinian research :[4] he presents a map of Jerusalem of about 1150, from the Library of Cambrai in France (figure 14),[5] a second, including the city's environs, of about the same antiquity, from the Royal Library of Belgium in Brussels (figure 15),[6] and three illustrated maps, one of about 1170, from the Library of the Hague (figure 13),[7] another of about 1180 (figure 19),[8] the third, also of the twelfth century, from the Library of Stuttgart in Germany (figure 16).[9]

Maps of Acco, which became the Crusader capital after Jerusalem had fallen into the hands of the Moslems in the thirteenth century, also began to appear in the Middle Ages. One such was drawn by the English monk Matheus Paris (Matthaeus Parisiensis) in the thirteenth century; he was one of the first scholars to study the history of Crusader Acco. The map belongs to a manuscript of Matthaeus, of which a copy is listed in the Library of Cambridge (figures 358-359).[10] Another map of Acco, dated 1330, is appended to the Latin work of the Italian historian Paulinus Puteolanus, and has survived in several copies, of which one is in the Library of St. Mark in Venice (figure 357).[11]

Among the many mediaeval maps of the Holy Land in pictured style, special interest attaches to a Latin specimen, from about 1300, in the Library of Florence,[12] showing: Bethlehem and the Tomb of Rachel (figure 161), Hebron and Abraham's Oak (figure 198), Gaza and its surroundings (figure 240), Haifa (figure 332), Nazareth, the Sea of Galilee (figure 437), Lake Hula and the sources of the Jordan (figure 458).

Marino Sanuto was a noble citizen of Venice, for many generations the main port of embarkation of pilgrims to the Holy Land. In 1310, about twenty years after the Crusaders had lost their last foothold in Palestine, Sanuto went east.

He travelled extensively through the countries of the Levant and made a thorough study of the situation in the Holy Land in contemplation of a renewed Crusade for the deliverance of the Holy Places from Moslem servitude. His final work, offered in homage to Pope John XII in 1321, [13] contained a map that showed the Jordan bisecting the Land in all its length, flowing first through the Sea of Galilee, then down to a Dead Sea of peculiar outline ; here, as Christian legend claims, the Jordan plainly derives its name from those of its two sources, the Ior and the Dan, and Lake Hula appears as Mei-Meron — the Waters of Meiron, a name long used by Christian pilgrims (figure 460). There are two smaller pictorial maps in Sanuto's manuscript : one of Jerusalem and roundabout (figure 22) and the other of Crusader Acco (figure 356).

Two other maps of Jerusalem were made during the fourteenth century ; today one is in the Bibliothèque Nationale of Paris (figure 20) [14], and the second in the Laurentianna Library of Florence (figure 21). [15]

A more varied choice of views, among them the Dead Sea and its shores (figure 219), Jaffa (figure 263) and Haifa (figure 334), characterizes the Latin map in a book written by William Wey, an Englishman who twice went the way of the pilgrimage, in 1458 and in 1462. [16]

A still wider selection of panoramas illuminates the great chart which the German voyager of 1483, Bernhard von Breidenbach, drew up to accompany his study of the Holy Land under Moslem-Mameluke rule (see Chapter II).

The Arab literature of the period, as always devoid of illustrations, provides no pictures of the Holy Land, except for a pictorial map of the fifteenth century, which presents the Temple court and, conspicuously in its centre, the Mosque of Omar. This the Moslems call the Dome of the Rock, after the sacred outcrop over which it is built, the Rock of Foundation of Jewish tradition. The Mosque of el-Aksa is drawn next to it (figure 67). [17]

As time went on, many more maps of the Holy Land were published, mostly pictorial and, more often than not, altogether imaginary, the cartographer's guiding purpose being to give prominence to the famous sites, heedless utterly of true proportions or geographical scales. In the sixteenth century, when Palestine was in the thrall of the Mamelukes, a few new maps, and some atlases as well, were issued. The first atlas desrving of the name, although far from recording exact contours, was a Latin compilation eked out with a collection of maps of the Holy Land, which was published by the German Jacob Ziegler in 1538 ; [18] the Dead Sea, for example, takes on a strangely elongated form (figure 220).

The Frenchman Antoine Regnault, a visitor in 1549, also included maps in his opus 'Discours du Voyage d'oultre mer au saint sépulchre de Jérusalem' (1573) ; significantly one of the Holy Land is at its beginning and one of the wanderings of the tribes of Israel in Sinai is at the end. [18*]

In 1555, an instructive map appeared, the labour of Adam Reisner, and seemingly the first German map of the Holy Land. [18**]

In 1572, a new edition of the Scriptures was published in London, known as the 'Bishop's Bible' ; one appendix was a pictorial map of Palestine, the first such to be printed in England; the cartographer, Humphrey Cole, carefully inscribed his name on his handiwork. [19]

In the Bibliothèque Nationale of Paris, among a collection of Latin maps drawn by an unknown cartographer and named after the famous geographer of the second century, Ptolemaeus, there is at least one pictorial map of Jerusalem which merits attention (figure 33). [20]

At the end of the sixteenth century the Dutch cartographer, Christian van Adrichom, who had visited the Holy Land in 1590, published a large collection of maps of the country and its capital, which signalize a definite improvement on previous attempts, although still nothing like precise. The Dead Sea, stumbing-block of most cartographers of the age, is drawn with a pointed end at its southern extremity and, in docile acceptance of the biblical narrative, with the five cities of sin plunged beneath its nauseous waters. Undoubtedly this was the model from which, a century later, Abraham the son of Abraham drew his own map of the Dead Sea which came out in 1695 in Amsterdam as adornment of a Passover Haggadah (figure 224). [21]

Although he never enjoyed the boon of a pilgrimage to the Holy Places, the English monk Thomas Fuller, a prolific writer, repaired his grievous omission by devoting himself to the study of the Holy Land, and so acquired a profound knowledge of all the pertinent literature. In 1650 he published a work fittingly entitled 'A Pisgah-Sight of Palestine', equating his own status to that of Moses, who from the height of Pisgah glimpsed only a distant view of the Land he would not have the joy to enter. Fuller's work is enriched with many a pictorial map: the most striking are the Dead Sea and the five accursed cities drowning in its waters (figure 223), the Sea of Galilee through which the Jordan passes in a separate flood with no mingling of waters, as the legend tells (figure 438), and Sinai and the path followed by the tribes of Israel on their way to the Land of Canaan (figure 488). [22]

Antonius Gonzales, a traveller in the year 1667, left an interesting account of his journeys, also handsomely illustrated (see Chapter III), and with a beautiful map of Mount Carmel, the first in literature, the altar of Elijah on its crest and dense pillars of smoke rising into the sky (figure 353).

Eighteenth century sightseers in Acco, then in Turkish hands, have bequeathed us maps of the town and its surroundings. The author of one was the Englishman Richard Pococke, in 1738 (figure 362), of another the German C. Niebuhr in 1766 (figure 363) [23]. Acco, besieged during Napoleon Bonaparte's brief incursion into Palestine in 1799, is drawn with great exactitude on a large French map which marks the lines of the investing army (figure 373) ;[23] an English edition of this map was published in the report of the party of Royal Engineers which toured the Holy Land in the first half of the nineteenth century to study, especially, the fortifications of the towns along the coast. [24]

1 Tanhuma, Kedoshim 10. Midrash Tehilim 50, 1.
2 L. Miller. Die Hereford Karte, 1903. G. R. Crone, The Hereford World Map. 1948.
3 Ebstorf Karte : K. Miller Mappae Mundi, V, 1896.
4 R. Röhricht Zeitschrift des Deutschen Palästina-Vereins—ZDPV.
5 Cambray (no. 437) : ZDPV, XIV, 1891, Ta. 4.

[6] Bruxelles, Bibliothèque Royale de Belgique (no. 9823-24, fol. 157). M. de Vogüé, Les Eglises de la Terre Sainte, 1860, p. 411.
[7] Haag, Bibliothèque Royale (sign 69) : ZDPV, XV, 1892, Ta. [8] ZDPV, XV, 1892, Ta. 1.
[9] Stuttgart, Staats-Bibliothek (Pass, no. 56, 57, 58) : ZDPV, XV, 1892, Ta. 4.
[10] Matthaeus Parisiensis Mss.: 1) London (1) Royal 14, C, VII, fol. 2a—5a. (2) Landsdowne 253, fol. 228. 2) Cambridge, Corpus Christi College (1) XVI (2) XXVI.
[11] Paulinus Puteolanus, Chronologia Magna de passagiis in Terram Sanctam.
[12] Florence, Bibliotheca Laurentiana : ZDPV, XIII, 1890, Ta. 1.
[13] Marino Sanuto Torselli, Liber secretorum fidelium Crucis: Bongars, Gesta Dei per Francos, ZDPV; XXI, 1898, Ta. 4-5.
M. de Vogüé, Les Eglises de la Terre Sainte, 1860.
[14] Paris, Bibliothèque Nationale (fonds latin no 8865, fol. 133) : ZDPV, XXI, 1898, Ta. 5.
[15] Florence, Bibliotheca Laurentiana (plat. LXXVI, no. 56, fol. 97 v) ; ZDPV, XXI, 1898, Ta. 8.
[16] The Itineraries of William Wey, 1857 ; ZDPV, XXVII, 1904.
[17] Ch. Schefer, Safer nameh, Relation du voyage de Nassiri Khosrau, 1881.
Al. Gayet, L'Art Arabe, 1893, p. 40.
[18] L. Ziegler, Quae intus continentur, 1532.
[18*] A. Regnault, Discours de Voyage d'oultre mer au saint sépulcre de Jérusalem, 1573.
[18**] A. Reisner, Jerusalem die alte Haubstat der Juden, 1563.
[19] Bishop's Bible : Canaan ... at this daye ... called the holie lande. H. Cole, 1572.
[20] Ptolemaeus : Paris, Biblothèque Nationale (fonds latin 4802).
[21] Christian van Adrichom, Theatrum Terrae Sanctae, 1590.
[22] Z. Vilnay, The Hebrew Map of Eretz-Israel, 1945, p. 17 (Hebrew).
T. Fuller, A Pisgah-Sight of Palestine, 1650.
[23] R. Pococke, Description of the East, 1743-5. C. Niebuhr, Reisebeschreibung, III, 1837, p. Ta. VIII.
[24] Papers of the Corps of Royal Engineers, VI, 1843.

V. ILLUSTRATIONS OF THE HOLY LAND IN HEBREW MANUSCRIPTS AND PRINTS

It was not until the Middle Ages that sacred shrines and historical sites of the Holy Land began to be illustrated in Hebrew literature. They were crude and unsophisticated drawings made by folk artists who had never beheld the places they drew. They could, then, give full rein to their imaginings, and, however adolescent their attempts, the very artlessness of them all the better expressed the love of the Jew for his faraway homeland and his longing for its hallowed spots.

The Book of Ezekiel is actually the first Hebrew text to mention and to describe a picture of Jerusalem: 'Thou also, son of man, take thee a tile, and lay it before thee, and trace upon it a city, even Jerusalem; and lay siege against it, and build forts against it, and cast up a mound against it; set camps also against it and set battering rams against it. [1]

The façade of the Temple of Jerusalem is reproduced on one side of a coin dating from Bar-Kochba's rebellion in 134 A.D. (figure 55). Rabbis of the Talmud refer to a coin struck with the image of 'David and Solomon on one side and Jerusalem the Holy City on the other side', [2] but so far no coin of that description has come to light.

The same Rabbis tell of a golden ornament, engraved with a picture of Jerusalem, with which Jewish women were wont to bedeck themselves in memory of the Holy City: it was known as 'Yerushalayim de-Dahava' — Jerusalem the Golden, and also as Ir-Zahav — City of Gold, one of Jerusalem's many Hebrew names. Rabbi Ovadia of Bartinoro explains the expression 'City of Gold' as follows: 'an ornament designed in the shape of a city like unto Jerusalem'.

It is told that second-century Rabbi Akiva prepared a 'City of Gold' for his wife, and the tale adds that 'Jerusalem was pictured on it'.[3] No such ornament has yet been discovered.

Frescoes of the third-century synagogue of Dura-Europos excavated on the banks of the Euphrates, in what was once Babylonia and is now Eastern Syria, show the Temple and the Wall of Jerusalem (figure 58) and various biblical events; one such event is the passage of the Red Sea with the Egyptians drowning in the waters while the tribes of Israel cross on dry land (figure 499). All the frescoes of Dura-Europos are now in the Arab Museum of Damascus.[4]

In the sixteenth century a number of pamphlets were written about the sacred shrines in Eretz-Israel. For the Jewish people, sundered then from its native soil for more than fifteen hundred years, they were the main source of information about a Fatherland that was so distant in geography yet so close to the nostalgic heart. For the fortunate few who had experienced the joy of visiting the Holy Land, the pamphlets were precious guides which companioned them on their journeys along historic paths to sites inseparable from dear memories of the past.

One of the most widespread was the Hebrew brochure entitled 'Lineage of Patriarchs and Prophets', written in 1537 and copied by Uri ben Shim'on of Zefat in 1564. It was first printed in 1659, with a Latin translation and a wealth of fictional pictures of the tombs of sanctified personages in Jewish history; Rachel (figure 163); the sons of Jacob and his daughter, Dinah; the kings of the House of David in Jerusalem (figure 136), and his father Jesse in Hebron; shrines of prophets of renown— Samuel, Isaiah, Zechariah, Hosea, Hulda, and Ezekiel in Babylonia; and the legendary tomb of Queen Esther in Kefar-Bir'am in Upper Galilee.

In the brochure are numerous reproductions of the monuments of men outstanding in the Mishna and the Talmud from the second to the fourth century, for example: the Cave of the Sanhedrin and of Simon the Just in Jerusalem; the Tombs of Rabbi Shimon and his son (figure 449*); of Hillel the Elder and his pupils in Meiron; of Rabbi Hanina son of Dosa and his wife in Arab, a village in Lower Galilee; and of Yosi the Galilean and his son, Ishmael, in the village of Dalton in Upper Galilee. There are also designs of the Temple in Jerusalem, the palace of King Solomon (figure 64), and the adjoining Gate of Mercy, which is the Golden Gate of Christian tradition.

In 1598, in the hamlet of Cassel Monferrato in northern Italy, an anonymous Jewish artist copied down the text of 'Lineage of Patriarchs and Prophets', and contributed to it new illustrations out of his own musings. Professor Cecil Roth published this remarkable manuscript in 1929, together with its pictures, both in Hebrew and in English translation. The illustrations represent for the most part the Holy Places in Eretz-Israel, such as: the synagogue of the Ramban (Nahmanides) in Jerusalem (figure 91), Jericho surrounded by its seven walls (figure 211), a view of the town of Gaza showing the relics of the temple of Dagon which Samson brought tumbling down on the heads of the Philistines (figure 239), and the holy tombs of Tiberias (figure 428).

A picture of Jericho surrounded by seven circular walls had appeared long before in a manuscript of the Bible, known after its original owner as the

Farhi Bible, which was written in 1366; it is in the Sassoon Library in England (figure 210). A similar representation of fortified Jericho, together with a picture of the accoutred tribes of Israel led by Joshua blowing the horn, appears in the book 'Zikaron be-Yerushalaim' — 'Remmebrance in Jerusalem, that it shall be a memento to the sons of Israel and an everlasting memory of the Lovely Land' — which was published in Turkey in 1743 ; the inscription above the picture is as follows : 'People of Israel, look and behold the miracle that is written in the 'Book of Hayashar', the wall of Jericho that crumbled down' (figure 212).

A leaflet entitled 'Epistle Telling the Lineage of the Righteous of the Land of Israel' was published in Venice, in 1626, with a description of the holy tombs, and seems to have met with great success in Jewish quarters, for it went through many reprintings in subsequent years. Ya'acov Babani, a Sephardi rabbi of Zefat, included the text of it in his book 'Zikaron Yerushalaim' — Memorial of Jerusalem , which came out in Amsterdam in 1759. The publisher had wished to enhance this with pictures of what it described, but, possessing none, put in, at random, decorations, circles and lines in bizarre and, in some cases, absurd semblance of the Holy Places. A picture of the Western or Wailing Wall appears here for the first time, with phrases above the tiers of stone : 'This is the form of the Western Wall,' and God's words to Solomon, 'Mine eyes and My heart shall be there perpetually' [4] (figure 74).

A small pamphlet entitled 'Kissaot le Beit-David' — Thrones of the House of David, written by J. A. Mehattof, appeared in 1646. It featured a rough and entirely concocted representation of fortified Jerusalem with the Mosque of Omar at its centre as symbol of the ancient Temple, and the following quotation : 'For there were set thrones for judgment, the thrones of the House of David'. [5] (figure 48).

Another book, printed about 1655, and written in Yiddish, gets its Hebrew title from Isaiah, 'And the ransomed of the Lord shall return and come with singing unto Zion.' [6] It carries on its front page a picture of the Holy City with the Hebrew rubric, 'The Holy Temple and Jerusalem' (figures 49-50). This drawing, which retains the original Latin explanation, was manifestly borrowed from a non-Jewish source. It is noteworthy that a similar drawing, with a like explanation, adorned the title-page of the English edition of Cranmer's Bible in 1540, and also the frontispiece of the Latin book 'Totius Terrae Sanctae', by Martin de Brion, which appeared in Paris in the same year. This last may be the original from which all later copies were made.

In the sixteenth and seventeenth centuries the Temple of Jerusalem often figures in Hebrew literature in the guise of the Mosque of Omar ; on the frontispiece of the book 'Zevah Pessah' — The Paschal Lamb, in the year 1545, it passses as the trademark of the Italian printer, Marco Antonio Justiniano; it also is present in the first edition of the 'Travels of Rabbi Petahia', printed in 1595, and, in the book 'Levush-Haora' — Garb of Light, of Rabbi Mordekhai Jaffe, printed in 1604 (figure 66), in 'Zikaron be-Yerushalaim' — Remembrance in Jerusalem already variantly cited, and in 'Rishon le Tsiyon' — First in Zion, by Rabbi Haim Ben-Attar, written and printed in Jerusalem in 1750 (figure 65).

A number of Passover Haggadahs in the Middle Ages essayed to portray the beloved shrines of Eretz-Israel. The famous Haggadah of Sarajevo (Yugoslavia), about the fourteenth century, presents 'make-believe' drawings of the Temple (figure 59), Mount Sinai and the revelation of the Law (figure 517), the transfer of Jacob's bones from Egypt to Hebron for burial in the Cave of Machpelah (figure 188), and Lot's wife turned into a pillar of salt at Sodom (figure 228). One, of the fifteenth century, which belonged to Baron Edmond de Rothschild and is now in the Bezalel Museum in Jerusalem, includes among its beautiful illustrations a picture of Sodom, upon which the Angel of God is hurling fire and brimstone ; it is edifying that, as here pictured, Sodom resembles a mediaeval Italian town (figure 227).

In a Haggadah of the year 1665 'with a few designs of all the omens', Jerusalem is sketched with the Messiah on a donkey drawing near, preceded by Elijah sounding the horn of redemption (figures 39-40), the tribes crossing the Red Sea and falling upon Jericho (figure 209),

An artistically finer picture of the Messiah dignifies a manuscript of the beginning of the seventeenth century (figure 41). Another Haggadah, which was first published in Amsterdam, in 1629, and reprinted many times, offers a still broader range of subjects ; among them the Egyptians drowning in the Red Sea (figure 500), and the holy sanctuary in Jerusalem in all its glory (figure 63). A pictorial map of Eretz-Israel is appended, and the doomed cities are shown sunken in the Dead Sea (figure 224). The illustrations, and the map as well, are the work of a single artist who styles himself 'Abraham, son of Jacob of the family of Abraham the Patriarch', but was in fact a Christian monk who adopted Judaism and took this unarguably Jewish name.

A manuscript Haggadah of about the year 1709 displays a curious picture of the Holy City within its fortified wall, with the prayer : 'Next year in Jerusalem' (figure 51) : Jerusalem, its wall and gates appear again in a Haggadah printed in Trieste in 1864 (figure 52).

Very illusory illustrations of the Holy City titivate marriage contracts (ketubot) of earlier days. Their purpose was to beautify the ketubot by decorative versions of those Hebrew portions of Jeremiah which are part of the traditional wedding ritual : 'Yet again there shall be heard . . . even in the cities of Judah, and in the streets of Jerusalem . . . the voice of joy and the voice of gladness, the voice of the bridegroom and the voice of the bride'.[7] Occasionally, the embellishment came from the Psalms : 'If I forget thee, O Jerusalem, let my right hand forget its cunning . . . If I set not Jerusalem above my chiefest joy'.[8]

A likeness of Jerusalem is also emblazoned on ketubot originating in Italian towns ; some of them have been reproduced in the relevant literature, as, for instance, a ketubah from Mantua, dated 1638, which is in the New York Public Library (figure 44). A lovely view of 'Jerusalem and mountains around her' illustrates a ketubah written in 1727 in the Italian village of Rivarolo (figure 45) ; a similar one, found in a ketubah of 1738, is preserved in the Jewish Museum in London, while yet a third, of 1776, comes from Ancona (figure 46).

A picture of Jerusalem, all tricked out with vine leaf tendrils and clusters of grapes, was printed in Mantua in the sixteenth century, on a large roll of bunting to festoon house and booth during the Feast of Tabernacles (figure 42).

Another picture of Jerusalem, on the background of the encompassing mountains, appeared in 1650 in a Yiddish booklet, now very rare, with the Hebrew title 'Darkei-Tsiyon' — Ways of Zion (figure 47).

The Jewish Museum in New York possesses a precious curtain of the Holy Ark of Italian origin, from the year 1681: Jerusalem is embroidered in its centre, with the Gate of Mercy (Golden Gate) showing clearly in the eastern wall; among the houses is conspicuous a large building in the style of the Mosque of Omar, as always typifying the Temple of old, and, above, the Psalms are cited: 'I set Jerusalem above my chiefest joy' [9]. Above Jerusalem on the curtain rises Mount Sinai, with another verse of the Psalmist set in a semi-circle around its peak: 'the mountain which God hath desired for His abode', [10] and two Tables of the Law. At the bottom, the artist has embroidered her own name: Simha the wife of Menahem Levi Meshulami 1681 (figure on page 32).

A new edition of 'Tsena u-Rena', a Yiddish translation of the Pentateuch, was issued in Amsterdam about 1766; one of the few extant copies is in the Schocken Library in Jerusalem. Among other themes, it presents the biblical account of Moses on Mount Sinai, the spies carrying great bunches of grapes from Hebron, Moses contemplating the Land of Canaan from Mount Nebo, the Holy Ark borne from Kiryat-Ye'arim to Jerusalem, Samson carrying off the gates of Gaza (figure 241), and the Prophet Elijah sleeping under a juniper bush in the desert, on his way to Mount Sinai.

In the nineteenth century, landscapes of Eretz-Israel began to be found in Hebrew books printed mainly in Jerusalem and in Zefat. Still childish and crude, they nevertheless portrayed Holy Places whose history was familiar to every Jew from early childhood, and, if he could not satisfy his yearning to fling himself down in worship at the hallowed sites themselves, he could at least seek vicarious comfort in looking upon their likeness. Pictures of Jerusalem and of other shrines were reproduced on napkins used to cover the Sabbath loaf, on paper sheets with which booths were made festive during the Feast of Tabernacles, and on miniature banners waved by children on Simhat Torah, the Rejoicing of the Law.

Naturally, Jerusalem is the focal theme of this popular art. Pictures of the Temple site, towards which Jews turn in prayer, are especially frequent. Ironically, the Temple itself, as we have seen, is set forth in the image of the Mosque of Omar, and the large dome stands out prominently on Mount Moriah. The Wailing Wall, a relic of the ancient western wall of the Temple area, is represented in manifold styles. Overlooking it are the Mosques of Omar and Aksa which now occupy the historic site (figures 80-85). Of particular appeal is the group of Jewish worshippers at the Wall, with passages from Isaiah and Jeremiah circling the picture. This illustration first appeared in the book 'Shalom Yerushalaim' — Peace of Jerusalem, by Shalom Adani, printed in Jerusalem in 1899 (figure 84).

In some instances there are also reproduced the monument to the kings of Davidic lineage, located, according to ancient belief, on the height known as Mount Zion (figures 139-141), the Tower of David which projects from the wall nearby (figures 132-135), and the main synagogues of the Old City: Hurva (figure 93), Tiferet Israel — Glory of Israel (figure 94), and the place of study known as Beit-El — Lord's House, centre of Cabbalist learning (figure 95).

The Mount of Olives rises east of Jerusalem and overlooks the Old City. According to legend, here the resurrection will take place in the fullness of time ; hence the desire of many Jews to be buried in its precious soil. Some books use it to illustrate Zechariah's description of the Lord's appearance on the Day of Judgment [11] : 'Then shall the Lord go forth . . . and His feet shall stand in that day upon the Mount of Olives' (figure 151). Zechariah's tomb is traditionally shown at the foot of the Mount, and is reproduced on the front page of the Jerusalem edition of 'Shevet Musar' — The Rod of Correction (1863), a popular work by Rabbi Shelomo Abraham Hacohen; the Wailing Wall and the Cave of Machpelah in Hebron are also reproduced in it.

The sepulchre of Shim'on Hazadik — Simon the Just — was a shrine deeply venerated by the Jews of Jerusalem. It was he who taught, 'Upon three things the world standeth : upon Torah, upon Worship and upon the practice of Charity'. [12] Each year the pious made the pilgrimage in their thousands to his tomb, until the Arab Legion of Jordan seized the area during the War of Liberation in 1948 ; some prints of Jerusalem include a picture of the monument.

The ancient town of Ramah, on a height in the vicinity of Jerusalem, is the traditional site of the Tomb of the Prophet Samuel, sanctified also in Arab folklore as en-Nebi Samwil. The Arab village built around the Tomb, which is often portrayed in writings published in Jerusalem, bears the same name. Here many Jewish pilgrims used to assemble to do homage to the Prophet's memory.

The Tomb of Rachel, on the highway to Bethlehem, was also once the cynosure of myriads of Jewish pilgrims (figure 173).

The Cave of Machpelah in Hebron, burial-place of the Patriarchs and Matriarchs of Israel, is pictured in several books, but the illustrations in many respects diverge from the building that now stands on the spot, and their only common feature are the towers on either side ; the Cave appears also on a seal of the Jewish community of Hebron (figures 190-191, 196).

Jericho, the first city captured by the Israelites when they invaded Canaan under Joshua, is known in Hebrew as Ir-Hatemarim — City of Palms ; consequently, it is always drawn in a setting of palmettos (figure 213). There are pictures, too, of the historic city of Shekhem standing in a narrow vale between Mount Gerizim and Mount Ebal. At the foot of Gerizim is Joseph's Tomb and, next to it, that of his sister Dinah, daughter of Jacob. The tomb of Hamor, recorded in the Torah as the founder of Shekhem, is situated on top of the mountain (figures 311-312). 'Hamor', meaning an ass in Hebrew, was seemingly regarded as an offensive name, and so the grave is often left unmarked in the drawings (figure 313).

Haifa, too, attracted devout and prayerful interest among Jewish pilgrims because of its nearness to Mount Carmel, with the Cave of Elijah on its ascent and the Tomb of Elisha on its crest (figures 348-351).

Pictures of Zefat, city of the mystics, and of Meiron close by, celebrated as the burial-place of Rabbi Shim'on son of Yohai, are printed in several books (figures 446-449). Zefat is divided from Meiron by a deep and rocky vale of famous wild beauty, Gei Hatahanot — Glen of the Mills (in Arabic: Wadi at-Tawahin); long ago, evidently, many busy millers channelled the flood waters of the ravine to grind the neighbouring corn. Gei Hatahanot is 'identified' in the picture by lone sails, although it is not known that any windmill ever turned on that exact spot (figure 450).

The frontispiece in a number of books printed in Zefat itself in the middle of the nineteenth century displays the building in Meiron where are the Tombs of Rabbi Shim'on son of Yohai and his son Elazar (figure 449). Great crowds gather from all over Israel to attend the annual ceremony of remembrance at the Rabbi's grave, and Jewish visitors from overseas take part enthusiastically. A few years ago, to mark the anniversary, a scroll was printed bearing a picture of the shrine at Meiron and that of Rabbi Yohanan ha-Sandlar (the cobbler) which adjoins it, and a poem lauding the saintly men of Meiron; the picture was, in fact, copied from a non-Jewish source (figure 451).

In the village of Peki'in, amid the mountains of Upper Galilee, west of Meiron, tradition sets the cave to which Rabbi Shim'on and his son escaped from the Romans, and where the Rabbi is reputed to have composed the Zohar, the standard text of Cabbalist theosophy ; a conjured etching of the cave is on the front page of 'Ben Yohai', a book printed in 1815 in praise of the renowned Shim'on. Legend has it that father and son lived in the cave for thirteen years, eating the fruit of a carob tree that grew at its entrance, and drinking from a spring that flowed miraculously at hand. Both tree and spring were figured on the seal of the Jewish community of Peki'in.

At the beginning of the nineteenth century Rabbi Joseph Schwarz of Germany settled in Jerusalem, and in 1832 began the writing of his 'Tevuot Haarets' — Crops of the Land, — first printed in Hebrew in Jerusalem in 1845, then in German (1852) and English (1858), with a few illustrations (figure 79). In 1837 he finished another labour ; on a large sheet he assembled illustrations of the principal Jewish shrines of the Holy City ; in the centre the Wailing Wall and the sacred buildings of the Temple area ; to the east the Mount of Olives with the Tomb of the Prophetess Hulda ; to the right of the Wailing Wall, the traditional Tomb of King David and the Jewish Quarter of the Old City, (figures 97, 144), on the left, twin views of the Tower of David as seen from outside and from inside the city (figures 134-135) ; on top a small plan of Jerusalem, the first such to appear in Hebrew (figure 98). This sheet purported to be, as the inscription of it says, 'A loving gift sent to my brethren who are in the Diaspora, the well-wishers of Zion and Jerusalem (may it be rebuilt soon in our days, Amen!), the year 1837. Made by the humble youth Joseph Schwarz. And I had it distributed among (the people of) Israel by my beloved brother, my master Rabbi Haim Schwarz, may his light shine . . . '

The influence of the work of Joseph Schwarz can be traced in an unusual tabernacle (succa) brought from Germany to the Bezalel Museum in Jerusalem : on its wooden panels are pictures of Jerusalem and of Holy Places that are clearly inspired by Schwarz's original design (figure 81). This booth belonged to the Daller family of Fishakh, a little town in Bavaria, and was safely conveyed to the Bezalel Museum on the eve of the Second World War, thanks to the tireless efforts of H. Feuchtwanger, a Jerusalem scholar and collector of Jewish ritual objects.

Many more scrolls depicting holy shrines and sites made their appearance in the nineteenth century. One, in manuscript, from the year 1800, is also in the Bezalel Museum. Another, in colour, from the year 1839, was presented to Sir Moses Montefiore on his visit to the Holy Land and is now kept in Jews' College in London. A third was the work of Haim Zev Ashkenazi, a Jerusalem printer (figure 53), and a fourth is by S. Pinie of Zefat, who printed a pictorial map of Eretz-Israel, in about 1875, both on paper and cloth, showing the main towns, the saintly tombs, Jerusalem with its shrines (figure 54), the Dead Sea, the Jordan and Jericho (figure 226), Haifa, Mount Carmel and Acco along the seashore (figure 348), Tiberias and its venerable sepulchres (figure 429), and Zefat itself and its environs (figure 446).

Rabbi Shaul Horenstein, renowned as the author of the Hebrew book 'Givat-Shaul', printed, too, colourfully naive drawings of sacred sites and shrines in the Holy Land, among them Shekhem and Joseph's Tomb (figure 311), Zefat and its revered graves (figure 447), and Meiron with the shrine of Rabbi Shimon and his son Elazar (figure 452).

The Jewish Museum of New York has among its most prized exhibits a large wooden 'Chair of Elijah', from about 1900 (figure 86), discovered in an unknown synagogue. Engraved copper plates adorn it : in the centre of the back is a carving of the Wailing Wall (figure 87), and around the seat are incised the Tomb of King David on Mount Zion (figure 140), the Tomb of Zechariah and the 'Hand' of Absalom, the monument over the Cave of Machpelah (figure 193), and palm-embowered Jericho (figure 214).

Pictures of Mount Sinai and the giving of the Torah are also to be found in Hebrew literature. One is of the fourteenth century, from the Sarajevo Haggadah (figure 517), another, dating back to 1723, appears in the 'Book of Customs' printed in Amsterdam (figure 518) and is reproduced with fair accuracy in the Yiddish edition of 'Tsena u-Rena' (figure 519) ; there is also one in a prayer-book of the beginning of the nineteenth century (figure 521).

[1] Ezekiel 4, 1. [2] Babli, Baba Kama 97b.
[3] Mishna, Shabat 6, 1. Babli, Shabat 29a ; Nedarim 50a ; Yerushalmi, Shabat 6, 1.
[4] E. L. Sukenik, The Synagogue of Dura-Europos and its Drawings, 1947 (Hebrew).
[5] Psalm 121, 7. [6] Isaiah 35, 10. [7] Jeremiah 33, 10—11. [8] Psalm 137, 5—6. [9] Psalm 137, 6.
[10] Psalm 68, 17. [11] Zechariah 14, 1—11. [12] Ethics of the Fathers, 1, 2.

AN ASSYRIAN BAS-RELIEF OF A BESIEGED CITY

1. An Assyrian Bas-Relief of a Besieged City About 700 B.C.

The mountain-top town is surrounded by a fortified wall, which is buttressed by a tall tower. As Assyrian soldiers charge, the defenders on the battlement discharge arrows and hurl stones at them. At the bottom of the bas-relief are vines and other trees, possibly palms. Below, fish swim in a river.

Above the tower, the concluding words of an Assyrian cuneiform inscription say: '...alammu I besieged and its booty I took'. '...alammu' may be, with a slight alteration, the last letters of 'Urusalimmu', the Assyrian form of the name Jerusalem. The river would be the Jordan, which the Assyrian forces had to cross on their way.

The bas-relief was unearthed during the excavation of Nineveh, capital city of the Assyrian king Sennacherib, whose siege of Jerusalem is described in the Bible. It is displayed in the British Museum.

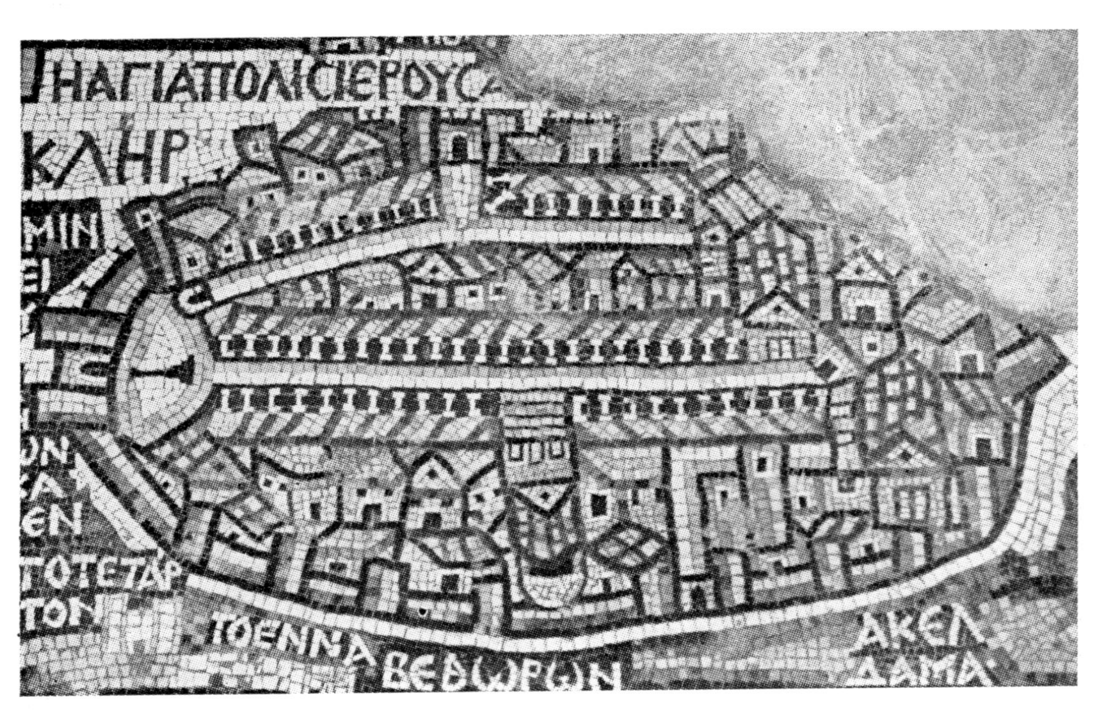

2. Jerusalem in the Map of Madaba Sixth Century

This pictorial map of the Holy Land, which includes the notable sites with their ancient names inscribed in Greek, is named after the town of Madaba in Transjordan, the biblical Medeba, where it was found by chance in 1896. It dates back to the sixth century, in the Christian-Byzantine era, and is preserved in the floor of the Orthodox Church where it was first discovered.

Explanation on the next page

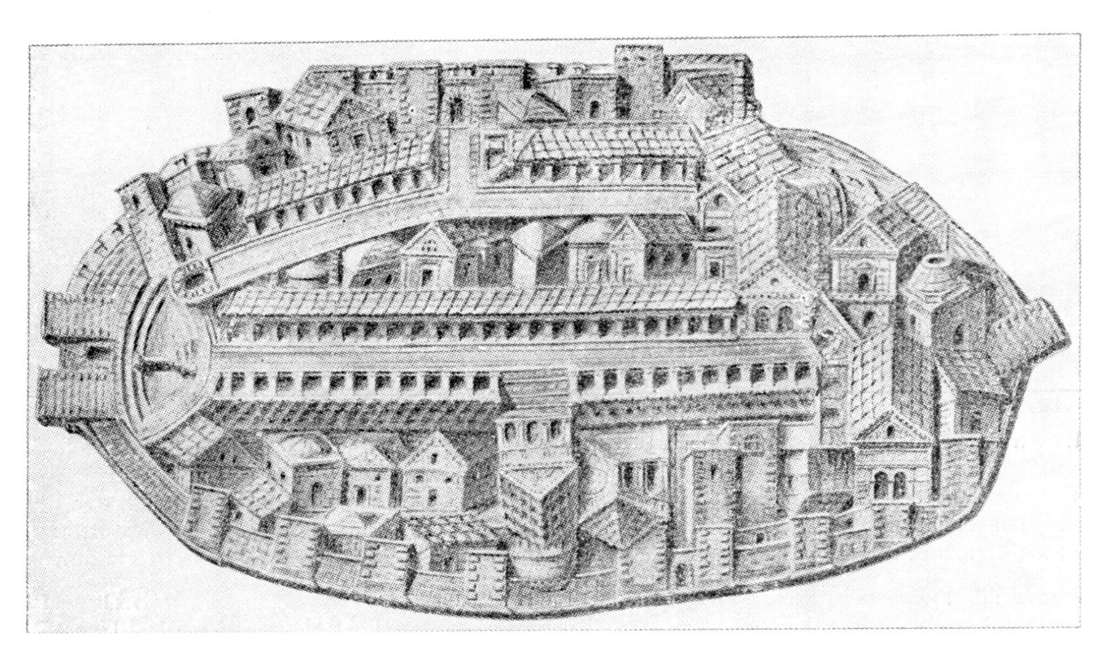

3. Jerusalem in the Map of Madaba Restoration

The map was restored in 1912 by Mauricius Gisler, a Benedictine monk at the Abbey of the Dormition on Mount Zion, Jerusalem.

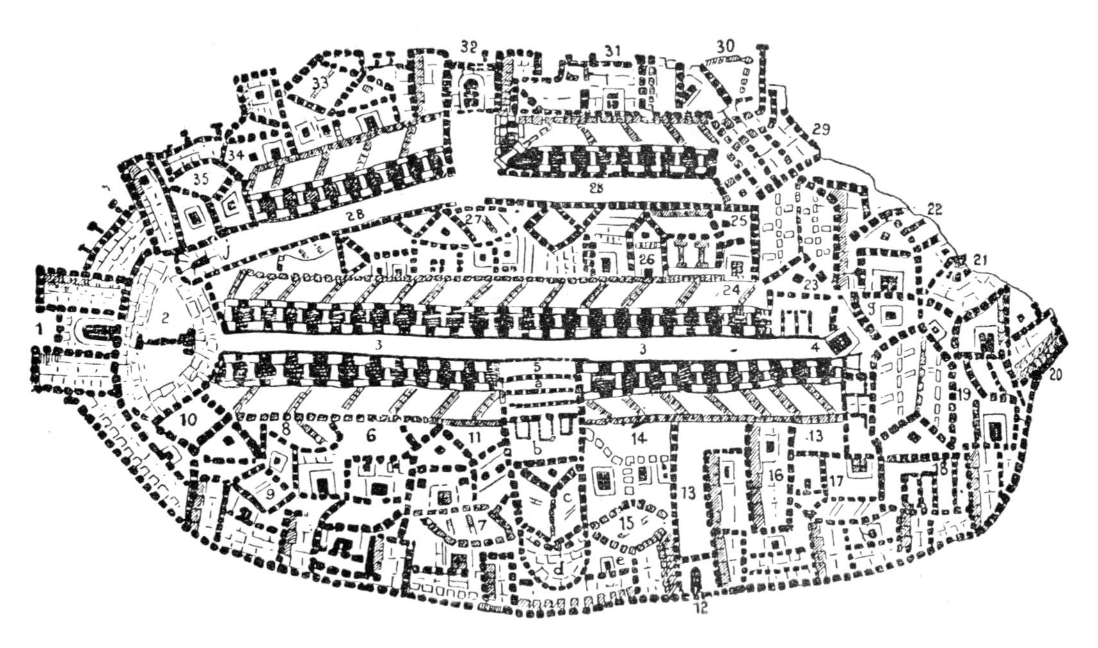

4. Jerusalem and its famous sites in the Map of Madaba

1) The northern gate, on the site of to-day's Damascus Gate. 2) A pillar opposite the gate marks the starting point of all measures of distances in the Holy Land. Possibly for this reason the gate is known in Arabic as Bab-el-Amud – Gate of the Pillar. 3) Main street, with rows of pillars, running from the northern to the southern gate. 4) The southern gate, on the site of the modern Zion Gate. 5) Church of the Holy Sepulchre, called by the Byzantines Anastasis or Resurrection. 6) Palace of the Byzantine Patriarch. 7) Building occupied by the priests officiating at the Holy Sepulchre. 8) The goldsmiths' market. 9) Church of St. Theodore. 10) Church of St. Serapion. 11) Church of St. Sergius. 12) The western gate on the site of the modern Jaffa Gate. 13) Public square. 14 – 15) Pools. One of them occupies the site of the pool contemporarily named after King Hezekiah. 16) Fortress, on the site of the Tower of David. 17) The house of Caiaphas, the High Priest in the time of Jesus. 18 – 19) Church of Holy Zion, which stood on the site of the present-day Mount Zion. It was a splendid building and famed as 'the Mother of all the Churches'. To-day, the site is occupied by the building which contains the so-called Tomb of King David and the Abbey of the Dormition. 20) Southern tower. 21 – 22) Churches next to the Pool of Siloam. 23) New Church – Nea, erected by Emperor Justinian. 24) Gate. 25) Courtyard. 26) Church of St. Sophia. 27) Church. 28) The eastern street, to-day's Valley Road, leads to 29) An unidentified structure, possibly the Wailing Wall. 30) Building bordering on the Temple Court. 31) The eastern gate, which is the Golden Gate or Gate of Mercy of Jewish tradition. 32) Other eastern gate, where to-day is St. Stephen's Gate. 33) Church of St. Anne, which still occupies the same spot; it belongs to the Catholic 'White Fathers'. 34) Church. 35) The Palace of Empress Eudocia, who came to Jerusalem in the year 449 and built the church which is named after her.

Two sites outside the wall of Jerusalem, but famous in Christian tradition, are indicated: Aceldam or Hakaldema (Field of Blood) and Gethsemane[1]. Another extra-mural site mentioned in the map is Beit-Horon, north of Jerusalem, on the ancient main road to the Coastal Plain. Left of Beit-Horon there is written in Greek, 'to Enna(ton)' – 'the ninth' (mile), and also, 'to Tetarton' – 'the fourth' (mile). They were stations on the highway leading from Jerusalem northwards to the Coastal Plain, with the indication of the distance from the capital in Roman miles.

On the left hand of Jerusalem, the name of the tribe of Benjamin is inscribed with the words of Moses' blessing: 'He covereth him all the day, and He dwelleth between his shoulders'[2].

1) Matthew 27, 8. Mark 14, 32. 2) Deuteronomy 33, 12.

JERUSALEM IN MOSAICS OF CHURCHES IN ROME

5. Jerusalem in the Church of Santa Pudenziana Fourth Century

A large picture of Jerusalem and its churches occupies the background of a mosaic of Jesus blessing his disciples and followers. In the centre is Mount Golgotha – Calvary, with the Church of the Holy Sepulchre.

Santa Pudenziana is the most ancient of Roman churches. It is built on the site of Pudens' House, where St. Paul was a guest on his visit from Jerusalem.

6. Jerusalem in the Cathedral of San Giovanni in Laterano Fifth Century

The picture is set in the upper part of the portico of San Venanzio. On the right – Jerusalem (next figure). On the left – Bethlehem (see: Bethlehem).

7. Jerusalem Fifth Century

See previous figure.

8. Jerusalem – Hierusalem Fifth Century

In a mosaic of the Church of Santa Maria Maggiore.

9. Jerusalem in San Lorenzo fuori le Mura — Outside the Walls — Sixth Century

Left of the arch is a picture of Jerusalem, with its name in Latin characters — Hierusalem. Right — a picture of Bethlehem with its name inscribed over the entrance gate. Above the arch are Christian saints. On the left stands Pelagius II, the founder of the church, holding a model of the building. The Church of San Lorenzo and its mosaics were completed in the year 578.

10. Jerusalem and Bethlehem, in a mosaic of San Vital of Ravenna — About 540

On the left is Jerusalem — Hierusalem, and on the right — Bethlehem.

11. Jerusalem and Bethlehem, in a mosaic of St. Peter of Rome Fifth Century

From the book, De sacris aedificiis a Constantino Magno constructis historia, by G. G. Ciampini, 1693, III, pl. XIII-

Jerusalem is surrounded by a wall reinforced by circular towers and pierced by gates. Within the town rises a pillar carrying a cross, which is surmounted by a human face representing Jesus.

Each of the six gates is designated by a serial number adjoining the name. At the west, Occidens, there stand, on the right the Gate of David : Porta I, David, on the site of the Jaffa Gate of to-day, on the left: Porta II, Ville Fullonis – Gate of the Fuller's House. The Fuller's House is unknown to-day; but the 'Way of the Fuller's Field', in Latin – Via Agri Fullonis, is recorded in the Holy Scriptures[1] and Josephus Flavius mentions the 'Tomb of the Fuller'[2].

On the left, facing north – Septent(ri)o, is the Gate of St. Stephen – P(orta) III Scti Stephani, today the Damascus Gate. Above, facing east, Oriens, the Gate of Benjamin opens – P(orta) IIII Benjamin, possibly on the site of to-day's Herod's Gate, which faces north towards the area occupied of old by the tribe of Benjamin. Next to it is the Small Gate – P(orta) Parvula, possibly on the site of the Dung Gate. Further to the right appears the Gate of the Tekuites–P(orta) VI Tecuitis, possibly on the site of the Zion Gate and named after the town of Tekoa, which lay south of Jerusalem. The Book of Nehemiah mentions its inhabitants, the Tekuites, among the builders of the Wall[3]. Above the Small Gate an inscription reads: 'From here one descends by steps to the Valley of Jehoshaphat' – ab hac pgd' (per gradus) ad vallem iosafat descenditur.

1) Kings II, 18, 17. Isaia 7, 3. 2) Wars, 5, 4, 2 3) Neh. 3, 5.

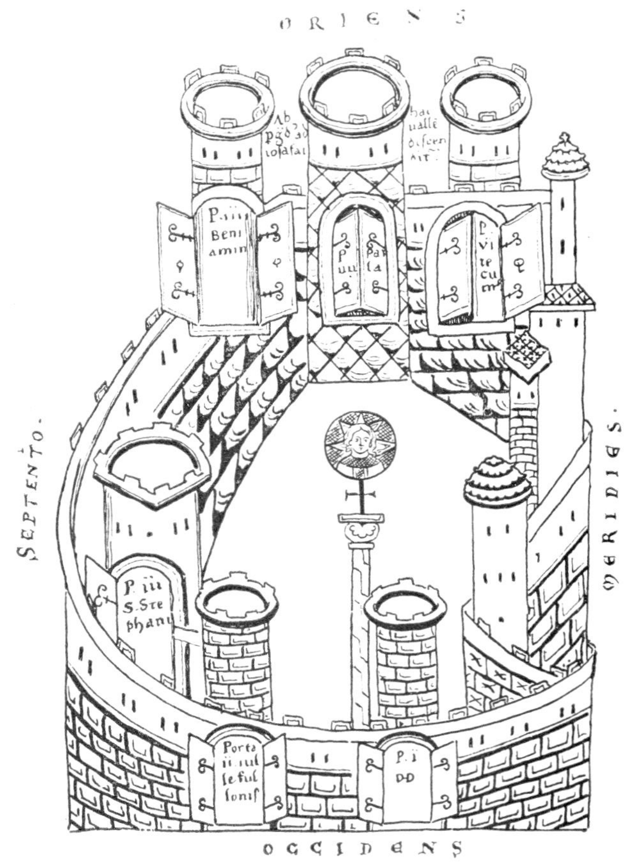

12. Map of Jerusalem Seventh Century

Attached to the travel book of Arculfus – 670.

13. Map of Crusader Jerusalem About 1170

Manuscript preserved in the Library of The Hague, Holland.

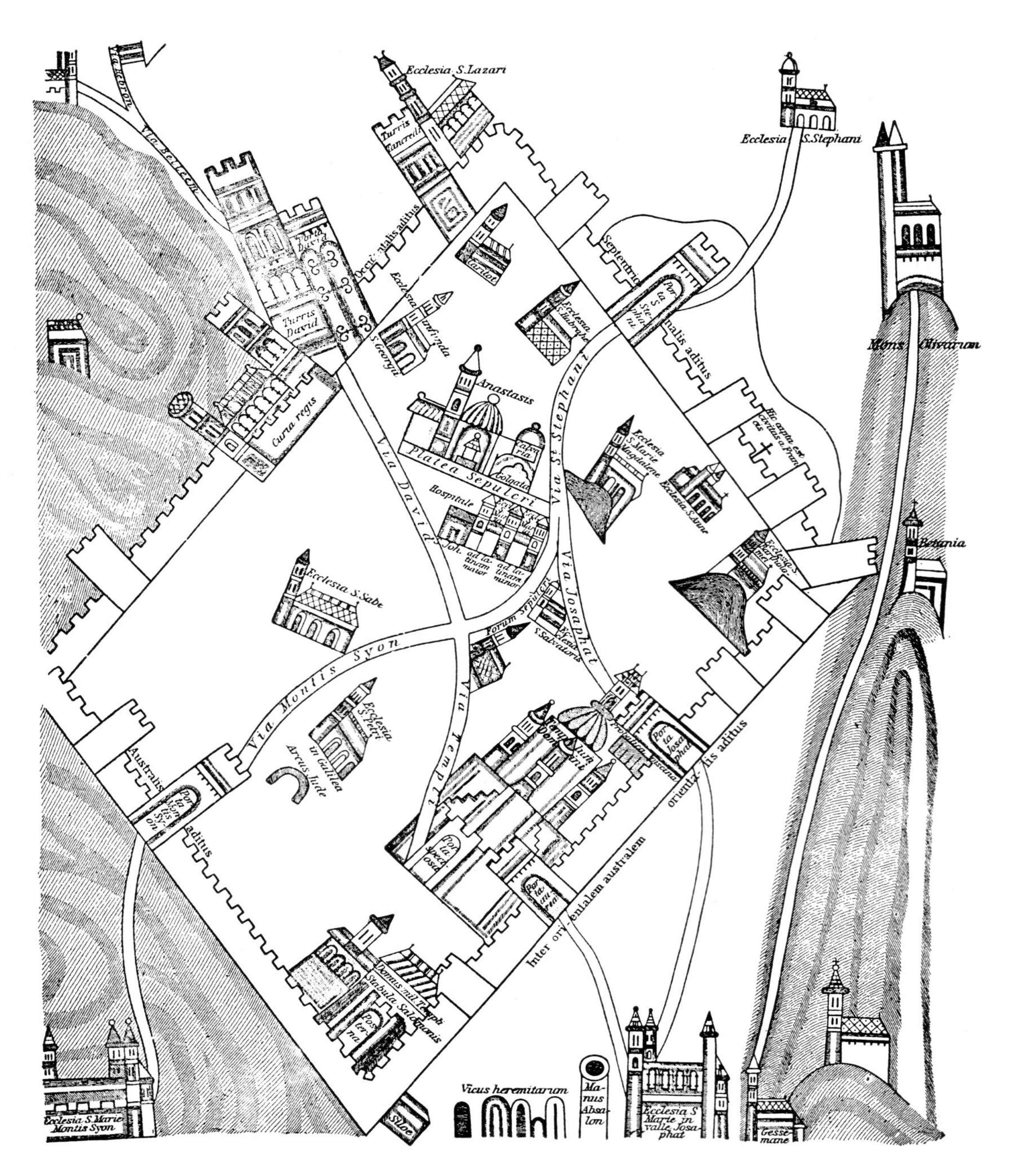

14. Map of Jerusalem of the Crusaders About 1150

The manuscript, illustrated in colours, is preserved in the public library of Cambrai (No 438).

Jerusalem is surrounded by a wall with gates and towers. At the top left stands the Tower of David – Turris David, and, to the right, the Gate of David – Porta David, on the site of the Jaffa Gate. The portals and their iron bolts are clearly drawn. On the left is the royal palace – Curia regis, the seat of the Crusader kings. Two important roads, to Bethlehem – Via Betleem, and to Hebron – Via Hebron, start from this gate.

From the Gate of David a main street – Via David, continues into the town and meets the Street of the Temple – Via Templi, which leads to Templum Domini – the Temple of the Lord – the Mosque of Omar of today. It is entered by the Gate of Beauty – Porta speciosa, mentioned in the New Testament. The southern end of the Temple Courtyard is filled by a large building – Domus mil(itum) Templi, and the Stables of Solomon – Stabula Salomonis, an underground structure known to this day, with its small postern gate – Posterna, situated at the place of the Single Gate which is now walled up.

The southern wall affords a passage at the Gate of Mount Zion – Porta Montis Syon, whence a road leads, outside the town, to the Church of St. Mary on Mount Zion – Ecclesia S. Marie Montis Syon, standing within the area now occupied by the Tomb of King David. Via Montis Syon traverses the town alongside the Church of St. Peter in Galilee – Ecclesia S. Petri in Galilea, next to the Arch of Judah – Arcus Jude. *

Farther on, the street Montis Syon passes by the Church of St. Saba – Ecclesia S. Sabe, dedicated to a famous monk of the fourth century, who lived in the monastery bearing his name that still survives in the Wilderness of Judah. Beyond again, the road leads to the Holy Sepulchre, identified by its Greek name Anastasis – Resurrection, built on the Hill of Golgotha – Golgota, in Latin – Calvaria. Across the Platea Sepulcri – the Square of the Tomb – is a shrine dedicated to St. Mary – Eccl(esia) S. Marie ad latinam maior (and) ad latinam minor, adjoining the Hospital of St. John – Hospitale S. Joh(annis). Next to the Holy Sepulchre is the Church of St. Salvador – Ecclesia S. Salvatoris, patron saint of today's large Franciscan monastery in the Old City of Jerusalem. North are the Churches of St. George – Ecclesia S. Georgii, and of St. Habrahe, a name unknown today.

At the corner of the wall there rises the Tower of Tancred – Turris Tancredi, perpetuating the memory of a Crusader knight who won fame in the conquest of Jerusalem from the Moslems. To this day remains of it are shown in the vaults of a school kept by the 'Frères' near the New Gate. Next to the tower is the Church of St. Lazarus – Ecclesia S. Lazari.

The northern section is divided by the Via S. Stephani, leading through the gate of the same name (today, Damascus Gate) to the church dedicated to the saint – Ecclesia S. Stephani, now occupied by the Dominican monastery.

In the north three churches are shown: St. Mary Magdalene – Ecclesia S. Marie Magdalene, St. Bartholemew – Ecclesia S. Bartholomei, and St. Anne – Ecclesia S. Anne. The last-named is still in existence; it belongs to the Catholic 'White Fathers'.

A large cross near the corner of the northern wall marks the spot where the Crusaders breached the wall in July 1099 – Hic capta est civitas a Francis.

St. Stephen Street joins Jehoshaphat Street – Via Josaphat, which bears into the Jehoshaphat Gate – Porta Josaphat, in the eastern wall. Another gate opening in this wall is the Golden Gate – Porta aurea, now blocked up – the Gate of Mercy of Jewish tradition.

From the two eastern gates, roads lead to the Church of St. Mary in the Valley of Jehoshaphat – Ecclesia S. Marie in valle Josaphat, which today belongs to the Greek Orthodox Church. Beside the church, on one side is Gethsemane – Gessemane, on the other – the Hand of Absalom – Manus Absalon, a monument well-known to this day, and farther on the Street of the Hermits – Vicus heremitarum, near the Pool of Siloam – Siloe.

To the east rises the Mount of Olives – Mons Olivarum, with Bethany – Betania. To the south, near Gethsemane, is an unidentified church; apparently it stood on the traditional site of Jesus' Ascension. Part of its ruins are still to be seen on the summit of Olivet.

*) A Crusader description of Jérusalem from the year 1231 also mentions the Street of the Arch of Judah – Rue de l'Arc Judas. Ernoul, L'estat de la Cité de Jérusalem: Michelant–Raynaud, Itinéraires à Jérusalem, 1882, p. 43.

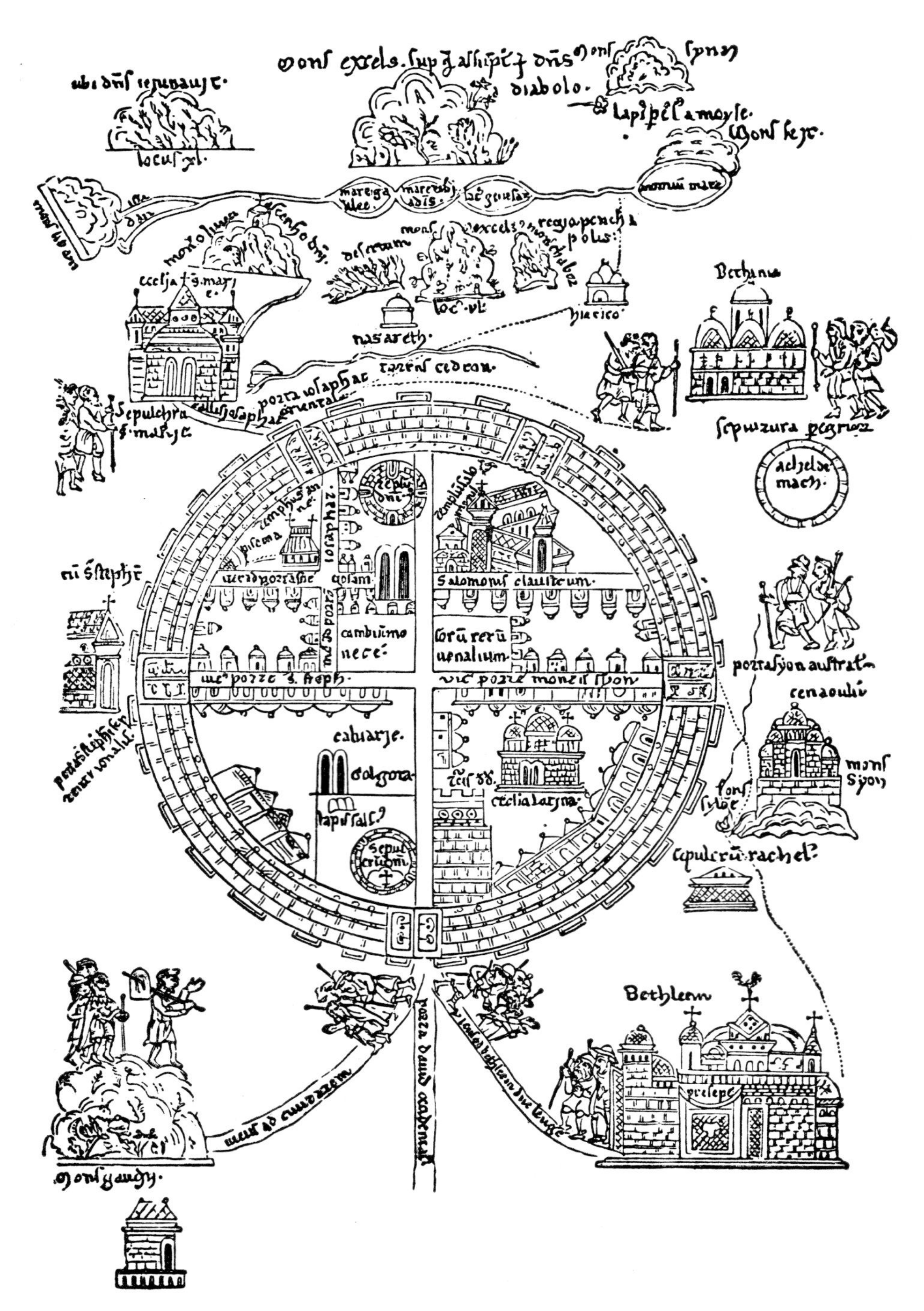

15. Map of Crusader Jerusalem and its Surroundings About 1150

Manuscript in mediaeval Latin preserved in the Royal Library of Brussels.
(Ms. No. 9823 – 24. Fol. 157)

Jerusalem is surrounded by a circular wall, with its tiers clearly outlined. Five gates are set symmetrically around. The town is divided into four equal quarters by two perpendicular streets. Important buildings are shown within and around.

Explanation on the next page.

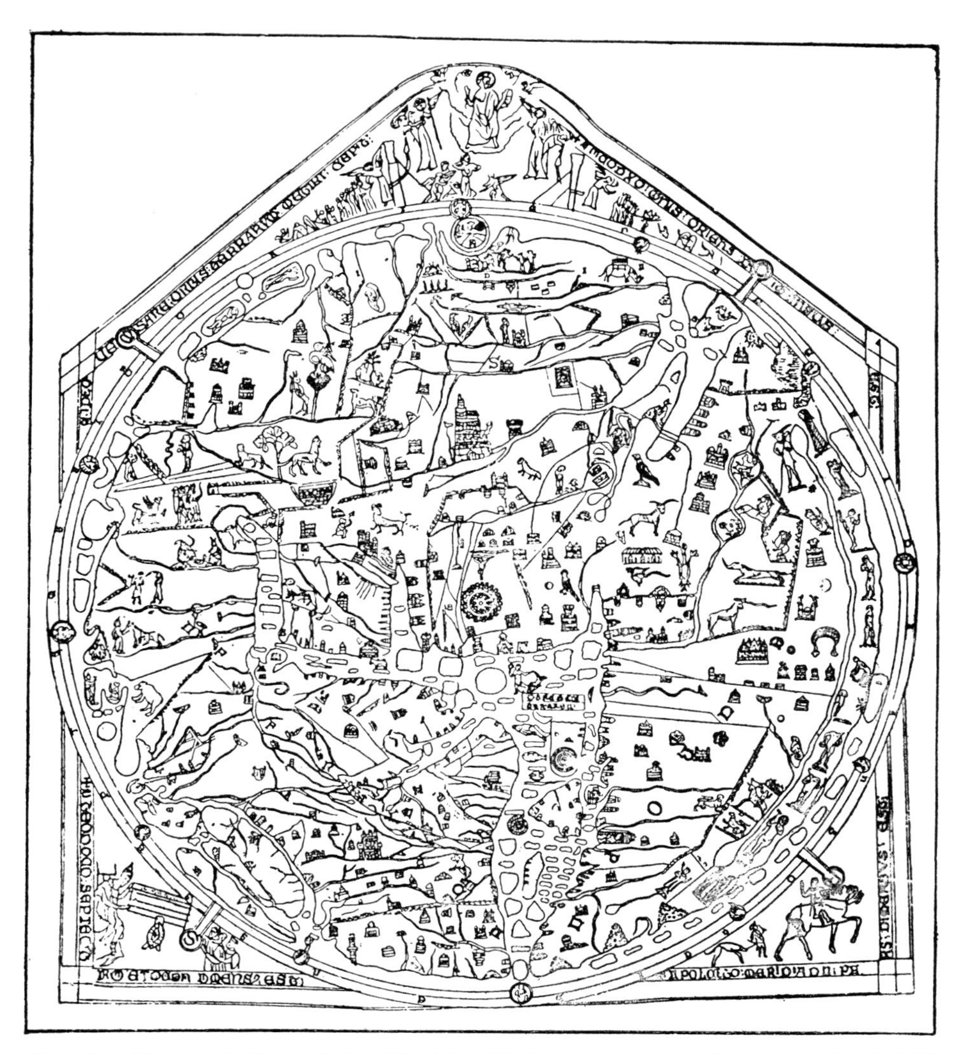

18. The Hereford Map of the World, with Jerusalem in the Centre About 1283

Preserved in the ancient cathedral of Hereford, England.
One of the oldest maps of the world.

Jerusalem is represented in the centre as a wheel-shaped circle. Various sites are indicated around it: the Mount of Olives, the Valley of Jehoshaphat, Bethlehem. The Coastal Plain shows the celebrated cities of Gerar, Gaza, Ashkelon, Yavne – indicated by its Greek name of Jamnia, Lod – Diospolis, Jaffa, Acre, and others.

The Jordan is pictured with its twin sources: Jor and Dan, and the Sea of Galilee. The Jordan takes the waters of the River Jabbok, shown descending from the Mountains of Gilead. In the south, Moses appears on Mount Sinai, and nearby is the track followed by the Israelites in their wanderings from Egypt to Canaan.

Around its border the map is decorated with pictures of plants and animals mentioned in the Holy Scriptures, a bird with a parrot's beak, another bird and next to it a horned deer, the legendary salamander which often recurs in folklore, a mandrake root in human form.

In the frame are various figures and inscriptions. At the bottom on the left hand is the name of the map's composer: Richard de Holdinghame e de Lafford. Both places are known in Lincolnshire to this day, the second as Saliford.

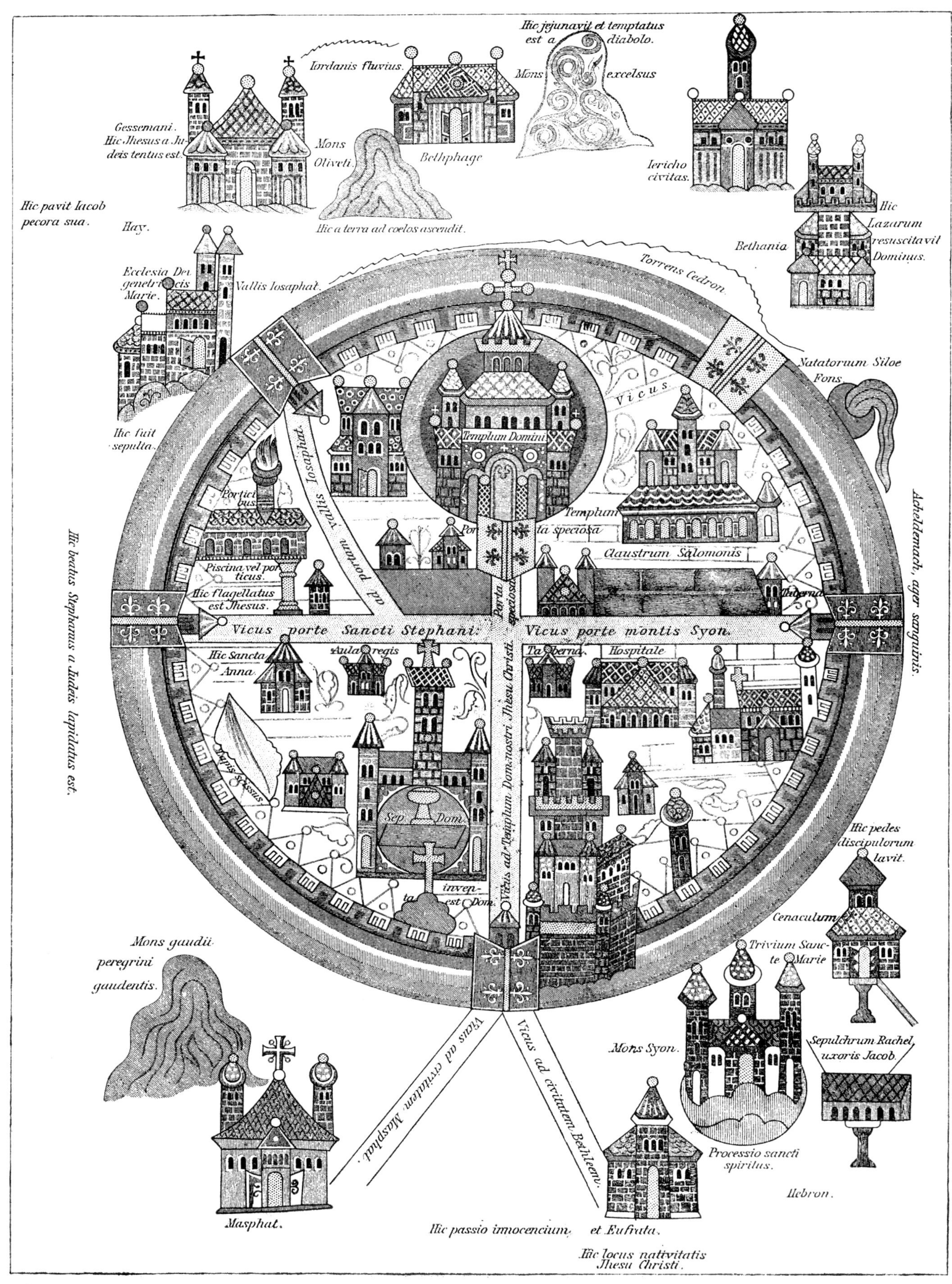

19. Map of Crusader Jerusalem — About 1180

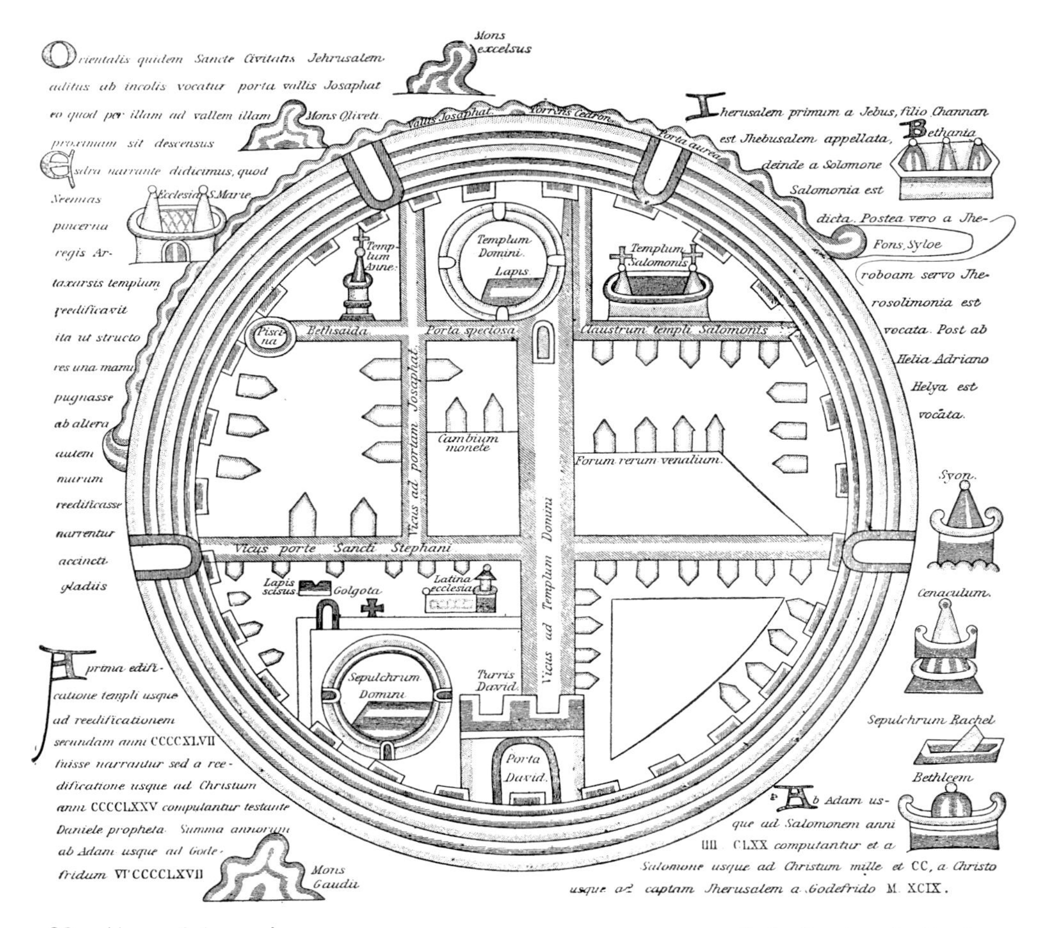

20. Map of Jerusalem Early Fourteenth Century

Jerusalem is enclosed within a circular wall pierced by five gates set symmetrically around it. All the sites usually mentioned in similar maps of the period appear: Porta David for today's Jaffa Gate, Sepulchrum Domini – the Holy Sepulchre, Templum Salomonis for the El-Aqsa Mosque, the Coenaculum, the Brook Kidron – Torrens Cedron, and so on. Two unusual additions deserve mention: the Stone — Lapis, designating the large rock which occupies the centre of the Mosque of Omar — Templum Domini, the same rock on which, legend tells, Abraham was ready to sacrifice his only son Isaac to the glory of the Almighty; and the Latin inscription that surrounds the map on all sides and purports to convey part of the history of Jerusalem from its earliest times until its conquest by the Crusaders under Godfrey de Bouillon, in 1099. It reads as follows:

> 'The eastern entrance to the Holy City, Jerusalem, is called by the inhabitants the Gate of the Valley of Josaphat, because by it one descends to that nearby valley.
>
> In Ezra's narrative we learn that Nehemiah, the cupbearer of King Artaxerxes, rebuilt the Temple in such a way that the workers, their swords by their sides, fought with one hand and built the wall with the other.
>
> From the first building of the Temple to its reconstruction there are said to have been 447 years, and from its reconstruction to Christ 475 years are computed according to the testimony of the Prophet Daniel. The total number of years from Adam to Godfrey is 6467.
>
> Jerusalem was first called Jerusalem after Jebus, the son of Canaan, then named Solomonia after Solomon. But afterwards it was called Jerosolimonia after Jeroboam, the servant (of Solomon). After that it was called Helya after Helia Hadrian.
>
> From Adam to Solomon there are 4170 years, and from Solomon to Christ 1200, from Christ to the capture of Jerusalem by Godfrey 1099.

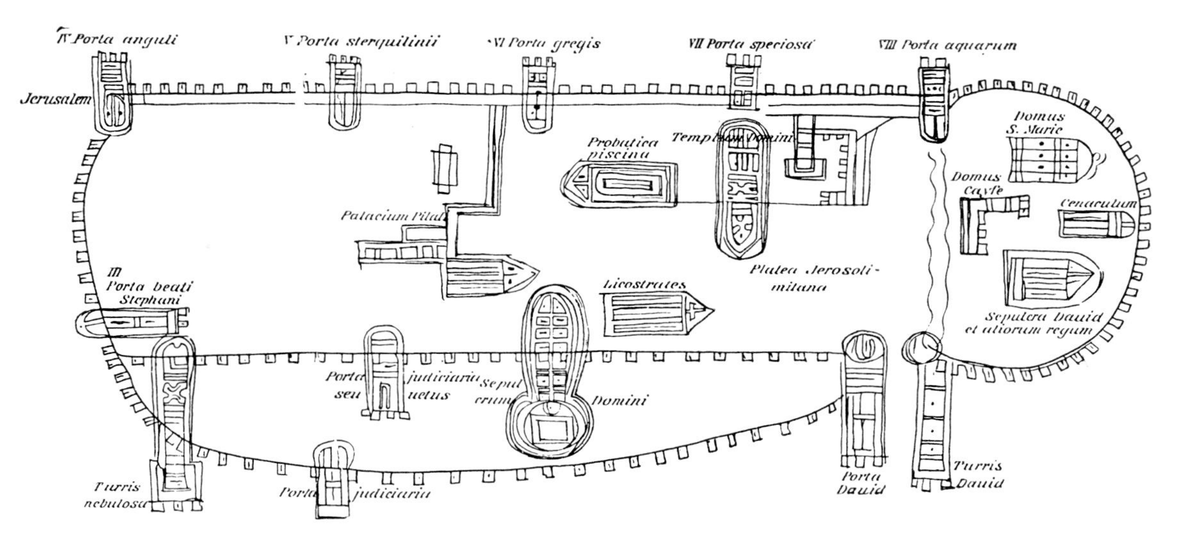

21. **Map of Jerusalem** About the Fourteenth Century

Manuscript preserved in the Laurenziana Library of Florence (Plut. LXXVI 56, fol. 97).

Jerusalem is surrounded by a fortified wall with its towers and gates; the largest is at the bottom of the picture, the Gate of David — Porta David, and protected by the Tower of David — Turris David; left of it, on the same side, is the Gate of Justice—Porta Judiciaria, and within the town another gate bearing the same name. Through the Gate of Justice, according to Christian tradition, the Romans led Jesus to crucifixion outside the city precincts; it is mentioned for the first time in the Christian literature of the Middle Ages.

Left of the Gate of Justice is a tower marked Turris nebulosa. The reference is of course to Nablus, the Arabic name of Shechem, and a corrupted form of the original Latin Neapolis — New Town; but the cartographer transcribed the sound of the Arabic word he heard into nebulosa, which means cloudy. Near the Tower of Nablus is the Gate of St. Stephen — Porta beati Stephani, by which, it is believed, the saint was taken out of the Holy City to be stoned to death. Today its site is occupied by the Nablus Gate, whence the road to Nablus starts.

Various gates mentioned in the Bible are indicated along the eastern wall under their Latin names: the Corner Gate — Porta anguli, the Dung Gate — Porta sterquilinii, the Sheep Gate — Porta gregis, and the Beautiful Gate — Porta speciosa of the New Testament. Near the last is the Gate of Waters — Porta aquarum. All these portals figure in the record of Nehemiah's night survey around the ruined wall of Jerusalem and the description of its restoration. [1]

The Mosque of Omar is pictured within the city and designated by its Crusader name, Temple of the Lord – Templum Domini. Next to it are the Sheeps' Pool – Probatica piscina, the Palace of Pilatus – Palacium Pilati, and the Holy Sepulchre – Sepulcrum Domini. In the same vicinity appears the Greek name Licostrates (sic: Lithostrates), the stone floor or pavement which is referred to in the New Testament tale of Jesus' trial by the Roman Procurator Pontius Pilatus in Jerusalem: 'and sat down in the judgment seat, in a place that is called Pavement but in Hebrew Gabbatha'.[2] To this day the stone floor is shown in the Old City of Jerusalem, in the Convent of the Sisters of Zion situated on the Via Dolorosa. In the south is the House of Caiaphas – Domus Cayfe, the High Priest in the time of Jesus;[3] today it is an Armenian church on Mount Zion. The House of Mary — Domus S. Marie, is indicated at the site of the present Abbey of the Dormition. Here, again according to Christian tradition, St. Mary fell into eternal sleep. Next is the Coenaculum, the Hall of the Last Supper, and underneath, a building marked: the tombs of David and other kings — Sepulcra David et aliorum regum.

According to this map, Mount Zion, now outside the area of Old Jerusalem, was, in the fourteenth century, encompassed by the city's wall (See next figure.)

1) Nehemiah 2, 13. 3, 1. 8, 1. 2) John, 19, 13. 3) John, 18, 28.

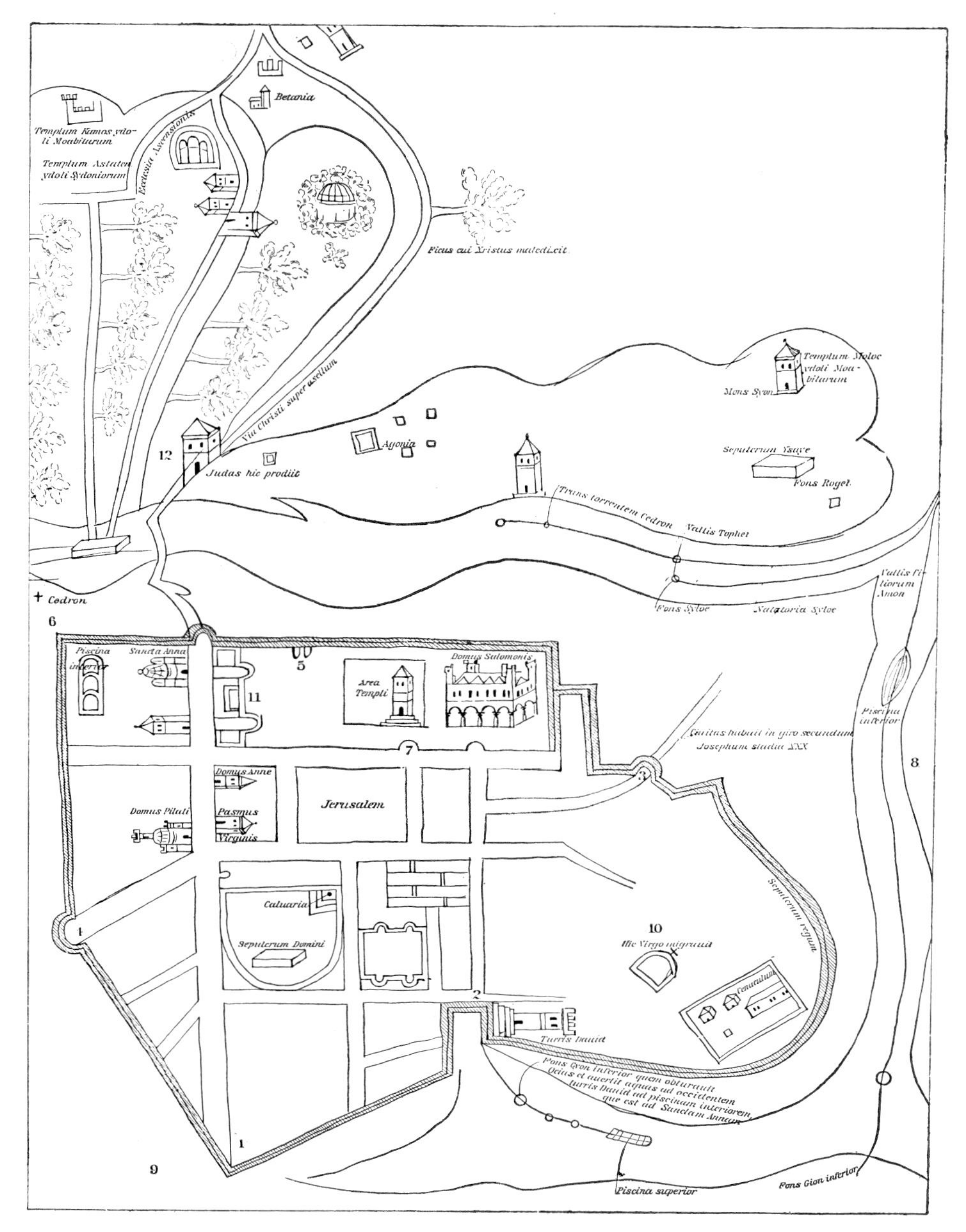

22. Map of Jerusalem and its immediate surroundings About 1310

Attached to the account of his travels, 'Liber secretorum fidelium Crucis', written by the Italian pilgrim Marino Sanuto Torselli, who visited Palestine in 1310.

The manuscript is preserved in the Library of the British Museum, London (Codex 27376).

Jerusalem is surrounded by a wall, whose outline is drawn in parts in straight and in parts in curved lines. Here again, the height known as Mount Zion, today outside the Old City, is, according to the map, within the walled territory.

In the centre, the Holy Sepulchre – Sepulcrum Domini, on the Hill of Golgotha – Calvaria. In the south-east, the Temple enclosure – Area Templi, and the Temple of Solomon – Domus Salomonis, the Crusader name of the Mosque of Omar.

Important Christian sites are indicated within the city: among them the House of Pilatus – Domus Pilati, the Roman Procurator in the time of Jesus, a building next to it marked the Virgin's Spasm – Pasmus Virginis, today an Armenian-Catholic church which marks the Fourth Station along the Via Dolorosa, the House of Anne (Mother of St. Mary) – Domus Anne, and the Church of St. Anne – Sancta Anna. Next is the Piscina interior, better known as the Pool of Bethesda, sacred to Christians. In the west is the Tower of David – Turris David. To the right stands the Hall of the Last Supper, in Latin Coenaculum; beside it there is written:

Continued on the next page

23. Jerusalem Beginning of the Fifteenth Century

From an English manuscript describing the 'Travels' of Sir John Maundeville in the East. Preserved in the Library of the British Museum, London (Add. 37049).

Continued from previous page

The Virgin wandered here — Hic Virgo migravit. This spot today carries the Abbey of the Dormition of the Benedictines, situated between the Tomb of King David and the present wall of Jerusalem.

Near the southern section of the wall the legend reads: Burial-place of the Kings — Sepulcrum regum. These are the tombs of the Kings of the House of David.

Near the Tower of David and outside the wall, a curved line indicates the Valley of Hinnom without naming it. Next to the tower is the Higher Pool — Piscina superior, named the Sultan's Pool today. At the foot of Mount Zion an inscription reads: The fountain of the Lower Gihon which Hezekiah stopped and diverted its waters to the west of the Tower of David, to the inner pool, which is next to the Church of St. Anne — Fons Gyon inferior, quem obturavit Ocias (?) et avertit aquas ad occidentem turris David ad piscinam interiorem, que est ad Sanctam Annam.

Underneath, on the right, is the Fountain of the Lower Gihon — Fons Gion inferior, and well above it the following inscription: The city had a periphery, according to Josephus, of 30 stadia—Civitas habuit in giro secundum Josephum stadia XXX. [1]

Above the Lower Pool — Piscina inferior, is the Valley of the Sons of Amon – Vallis filiorum Amon; on the left the Pool of Siloam – Natatoria Syloe, and the Fountain of Siloam — Fons Syloe. A little above, the Valley of Tophet – Vallis Tophet, is indicated. Beyond the Brook Kidron — Trans torrentem Cedron, rises Mount Zion — Mons Syon, carrying the Temple of Moloch, deity of the Moabites – Templum Moloc ydoli Moabitarum. Next to it stands the Tomb of Isaiah – Sepulcrum Isaye, which was well known to the pilgrims of the Middle Ages; in its vicinity the biblical Fountain of Rogel — Fons Rogel, called today in Arabic Bir-Ayoub – The Well of Job, emerges in the river-bed of the Brook Kidron. The Mount of Olives, rising to the east, bears no name; it is covered with trees and on it stand many handsome buildings to which lead various roads. The place where Jesus hid from the Roman soldiers is indicated – Agonia. Next to it is written: Here Judas betrayed – Judas hic prodiit.

From a two-storeyed house a road ascends the mountain along the way taken by Jesus riding the ass – Via Christi super asellum. The road passes by the fig-tree Jesus cursed—Ficus cui Xristus maledixit. Nearby stands the Church of the Ascension—Ecclesia Ascensionis. Next to it is another building marked: Temple of Kamos, the Moabites' deity – Templum Kamos ydoli Moabitarum, and Temple of Ashtoret, the Sidonians' goddess – Templum Asta(r)ten ydoli Sydoniorum. At the top is Bethany – Betania.

1) According to Flavius 'The whole circumference of the city was thirty-three furlongs', 'Wars' V, 4, 3

24. Jerusalem Fifteenth Century

Manuscript preserved in the Bibliothèque Nationale, Paris. (Ms. francais 9087, fol. 85).

View of Jerusalem from the south. Among the houses topped with cupolas, the Mosque of Omar with its large dome, between tall minarets. Right, the Mosque of Aqsa and its smaller cupola. Left, the Holy Sepulchre with its dome strangely hollowed out.

At the bottom of the picture, on the site of the present Mount Zion, is a group of houses similarly roofed with cupolas, and among them the building in which Jewish tradition shows the Tomb of King David with the Hall of the Last Supper on the upper storey. On the left a house encircled by a wall is apparently the church named by mediaeval pilgrims after Caiaphas, the High Priest in Jesus' time. Today its place is taken by an Armenian church. The winding road at the bottom which leads to the Holy City comes from Bethlehem.

25. Civitas Jherusalem Fragment of a pictorial map of the Holy Land attached to the 'Peregrinationes' of the German pilgrim Bernhard von Breidenbach 1483

Jerusalem is pictured as seen from the east, from Olivet, unlike the rest of the map in which the Holy Land is represented as seen from the west, from the Sea.

In the centre rises the Mosque of Omar with a pointed cupola, while in reality it is covered by a rounded dome. It is inscribed with the name – Templu(m) Salomonis, and stands in a large courtyard with the smaller Mosque of Aqsa topped by a proportionally smaller cupola similarly pointed, pictured in the far left-hand corner and marked Templu(m) Symeonis – Temple of Simeon. This is apparently the Simeon of the New Testament who, in the Great Temple, met St. Mary carrying the infant Jesus, and hailed him as the future Messiah. Between the two mosques appears the inscription: Dome anne – House of Anne, the mother of St. Mary. To the right of the Mosque of Omar stands the large church of the Holy Sepulchre – Templu(m) gloriosum Domini Sepulchri. On its left another house is marked: Hospital where pilgrims coming to Jerusalem rest – Hospitale in quo peregrini Jerosolimam venientes reponuntur.

Farther left, by the side of the point of the Mosque of Omar, stand the buildings of the fortress named Tower of David – Palaciu(m) quondam a christianis constru(c)tum et palacium David appellatum.

Still farther left another church is marked: The place where St. James was beheaded – Locus ubi decapitatus fuit jacobus minor. This is the Armenian church extant to this day, and built, according to Christian tradition, on the site of the execution of James the Galilean, son of Zebedee, who, as the New Testament recounts, was put to death by the emissaries of King Herod Antipas, about 44 A. D.: 'And he killed James... with the sword'.[1] On the left Mount Zion is pictured – Mons Syon, with several buildings on it, one of which is marked: House of the Virgin Mary – Domus Virginis Marie. Next to it is the Coenaculum. The House of Caiaphas – Domus quondam Cayphe, today an Armenian church, is also indicated. Below Mount Zion the word Tomb – Sepulchrum, marks the many burial caves cut in the rocky sides of the Valley of Hinnom running down from Mount Zion to the Brook Kidron.

Along the eastern wall of the town, which also borders the Temple courtyard, the name Civitas Iherusalem is written in large characters. To the right appears the Gate of Mercy, the Golden Gate of Christian tradition. Beyond the wall, to the left, the Valley of Jehoshaphat – Vallis josaphat, stretches along the Brook Kidron. Above rises the Mount of Olives with important Christian sites at its foot, among them the Tomb of St. Mary – Sepulchrum Marie Virginis.

1) Acts 12, 2.

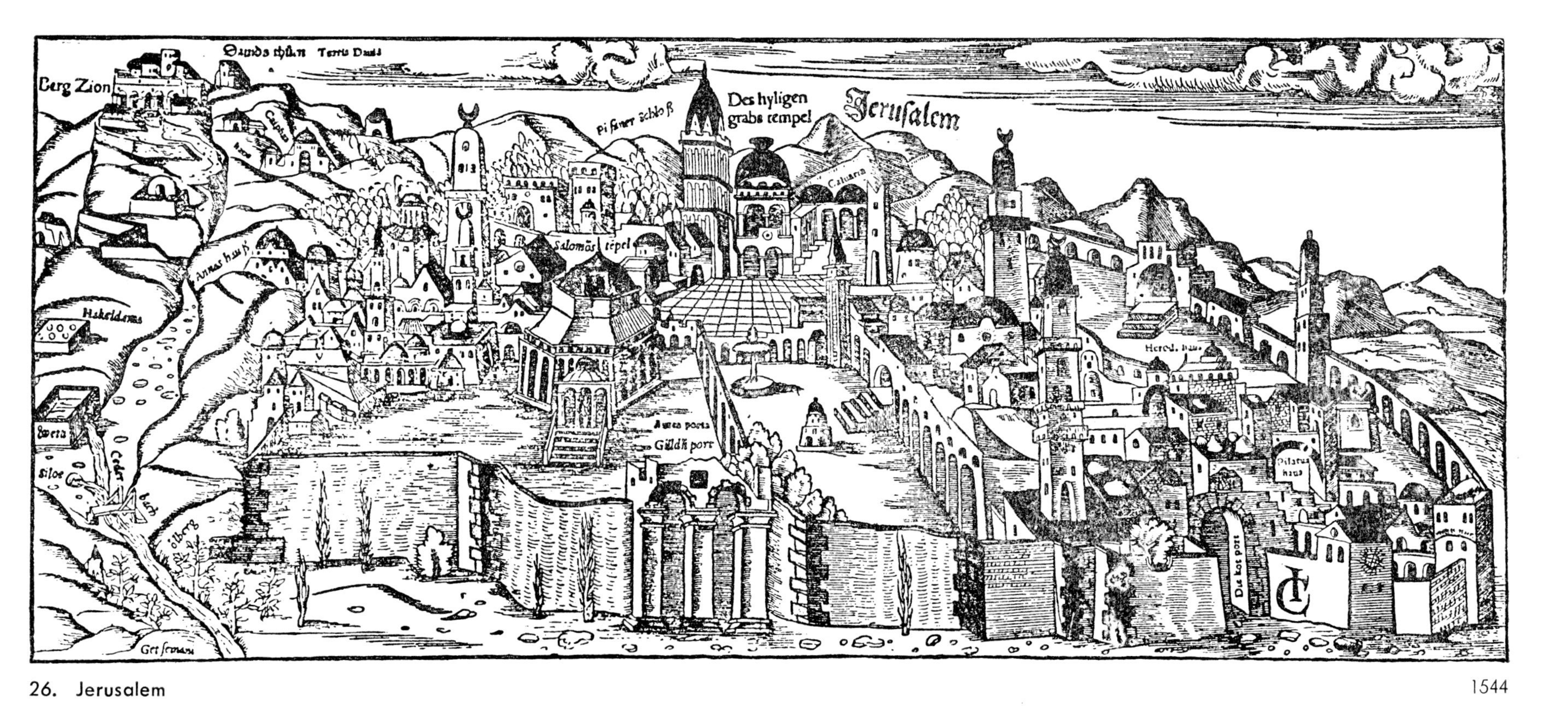

26. Jerusalem 1544

Attached to the book of the German, Sebastian Münster, 'Cosmografey oder Beschreibung aller Laender', printed in 1544, at Basle.

The illustration is the work of a German artist. Most of the names are written in German and only a few in Latin. The eastern wall is at the bottom with the Gate of Mercy, known to Christendom as the Golden Gate, in Latin – Aurea porta, in German – Güldn port. To the right is the Lions' Gate, called in German the Red Gate – rot port. Beyond the wall rises the Mosque of Omar marked: Temple of Solomon – Salomos Te(m)pel. Above, to the right, is the Church of the Holy Sepulchre – Des hyligen grabs tempel. Next to it stands the Tower of David, indicated by its Crusader name: The Pisan Castle – Pisaner Schloss. In the top left-hand corner the name Turris David, in German – Davids thurm, appears above the alleged royal tomb on Mount Zion – Berg Zion. A beautiful gate is pictured in the northern wall; although it bears no name it is easily identified as the Damascus Gate.

At the bottom right-hand corner the artist has inscribed his monogram.

27. Jerusalem 1581

Illustration found in the book of the German pilgrim, Solomon Schweigger, 'Reyssbeschreibung aus Teutschland nach... und Jerusalem', printed in 1608.

Jerusalem as seen from the east, from the top of the Mount of Olives. Among the clustered houses of the town the most important buildings are indicated by letters of the alphabet: A. Mosque of Omar, on the site of the Great Temple. – B. Holy Sepulchre. – C. Jaffa Gate. – D. Tower of David. – E. Zion Gate. – F. Dung Gate, and the road leading to the Brook Kidron. – G. Gate of Mercy, or Golden Gate, with its two portals. – H. Lions' Gate or St. Stephen's Gate. – I. Herod's Gate. – M. The building erected on King David's Tomb, with the Coenaculum. – N. The Brook Kidron, dividing Jerusalem from Olivet.

28. Jerusalem 1588

Explanation on the next page

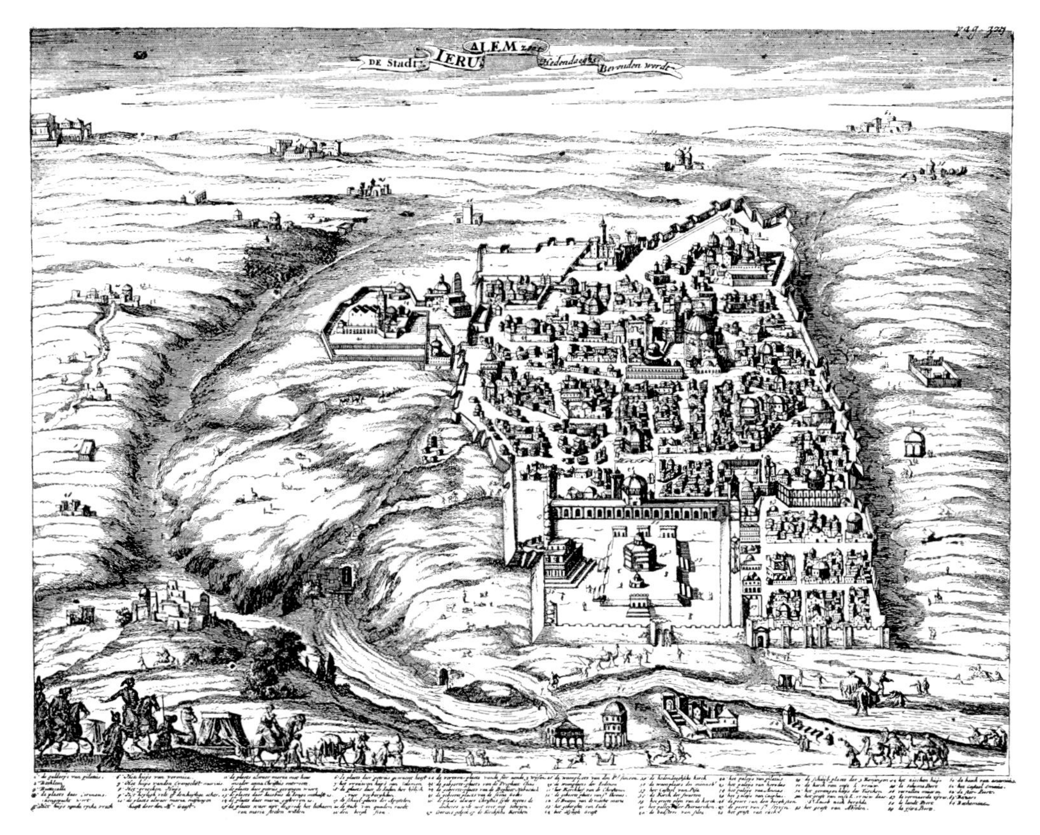

29. Jerusalem and its surroundings 1593

Illustration from the book of the Italian monk, Bernardino Amico, 'Trattato delle piante et Imagini de sacri edifizi di Terra Santa', printed in 1609.

View of Jerusalem from the Mount of Olives. The Temple area and its various buildings are clearly drawn. At the top, on the left, the traditional site of the Tomb of King David appears outside the wall. This is the first illustration which shows the Jewish quarter in the Old City; serial number 29 of the legend inscribed at the bottom of the map carries the explanation: Where the Hebrews live – dove abitaio gli Ebrei.

Continued from previous page

Illustration from the book of the Frenchman, Henri de Bouveau, 'Relation journalière du voyage du Levant', printed in 1615.

The top is inscribed with the words of the Prophet Ezekiel: 'This is Jerusalem! I have set her in the midst of the nations, and countries are round about her'.[1]

Jerusalem is seen from the east, from the heights of the Mount of Olives. In the foreground is the eastern wall with the Gate of Mercy in its middle; on the right, the Lions' Gate; in the northern wall, on the right, the Damascus Gate – Porta Damascena. In the western wall, on top, the Jaffa Gate, here again named Tower of the Pisans – Castrum Pisanor(um), after the provenance of the Italian Crusaders who restored and fortified it. In the southern wall, on the left-hand side of the picture, the Gate of Zion, here called Gate of Judah—Porta Judaica; next to it the Tomb of King David, and the Coenaculum. (See, further, a special enlargement of this section under the title Tomb of King David). At the bottom appear various types of Jerusalemites, men and women, garbed in sixteenth century costumes.

The box at the bottom left-hand corner reads: 'The Holy City of Jerusalem, by far the most famous city of Judah and the entire Orient which in its dimensions and magnificence is conspicuous in this age of ours'.

1) Ezekiel 5, 5.

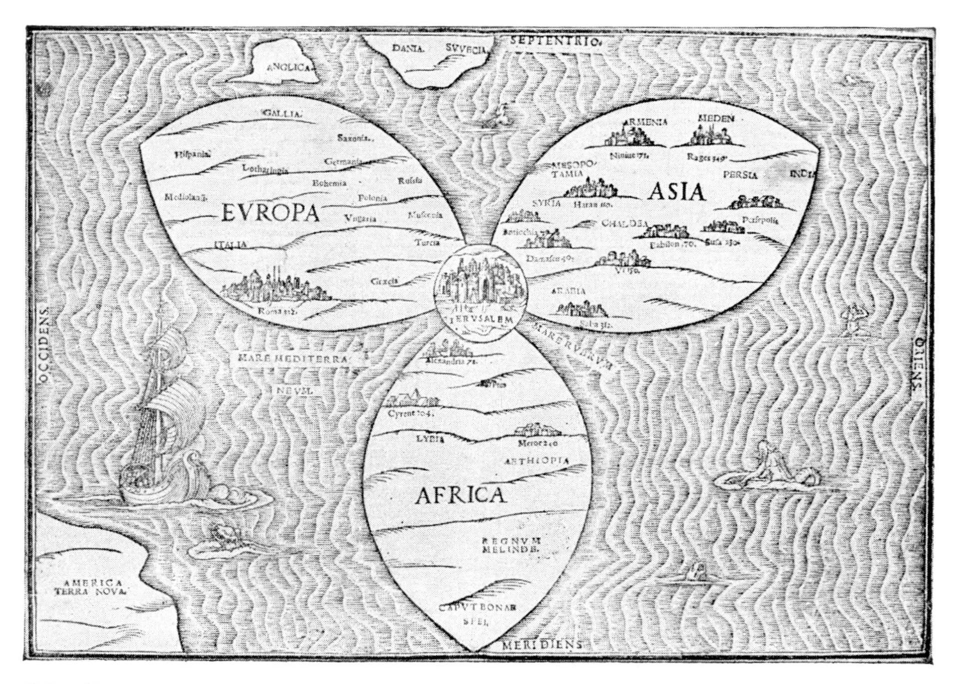

30. Map of the world with Jerusalem in the centre 1585

The world is represented in the shape of a three-leaved clover with a picture of Jerusalem in the centre. From Jerusalem the three continents spread out: to the right — Asia; to the left — Europe and the city of Rome; below — Africa with the Cape of Good Hope at its southern tip. In the bottom left-hand corner, part of a fourth continent shows: America Terra Nova — America the New Land. America was discovered about a hundred years before this map was drawn.

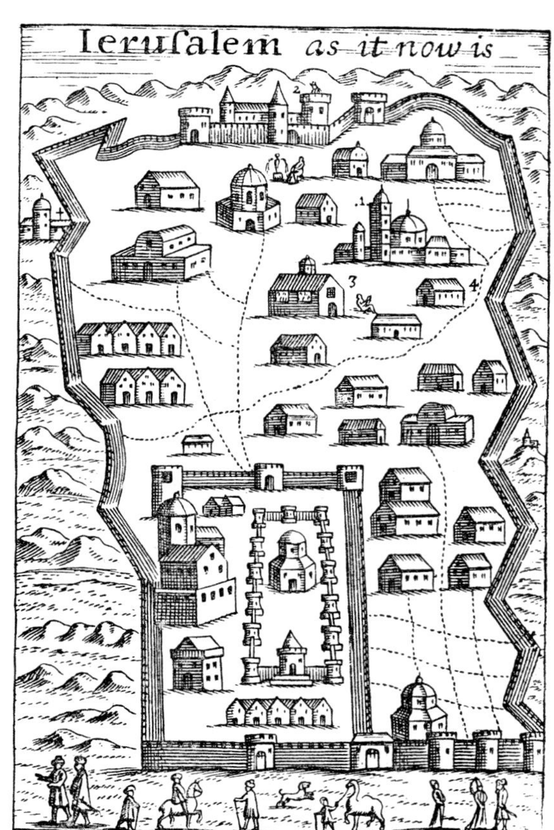

31. Jerusalem About 1600

Within the town: the Temple Area, the Holy Sepulchre (1), the Tower of David, called House of David (2), St. Mary's House (3), and others.

32. Hierusalem Sixteenth Century

From the book of the Italian traveller, Pietro Antonio, 'Guida fedele alla Santa Citta di Gierusalemme'. The Mosque of Omar, inscribed: Temple of Solomon — Templum Salamonis, the Church of the Holy Sepulchre — Sepulcru (m) Christi, the Western Wall, with the Golden Gate — Porta Aurea.

33. Hierusalem, from a translation of Ptolemy, Bibliothèque Nationale (Latin 4802). Sixteenth Century Jerusalem from the Mount of Olives. In the wall below, the Golden Gate – P. aurea, and on the right, the Gate of St. Stephen – P. S. Stefani. Within the wall the Mosque of Omar, named Temple of Solomon – Templu(m) Salomo(n)is, and the Mosque of Aqsa – Templu(m) dei. To the right, the House of Pilatus – Dom Pilati, the Church of St. Anne – S. Anna, the Holy Sepulchre – Sco sepulcro, on Golgotha – Monte calvario. Underneath, buildings named after St. Angelus – S. angelus, and St. Jacob – S. iacobus, next to the Roman Gate – Porta romana, the site of the present Damascus Gate. To the left a pilgrims' hostel – Hospicium peregrinor(um). Top centre, the castle of King David – Castello de david rege, and to its left Mt. Zion – Monte Sion, within the wall. Mount Zion also carries the Hall of the Last Supper. In the bottom left the Brook Kidron – Cedron torrens, runs through the Valley of Jehoshaphat – Vallis iosaphach, right, the town Em(m)aus.

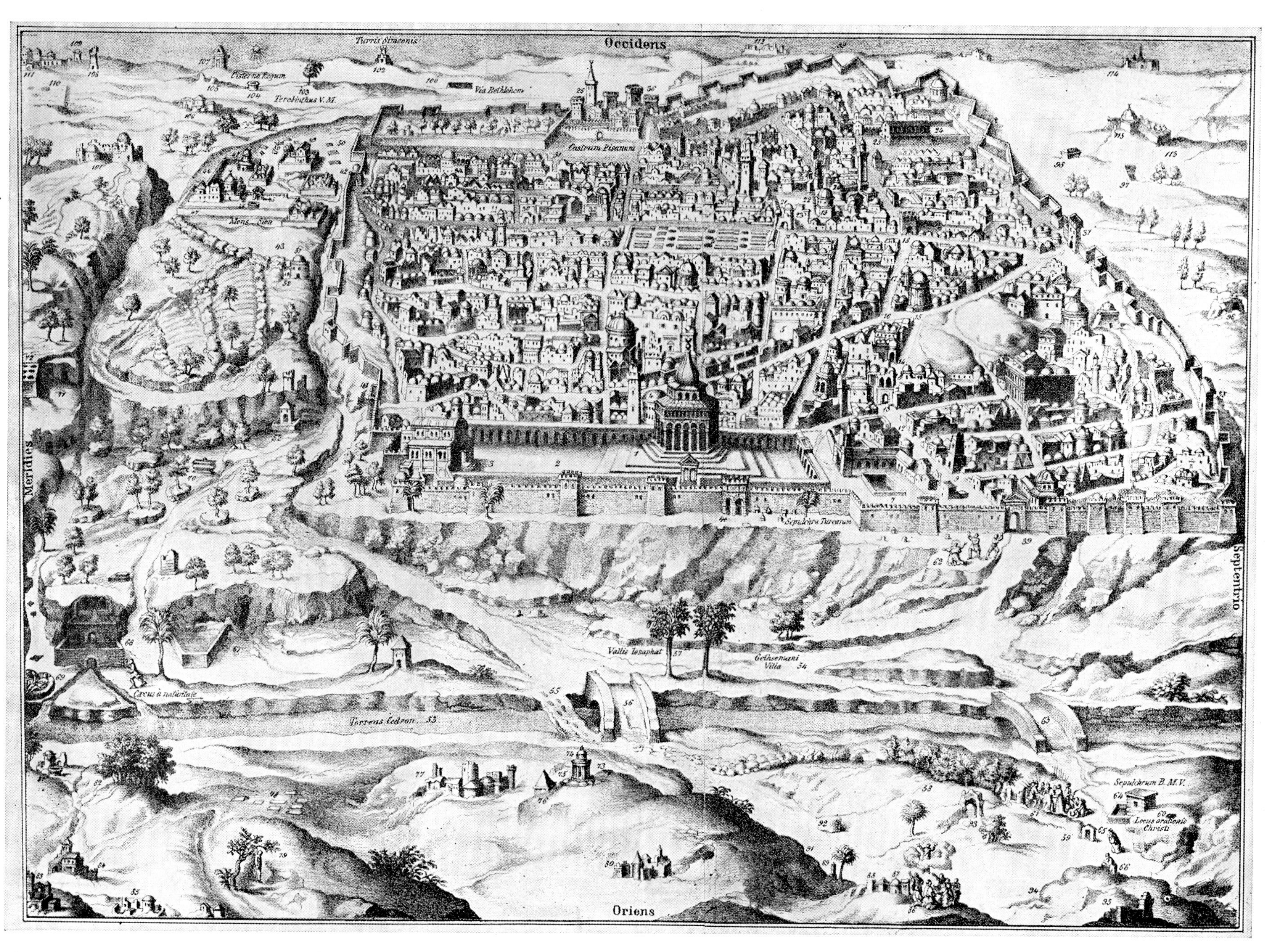

34. Jerusalem, view from the Mount of Olives

1618

From the book of the Italian monk, Francesco Quaresmus, 'Elucidatio Terrae Sanctae historica, theologica, moralis', printed in 1639.

35. Jerusalem — Seventeenth Century

36. Jerusalem and its holiest and most important buildings 1819

From the book of W. R. Wilson, 'Travels in the Holy Land', printed in 1822.

The dotted line indicates the direction of the ancient wall (A). On the left, on the top of the hill called Zion, the Building (B) on the Tomb of King David and the Coenaculum. Within the town, on top of a height – Mount Golgotha, a church (C) built over the Holy Sepulchre. Below is the Temple Area enclosed within a wall, with the Mosque of Omar (D) on the right and the Mosque of Aqsa on the left. The Golden Gate (E) is at the bottom of the picture, the Gate of Jaffa (F) at the top and the Damascus Gate (G) on the right. Within the town, along the wall of the Temple courtyard, is the Pool of Bethesda (H).

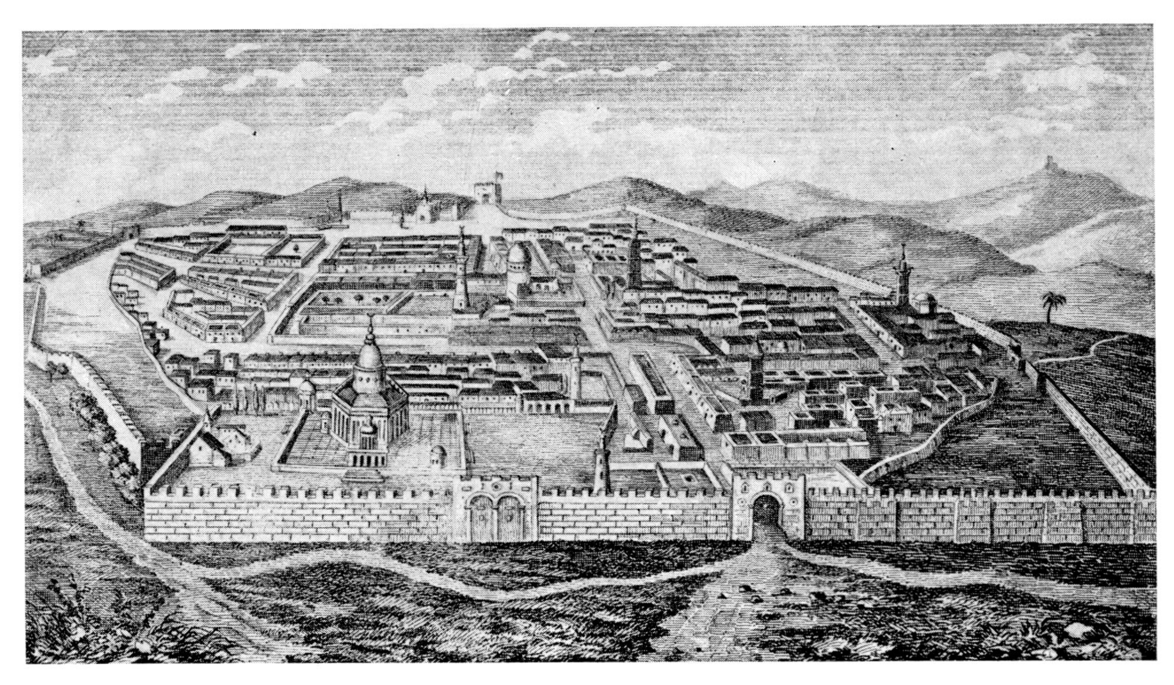

37. **Jerusalem** From the book of travels of Israel Josef Binyamin. 1850

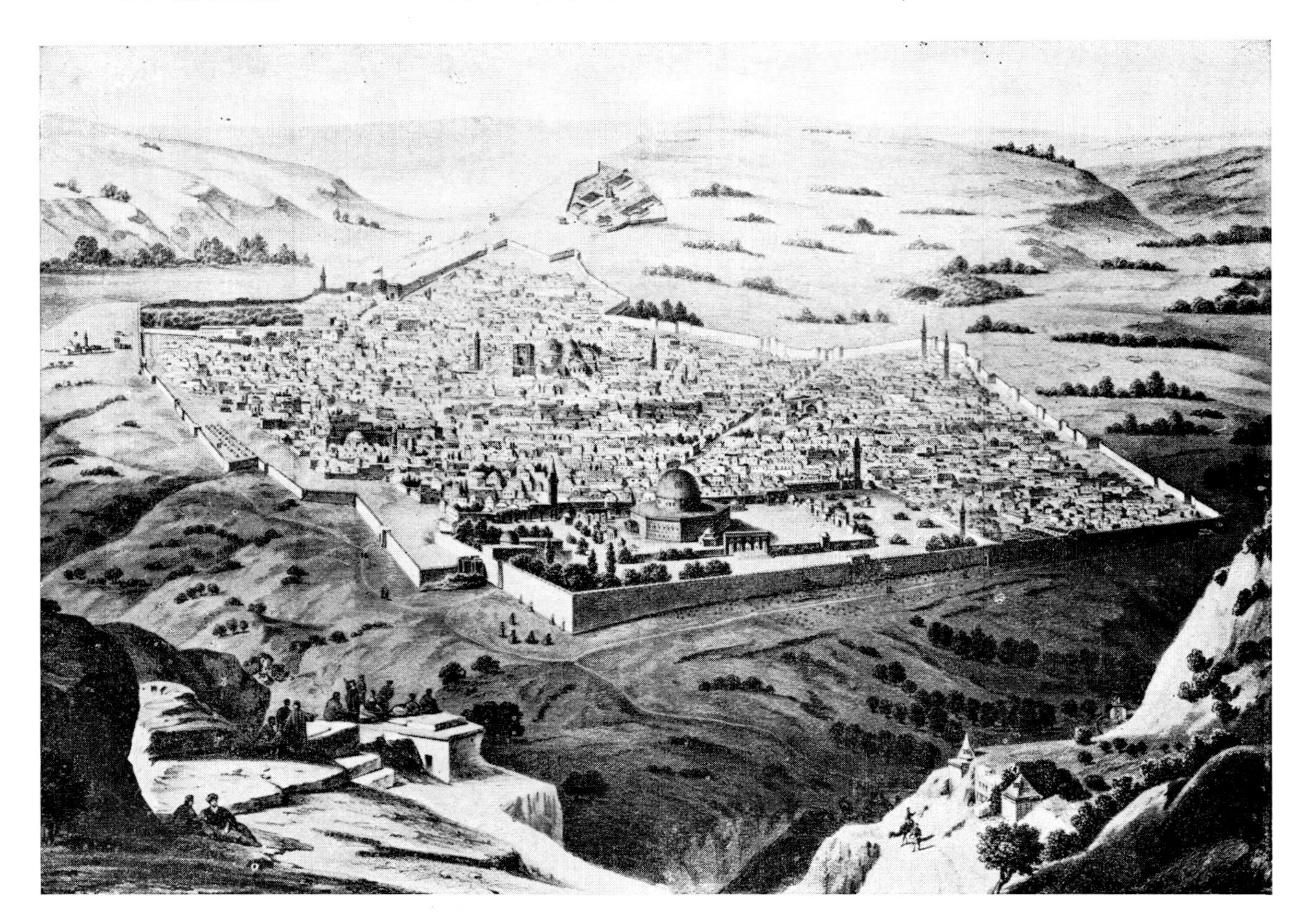

38. **Jerusalem** 1867

From the book of A. Graf Wartensleben, 'Jerusalem Gegenwärtiges und Vergangenes', printed in 1868.

View of Jerusalem from the Mount of Olives, seven years after the first Jewish suburb was built outside the walls of the Old City. This venturesome suburb – Mishkenot-Shaananim – was the nucleus of the new town of Jerusalem which today covers the hills rising west of the town. Beyond the wall, at the top of the picture, the Russian Compound is drawn alongside the highway to the port of Jaffa – the Jaffa Road, today the main artery of the New City.

39 – 40. The Messiah, riding an ass, is approaching Jerusalem

From a Passover Haggadah printed in Venice, in 1665.

From a Passover Haggadah, Frankfurt-an-der-Oder, 1753.

Elijah the Prophet walks in front of the Messiah and blows the trumpet of Redemption. They approach the eastern gate of Jerusalem, the Gate of Mercy of the Jews and the Golden Gate of Christian tradition. In fulfilment of prophecy, Jews from the whole world flock to the Holy City, coming forth joyously to welcome the Redeemer: 'Thus saith Lord God: I will even gather you from the peoples, and assemble you out of the countries where ye have been scattered, and I will give you the land of Israel'.[1]

1) Ezekiel 11, 17.

42. Jerusalem Sixteenth Century

Printed on a paper sheet, in the town of Mantua, Italy.

41. Jerusalem, the Messiah is coming

Beginning of the Sixteenth Century

42. Picture of Jerusalem, embroidered on the curtain of the Holy Ark 1681

From an Italian Synagogue; now displayed in the Jewish Museum, New York.

In the centre: an imaginary picture of Jerusalem represented with its fortified wall and gates. The Temple appears under the guise of the modern Mosque of Omar with the following verse embroidered in Hebrew characters on top of it: 'I set Jerusalem above my chiefest joy'.[1]

Above Jerusalem rises Mount Sinai with another verse from the Psalms set in a semi-circle around its peak: 'the mountain which God hath desired for His abode'.[2] The two tablets of the Law recline on the cloud through which God spoke to Moses: 'And the Lord said unto Moses: Lo, I come unto thee in a thick cloud'.[3] On top of the cloud a fourth biblical verse reads: 'The Lord spoke with you face to face in the mount out of the midst of the fire'.[4]

Under Jerusalem is the name of the embroideress: 'Made by the hand of the Lady Simha, wife of Menahem Levi Meshulami, in the year 1681'. 'He shall receive a blessing from the Lord'.[5]

1) Psalms 137, 6. 2) Psalms 68, 17. 3) Exodus 19, 9. 4) Deuteronomy 5, 4. 5) Psalms 24, 5.

44. Jerusalem 1638

This illustration decorates a ketuba which was written in Mantua, Italy.
Preserved in the Public Library of New York.

Jerusalem appears as a mediaeval fortified city with beflagged towers and a drawbridge on each side.

45. Jerusalem 1727

In the centre the Mosque of Omar stands out as a symbol of the Temple in olden days. Mountains are drawn at the back of the Holy City and over them appear the words of the Psalms: 'As the mountains are round about Jerusalem...' [1]

This illustration decorates a ketuba written in Rivarolo, Italy.
It was preserved in the collection of Jewish art of the Jewish Community of Berlin.

46. Jerusalem 1776

Above the picture of Jerusalem the words of the Psalms: 'If I forget thee, Jerusalem, may my right hand forget its cunning'. [2]

This illustration appears in the margin of a ketuba written in Ancona, Italy.

1) Psalms, 125, 2. 2) Psalms, 137, 5.

47. Jerusalem and the surrounding mountains 1650

From the book 'Darkei-Tsiyon'— Ways to Zion, by M. Porges (Präger).

49. Jerusalem About 1655

The frontispiece of the Hebrew pamphlet entitled: 'And the ransomed of the Lord will return and come singing to Zion'. (Next figure)

48. Jerusalem About 1646

From the book: 'Kisaot le beit - David' – Kings' Thrones of the House of David, by J. Asahel Mehattob (Leon de Bene), printed in Verona, Italy.

Around the picture the words of the Psalms: 'For there were set thrones for judgment, the thrones of the house of David'. [1]

1) Psalms, 122, 5.

Explanation to illustration 47

Below is Jerusalem, on top of 'Mount Moriah', with the words of the Psalmist: 'As the mountains are round about Jerusalem, So the Lord is round about His people'. [1]

Above are 'Mount Zion', the 'Mount of Olives' and the 'Mount of Ein-Eitam', which rises south of the Holy City, near Bethlehem. On top, the following verse is inscribed: 'This is the Gate of the Lord, the righteous shall enter into it'. [2]

1) Psalms 125, 2. 2) Psalms 118, 20,

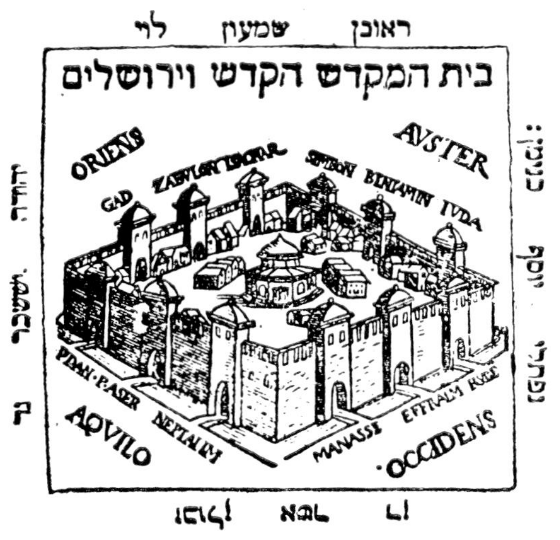

50. Jerusalem About 1655

At the top, in large Hebrew characters: 'The Holy Temple and Jerusalem'. Around the margin: the tribal names in Hebrew. Obviously this picture was copied from a non-Hebrew book, and the copyist, retaining the Latin inscriptions, added the Hebrew equivalents.

A similar drawing, with a like explanation, appears on the title page of the English edition of Cranmer's Bible, printed in 1540.

51. Jerusalem About 1709

From the manuscript Passover Haggadah by Arieh Leib, 'priest and scribe in Trèves', in the possession of A. Brandstaetter, Tel-Aviv.

In large Hebrew characters, the blessing: 'Leshana Habaah Biyerushalaim' – Next year in Jerusalem.

52. Jerusalem 1864

From a Passover Haggadah printed in Trieste, Italy.

In the bottom right-hand corner the artist has inscribed his initials in small characters: C. K(irchmayr).

53. Jerusalem and its Holy Places About 1850

Printed on a large sheet of paper (63/51 cms.) which portrays the sacred tombs of the Holy Land. Published in Jerusalem by the printer Zev Ashkenazi. Undated.

Left: the Mosque of Omar symbolizing the 'Holy Temple'. Centre: the 'Wailing Wall'. Right: the Mosque of Aqsa under its Hebrew name 'Midrash Shelomo' – King Solomon's House of Study. At the top: the monument called 'Hand of Absalom', the 'Tomb of Kalba Savua' (the Hebrew name for the Cave of the Tombs of the Kings), and the Tomb of 'Rabbi Yehuda Hassid' – the Pious.

54. Jerusalem and its vicinity 1875

A section of a pictorial map entitled: 'The shape of the Holy Land and its borders with all... its towns and villages', by Rabbi Haim Solomon Pinie of Tsefat (Safad), Galilee.

Among the dwellings of Jerusalem the Wailing Wall stands out conspicuously. Left: the Mosque of Omar, which indicates, as is written above it, the 'site of the Holy of Holies'. Right: the Mosque of Aqsa with the indication: 'House of Study of Solomon, King of Israel'. To its right the 'Houses of Jerusalem' and Mount 'Zion' carrying the 'Tomb of King David, King Solomon and all the Kings of the House (of David)'. To the east, the 'Mount of Olives' with the tomb of 'the Prophetess Hulda' and the 'Cave of Haggai and Malachi' prophets of Israel. At its foot, on the right, the 'Hand of Absalom', and 'Zechariah the Prophet'. Farther right, 'Bethlehem' and '(the tomb of) Our Mother Rachel'. At the bottom of the picture, on the left: '(the tomb of) the Prophet Samuel and his father', 'Simon the Just', '(the) Seventy (judges of the) Sanhedrin', 'the Courtyard of the Guard' of Jeremiah the prophet', '(the) Son of Kalba Savua'; on the right: '(A)bu Gosh', the Arab village west of Jerusalem, on the highway to Ramla, which is indicated farther on by the inscription: 'Town of Ramla, that is Gat'.

55. Facade of the Temple 134

Jewish coin from the time of the rebellion of Shimon Bar-Kokhba.

56. Plan of the Temple

Sixth Century

Set in an ancient colourful mosaic floor which was unearthed in the ruins of a Byzantine Church found on Mount Nebo in Transjordan.

At the bottom: entrance to the Temple courtyard. Within the courtyard, the sacrificial fire burning on the altar placed opposite the entrance to the Holy of Holies, flanked on each side, with two columns.

Length of the mosaic: 85 cms; width: 47 cms.

Four columns with the letters of the name Shim'on, in ancient Hebrew characters, on the sides. On the right: Sh, M; on the left: O, N; on top: a star, possibly the emblem of Bar-Kokhba, a nom de guerre meaning 'Son of the Star'.

The reverse carries the Hebrew inscription: 'Leherut Yerushalaim' – To the liberty of Jerusalem. A similar impression appears on other coins of the period.

57. The Roman conquest of Jerusalem Bas-relief from the year 700

Carved on the side of a casket made of whale-bone. Found in northern England, Northumbria, and preserved in the British Museum, London. It was presented to the Museum, in 1857, by its director, Sir A. Wollaston Franks, a well-known collector of antiquities, and is known by his name, the 'Franks Casket'.

The panel is divided into cn upper and a lower section. In the centre, an arched structure represents the Temple. Within it is the Ark of the Covenant with two bird-like figures, representing the Cherubim, on either side. Above the Cherubim, and in the centre of the roof of the Temple, the carving of a dove represents the Divine Spirit.

Upper section, left: a line of Roman soldiers carrying lances. Over this scene is written in Runic letters and in Anglo-Saxon the words: Her fegtath Titus and Giuthea su(mae) – Here fought Titus and some Jews. On the right: people are seen leaving the city and over them is written in faulty Latin: Hic fugiant (sic: fugiunt) Hierusalim afitatores (sic: habitatores) – here the inhabitants fly from Jerusalem.

In the lower section: the judge sits on a throne; the Jewish prisoners, next to him, are guarded by a soldier armed with a lance. Underneath, the word Dom – Judgment. On the right Jews are led into captivity with the word Gisl, hostage, carved in the bottom right-hand corner.

58. The Temple and the Wall of Jerusalem Third Century

A picture on the wall of the ancient synagogue in the ruins of Dura-Europos, the present Tel Salahiya, on the bank of the River Euphrates, in the extreme east of Syria. Preserved in the Arab Museum of Damascus.

59. The Temple Thirteenth Century

From the Passover Haggadah of Sarajevo, Yugoslavia.

60. Picture of the Temple Fourth Century

Adornment at the bottom of an antique plate brought to light in Rome, in the ancient cemetery of Via Labina. Preserved in the Vatican Library.

In the middle, the sanctuary, and in front of it, the seven-branched candlestick (menora), and sacred vessels. Around the margin of the plate, in Greek: 'House of Peace, Bless the children of Thy house'. Apparently, House of Peace, is another appellation of the Temple of Jerusalem.

אַדִּיר הוּא יִבְנֶה
בֵּיתוֹ בְּקָרוֹב:
בִּמְהֵרָה בִּמְהֵרָה.
בְּיָמֵינוּ בְּקָרוֹב:
אֵל בְּנֵה. אֵל
בְּנֵה. בְּנֵה בֵיתְךָ
בְּקָרוֹב:

61. An imaginary picture of the Temple About 1750

From the Passover Haggadah, printed in the book 'Seder Birkat Mazon' – 'Grace after Meals', published in Prague.

In large Hebrew characters, on the side, is the following verse of a Passover chant: 'O, may He who is most mighty soon rebuild His house, speedily, speedily, soon in our days. O God, rebuild it, O Eternal, rebuild it, rebuild Thine house in good time'.

62. The Temple Seventeenth Century

Protected by four circular walls.

From 'Yosifon', a Yiddish version of the works of Josephus Flavius, printed in Basel.

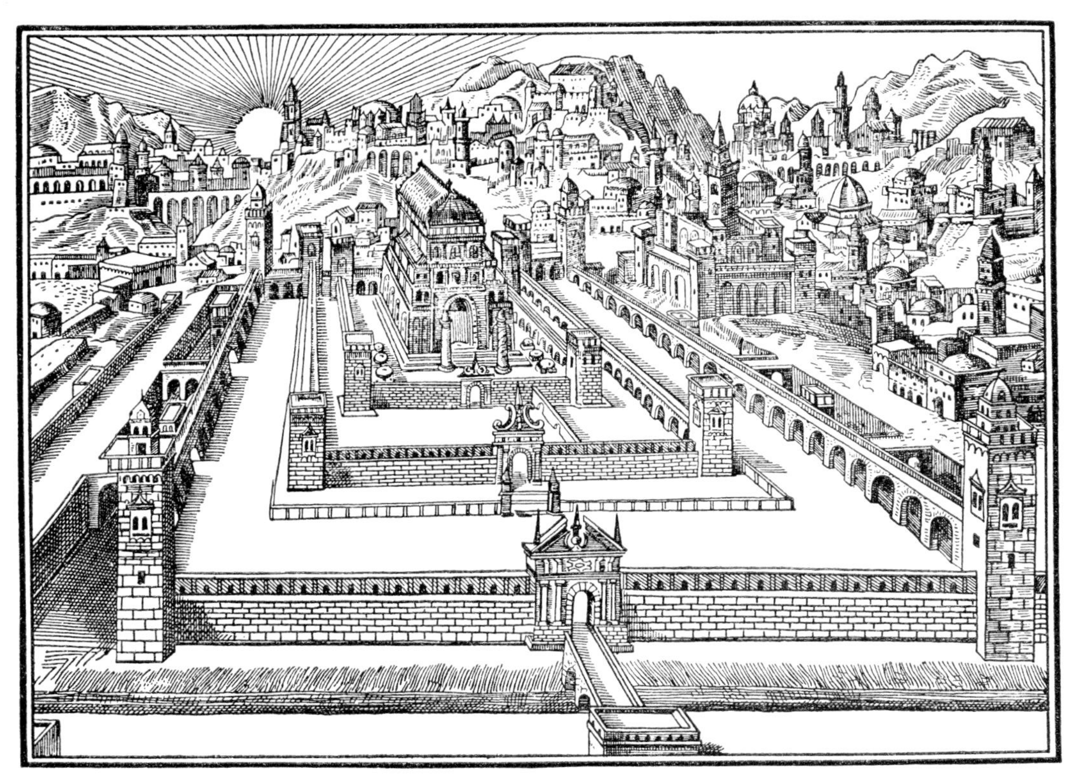

63. The Temple 1629

From a Passover Haggadah, printed in Amsterdam.

Underneath the picture, the legend written in Hebrew: 'Aspect of the Temple and the city of Jerusalem. May it be built and restored soon, in our days, Amen. May it be the Almighty's wish'.

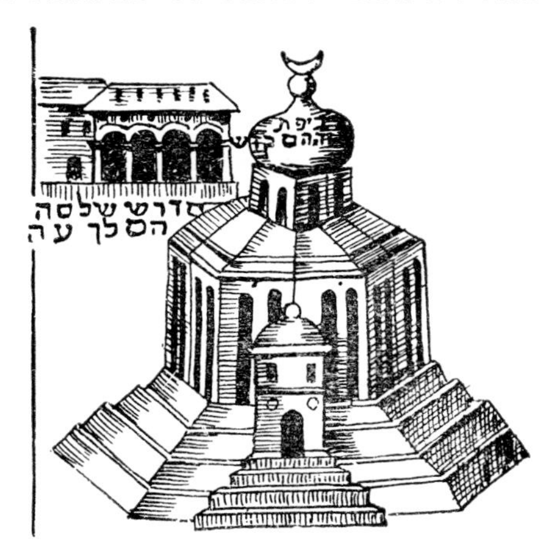

64. The Temple About 1537
From the Hebrew pamphlet 'Yihus Avot ve-Neviim' – 'Lineage of the Patriarchs and the Prophets', printed in 1659.
On the cupola the words: 'Dome of the Temple'.
Left: under a columned building, the inscription: 'The House of Study of King Solomom (Peace be upon him)', the Hebrew name of the Mosque of Aqsa.

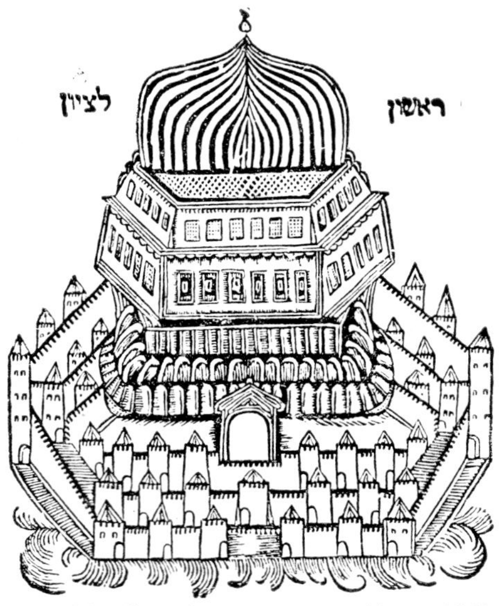

65. The Temple About 1750
An illustration from the book: 'Rishon-le Tsiyon'—First in Zion, by Rabbi Haim Ben-Attar. Written in Jerusalem and printed in Constantinople, in 1750.

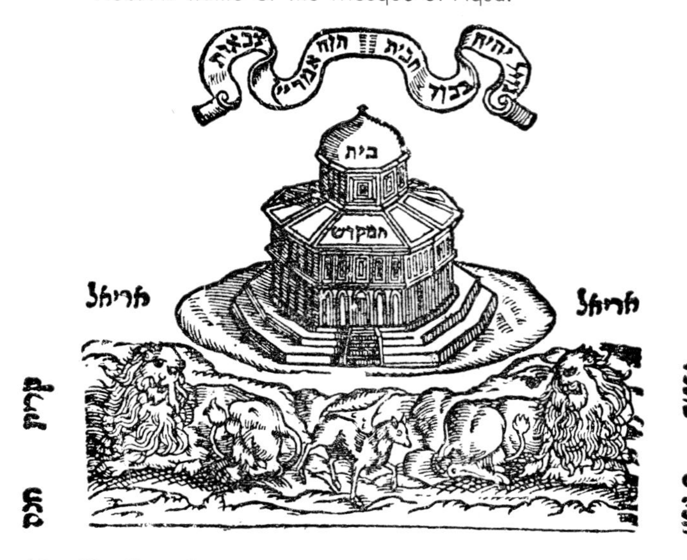

66. The Temple 1604

From the Hebrew book, 'Levush Haora' – Garb of Light, by Rabbi Mordekhai Yaffe, printed in Prague.

Above the Temple are written the words of the Prophet Haggai:

'The glory of the latter house shall be great . . . saith the Lord of hosts'. [1]

On the sides, the prophecy of Isaiah: 'Ah, Ariel, Ariel, the city where David encamped'. And on the right the artist added the words: 'God will restore her'. [2]

Ariel, in Hebrew – Lion of God, is one of the names of the Temple of the Lord in Jerusalem, of which the Sages said: 'The Sanctuary was narrow behind and wide in front and it was like unto a lion'. [3] As a reminder of this style, the artist drew lions in the foreground of the picture.

1) Haggai 2, 9. 2) Jsaiah 29, 1. 3) Mishna, Middot 4, 7.

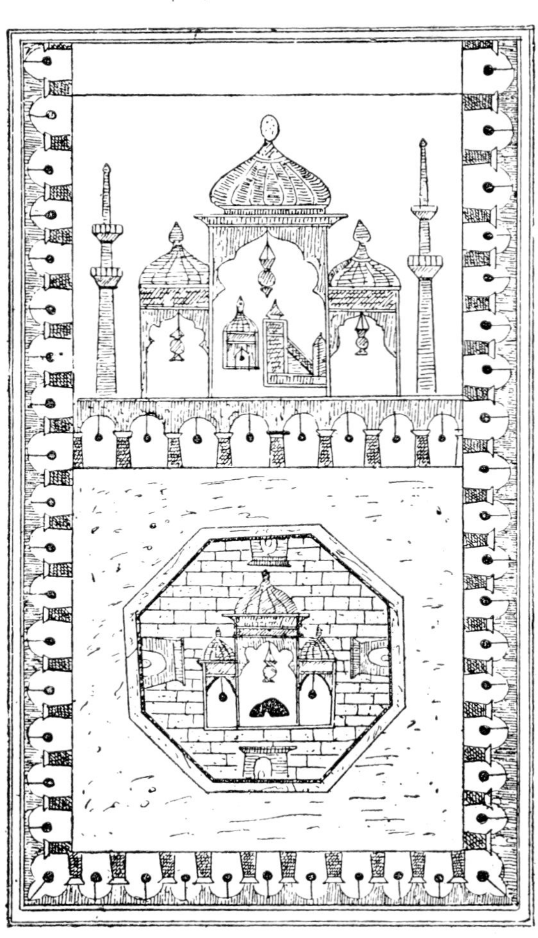

67. Mosques in the Temple Area Fifteenth Century
The work of a Moslem draftsman. Manuscript preserved in the Bibliothèque Nationale, Paris.
Below: The Mosque of Omar with its four gates and the Rock of Foundation in the centre.
Above: The Mosque of Aqsa with the pulpit.

68. The Temple Mount and the Mosque of Omar (Dome of the Rock) 1852

From the book, 'Jérusalem et la Terre Sainte', by G. D(arboy), printed in 1852

69. The Mosque of Omar 1565

From the book, 'Reiss... nach Hierusalem', by J. Helffrich, printed in 1577.

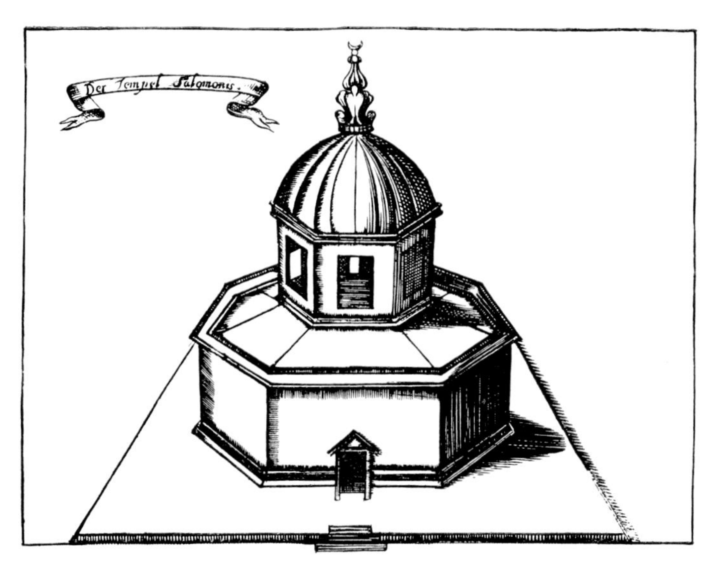

70. The Mosque of Omar 1675

From the book, 'Orientalische Reise-Beschreibung', by Otto Friedrich von der Gröben, printed in 1694.

The Mosque as Solomon's Temple, in German: 'Der Tempel Salomonis'.

71. The Mosque of Omar – Interior View About 1860

From the book of the German writer Ph. Wolff, 'Jerusalem', printed in 1862.

This illustration originally appeared, in colours, in the book of the American missionary, J. T. Barclay, 'City of the Great King', which was printed in 1858.

In the centre of the mosque, surrounded by a railing, rises the 'Holy Rock', the 'Stone of Foundation' of Jewish tradition.

72. The Mosque of Omar – the Cave in the Stone of Foundation 1880

From the book, 'Picturesque Palestine', by the English explorer Ch. W. Wilson, printed in 1880.

THE WAILING WALL

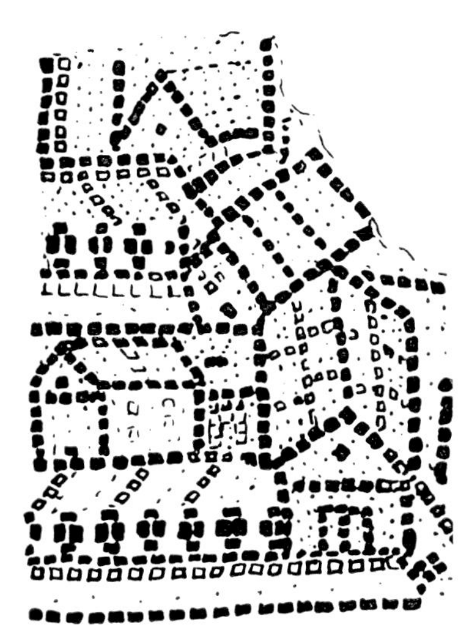

73. The Wailing Wall About 600

Part of the Map of Madaba.

See figure 4, number 29, page 3.

76. The Wailing Wall 1900
On the seal of a Jerusalem communal organization.

74. The Wailing Wall 1743

An illustration found in the Hebrew book: 'Zikaron B'Yerushalaim' — Memory in Jerusalem, by I. Poliastro, printed in Constantinople.

The first illustration of the Wailing Wall in Hebrew literature.

On top, 'This is the form of the Western Wall', and also, 'Mine eyes and My heart shall be there perpetually', an excerpt from the prayer of King Solomon at the consecration of the Temple.[1]

1) Kings I, 9, 3.

75. The Wailing Wall 1912
Pictured on a tombstone found in Eastern Europe.

77. The Wailing Wall 1900

Pictured on a Mezuza (talisman for doorpost).

Preserved in the Jewish Museum of New York.

On top: the Tomb of Rachel.

78. The Wailing Wall and buildings around it 1850
Often used as a decoration for the frontispiece of books printed in Jerusalem in the middle of the nineteenth century.

79. The Wailing Wall and the buildings surrounding it 1850
From the English edition of the Hebrew book 'Tevuot Haarets' – Harvest of the Land (of Israel), written by the Jerusalem Rabbi J. Schwarz and printed in 1850.

The foreground depicts the stonework of the Wailing Wall. Left: the Mosque of Omar. Underneath: the Gate of the Chain (in Arabic: Bab es-Silsileh), the main entrance to the Temple courtyard. Right: the Mosque of Aqsa or House of Study of King Solomon. Beyond the eastern wall rises the Mount of Olives, on its peak the building where the tomb of the Prophetess Hulda is traditionally shown.

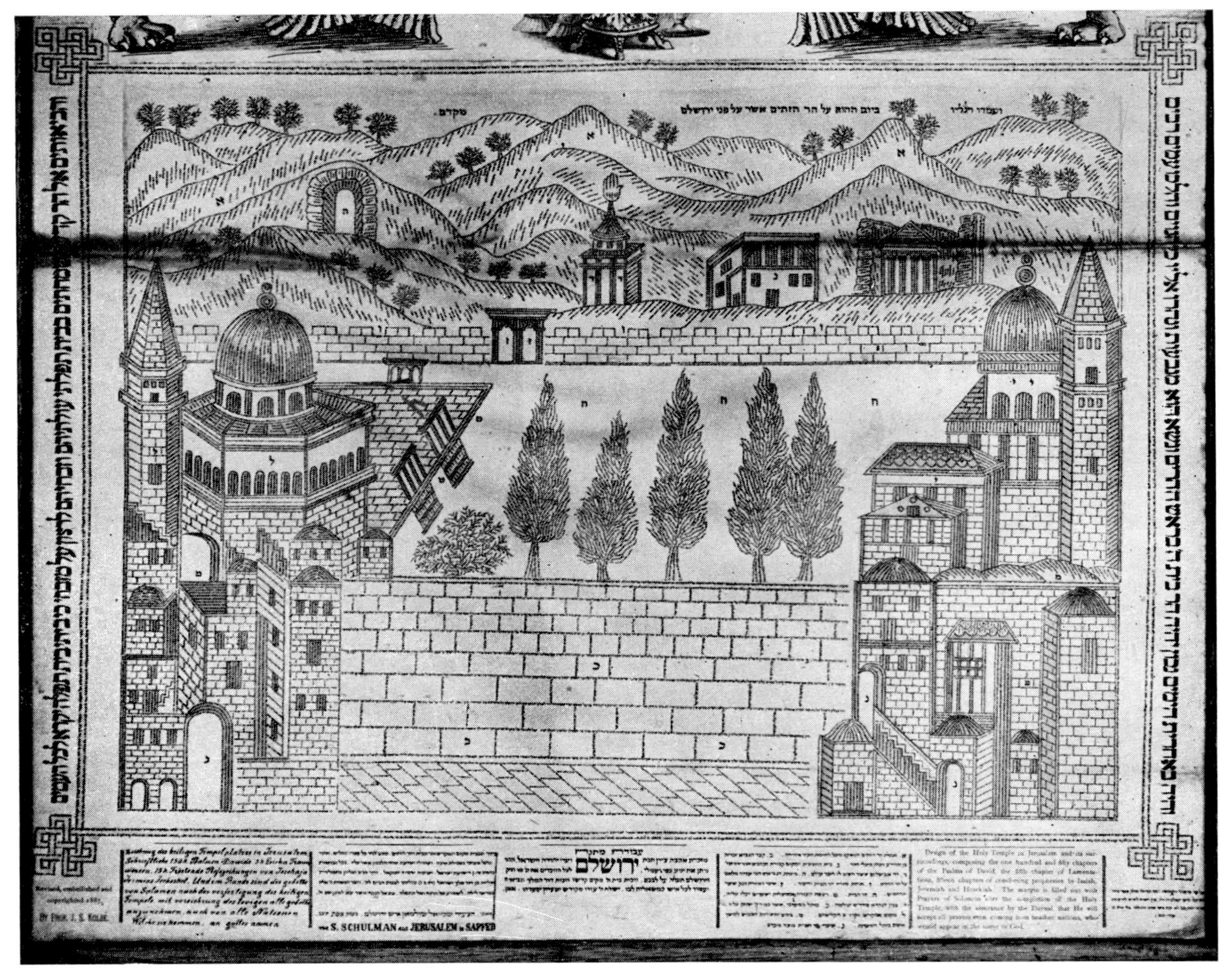

80. The Wailing Wall and the buildings in its vicinity, by Shemuel Shulman, a native of Jerusalem 1887

As the artist writes at the bottom of the sheet, the drawing was done from the indications given in 150 Psalms, in the fifth chapter of Lamentations and in 15 chapters from the prophecies of Isaiah, Jeremiah and Ezechiel. The prayer uttered by King Solomon at the consecration of the Temple is written around the margin. [1]

In the centre, the Wailing Wall; on its right the Mosque of Omar, representing the Temple, and, left of that, the Mosque of Aqsa. In the wall surrounding the Temple area appears the Golden Gate. Beyond, rises the Mount of Olives, with the words of the Prophet Zechariah: 'And His feet shall stand in that day upon the mount of Olives'. [2]

At the foot of the Mount of Olives, sites famous in Jewish tradition: the Tomb of the Prophet Zechariah, the House of Hofshit and the 'Hand' of Absalom, the rebellious son of King David. On the left, the Cave of the Prophets, where tradition places the tombs of Haggai and Malachi, the last prophets of Israel. 1) Kings I, 8. 2) Zechariah 14, 4.

81. Jerusalem and its Holy Places, with the Wailing Wall in the centre About 1830

Explanation at bottom of opposite page.

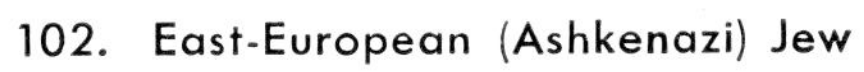

102. East-European (Ashkenazi) Jew 1917

103. Yemenite Rabbi 1917

104. Yemenite Beggar 1917

105. Persian Jew 1917

All the illustrations on this page are taken from the book of the famous Swedish traveller Sven Hedin, 'Jerusalem', printed in 1918.

106. A Jew 1565

From 'Reiss... nach Hierusalem', by J. Helffrich printed in 1577.

107. Jew in Prayer About 1900

108. Husband and wife About 1842

From the book of Mrs. Ewald, 'Jerusalem and the Holy Land, being a collection of... views... from drawings', printed in 1845.

109. Bukharian Jewess 1917

Picture drawn by Sven Hedin.

see previous page.

110. A Street in the Old City About 1851

J. J. Bourassé 'La Terre-Sainte', 1877.

111. An Arab barber About 1880

From 'Jerusalem', by F. de Saulcy, printed in 1882.

112. A water-carrier 1880

113. Jewish money-changer 1880

From the book of P. Lortet mentioned on page 50.

114. **Arab Sheikhs** About 1600

From the book of the Italian pilgrim, Bianco Noé, 'Viaggio da Venetia al sancto Sepolcro', printed in 1640.

115. **Governor of Jerusalem** 1565

From 'Reiss... nach Hierusalem', by J. Helffrich, printed in 1577.

116. The Greek Patriarch

117. Head of the Armenian Church

118. Head of the Maronite Church

Heads of the Christian Churches in Jerusalem in 1631

From the book of Eugène Roger, 'La Terre Sainte', printed in 1646.

119. Christian Family in Jerusalem 1845

A drawing of W. H. Bartlett in H. Stebbing's, 'The Christian in Palestine', 1847.

120. View from within the old City 1878

The Turkish flag floats on top of the Tower of David seen on the right. Opposite, the United States flag on top of the building of the U.S. Consulate. Between the two starts, the road leading to the Armenian Quarter stretching to the south.

121. The Holy Sepulchre About 600

The Holy Sepulchre as it is pictured in the Map of Madaba. Below, the facade of the building with its three portals opening on to a large courtyard.

see illustration 2, page 2.

122. The Holy Sepulchre
Twelfth Century

A Crusader seal. Around the edge, in Latin: Sanctissimi Sepulchri – the Most Sacred Sepulchre.

123. The Holy Sepulchre 1586

'Sepulchrum Christi' in J. Zuallart's, 'Il devotissimo Viaggio di Gierusalemme', printed in 1587.

124. Church of the Holy Sepulchre – Outside View 1483

From the book of Bernhard von Breidenbach, 'Peregrinationes', printed in 1486.

The Latin inscription at the top reads: 'Haec est dispositio et figura templi dom(in)i sepulchri ab extra' – This is the arrangement and appearance of the Church of the Lord's Sepulchre from the outside.

125. The Church of the Holy Sepulchre – Outside View 1842
W. H. Bartlett, 'Walks about the City and Environs of Jerusalem', 1844.

126. Holy Sepulchre – Interior View 1681
'Reyzen van Cornelius de Bruyn door de... Syrien en Palestine', 1688.

127. The Golden Gate 1845

A drawing of W. H. Bartlett in H. Stebbing's 'The Christian in Palestine', 1847.

128. Damascus Gate 1842

A drawing of the English painter W. Tipping.

129. **Jaffa Gate** About 1882

From Ch. W. Wilson's, 'Picturesque Palestine', 1882.

On the left, the deep moat which surrounded the Tower of David, rising left, outside the picture. In 1898, in preparation for the visit of the German Emperor, Wilhelm II, the Turks filled in the moat and, next to the Gate, through the part of the wall showing to its left, opened a direct entrance into the Old City.

130. **Jaffa Gate and the Tower of David** A drawing of W. H. Bartlett 1842

131. The Tower of David 1830

I. J. S. Taylor. 'La Syrie, l'Egypte, la Palestine et la Judée', 1839.

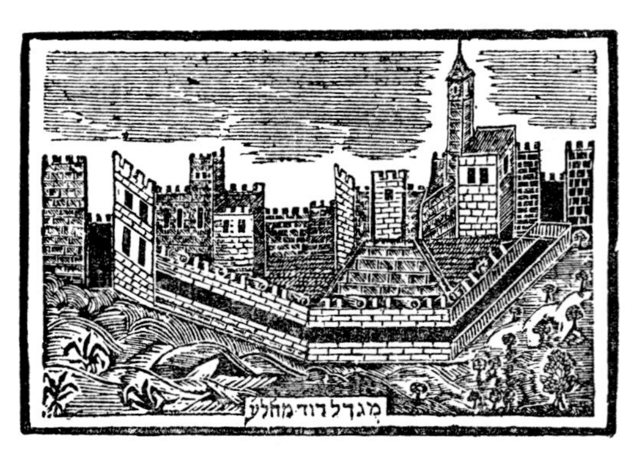

132. The Tower of David, 1900
View from outside the town
Decorative picture used in several Hebrew books printed in Jerusalem.

133. The Tower of David, on a Crusader seal About 1150

Left: the Tower of David and the Gate of David, at the site of today's Jaffa Gate. The tower is flanked on the left by the Church of the Holy Sepulchre and, on the right, by the Mosque of Omar, here a Crusader church. Around the edge: Civitas Regis Regum Omnium – City of the King of All Kings.

Right: Baldwin enthroned as King of Jerusalem.

134. The Tower of David, View from outside the town 1850

135. The Tower of David, View from inside the town 1850

From the German translation, printed in 1852, of the book of Rabbi Joseph Schwarz.
Cannons are seen in the embrasures of the wall.

136. **Tomb of the Kings of the House of David** 1537

From the Hebrew book, 'Lineage of the Patriarchs and the Prophets'.
First printed in 1659.

137. **Tomb of King David** Section of a picture from the year 1586

From the book of J. Zuallart, 'Il devotissimo Viaggio di Gierusalemme', 1587.

The letter A indicates a small cupola, possibly the same one that covers the building today.

138. **Tomb of King David** 1588

Section of the picture of Jerusalem on page 24, no. 28.

139. **Tomb of the Kings of the House of David** About 1900

Illustration used for the decoration of books printed in Jerusalem and of 'Simhat-Torah' flags waved on the 'Rejoicing of the Law', the last day of Succot, the Feast of Tabernacles.

140. **Tomb of King David** About 1900

Engraved on a brass tablet set in the 'Chair of Elijah'.

See illustration no. 86, on page 46.

כי בחר ה' בציון אוה למושב לו .

141. **Tomb of David** 1900

An illustration often found in books printed in Jerusalem at the end of the nineteenth century. Below, the words of the Psalms: 'For the Lord hath chosen Zion, He hath desired it for His habitation'.[1]

1) Psalms 132, 13

142. The Tomb of King David 1837

L'Abbé Gr(and) et M. A. Egron, 'La Terre Sainte', 1837.

143. Tomb of King David 1853

By the English painter W. H. Bartlett, in 'Jerusalem Revisited', printed in 1588.

144. The Tomb of King David 1837

Detail of the decorated paper sheet mentioned above.

(see figures 97 – 98).

145. The Cenotaph attributed to King David About 1860

Moslem worshippers at the tomb.

'Jerusalem und das Heilige Land' by J. N. Sepp, 1873.

146. The area of the New City of Jerusalem before its construction 1586

From the book of J. Zuallart, 'Il devotissimo Viaggio di Gierusalemme', 1587.

Right: the western wall of the Old City and the Tower of David with the Jaffa Gate to its left. Below: the Pool of Mamillah (A); higher up, a building roofed in cupolas (B) marks a tomb sacred to Moslems. To its upper left a group of pilgrims (C) advances towards the Holy City. Below them, a circular building (D) represents a holy tomb, perhaps the one named Nebi Ukhasha which, today, stands in the centre of the New City, in the quarter named Zichron-Moshé, on Strauss Street.

Behind the Old City rises the Mount of Olives (E). On the left, on the top of a mountain range (F), the tomb of the Prophet Samuel – Arabic: An-Nebi Samuil, which dominates the highway to Jerusalem.

147. The Pool of Mamillah and its vicinity 1850

From the book ot J. T. Barclay 'The City of the Great King', 1858.

In the background, the western wall of the Old City with the Tower of David in its centre; next to it the Jaffa Gate.

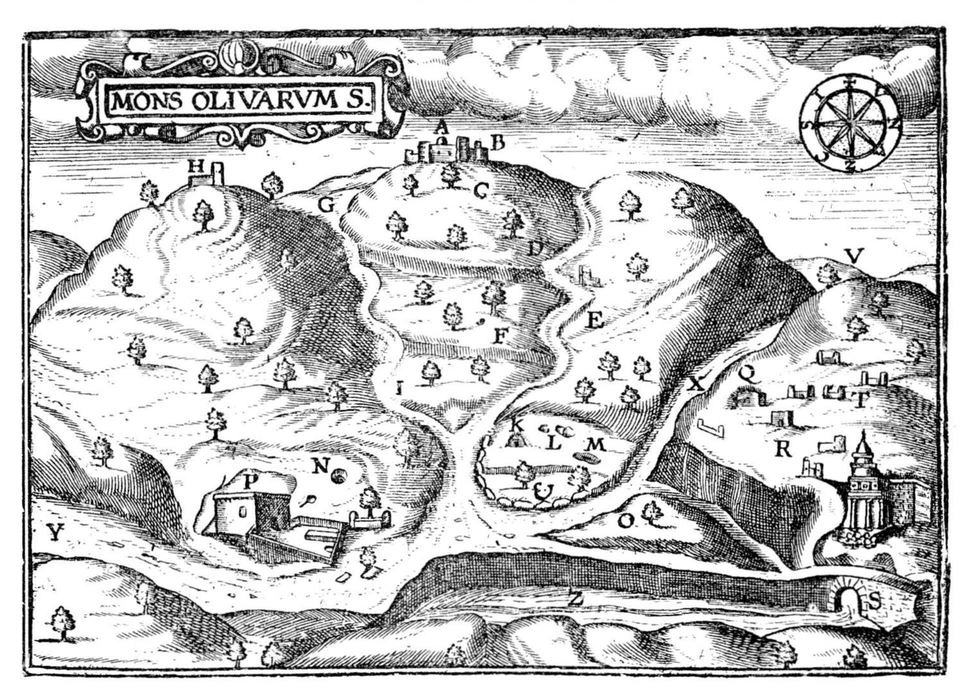

148. The Mount of Olives – Mons Olivarum S(acer). 1586

From the book of J. Zuallart, 'Il devotissimo Viaggio di Gierusalemme', 1587,
On the summit, the Church of the Ascension (A). To its right the tomb of the Prophetess Hulda (B) by Jewish tradition. At the bottom, the Brook Kidron (Valley of Jehoshaphat) spanned by a bridge (S), and, near by, the 'Hand' of Absalom (R).

W. R. Wilson, 'Travels in the Holy Land', 1824.

On the summit, the Church of the Ascension (A); at the foot, the Church of the Tomb of Mary (B). Several pathways wind up the steep mountain-side. The road to the right leads to Bethany, Jericho and the Dead Sea. At the bottom a bridge spans the Brook Kidron (G). Above the bridge, on the right, is the Jewish cemetery (F).

149. The Mount of Olives 1819

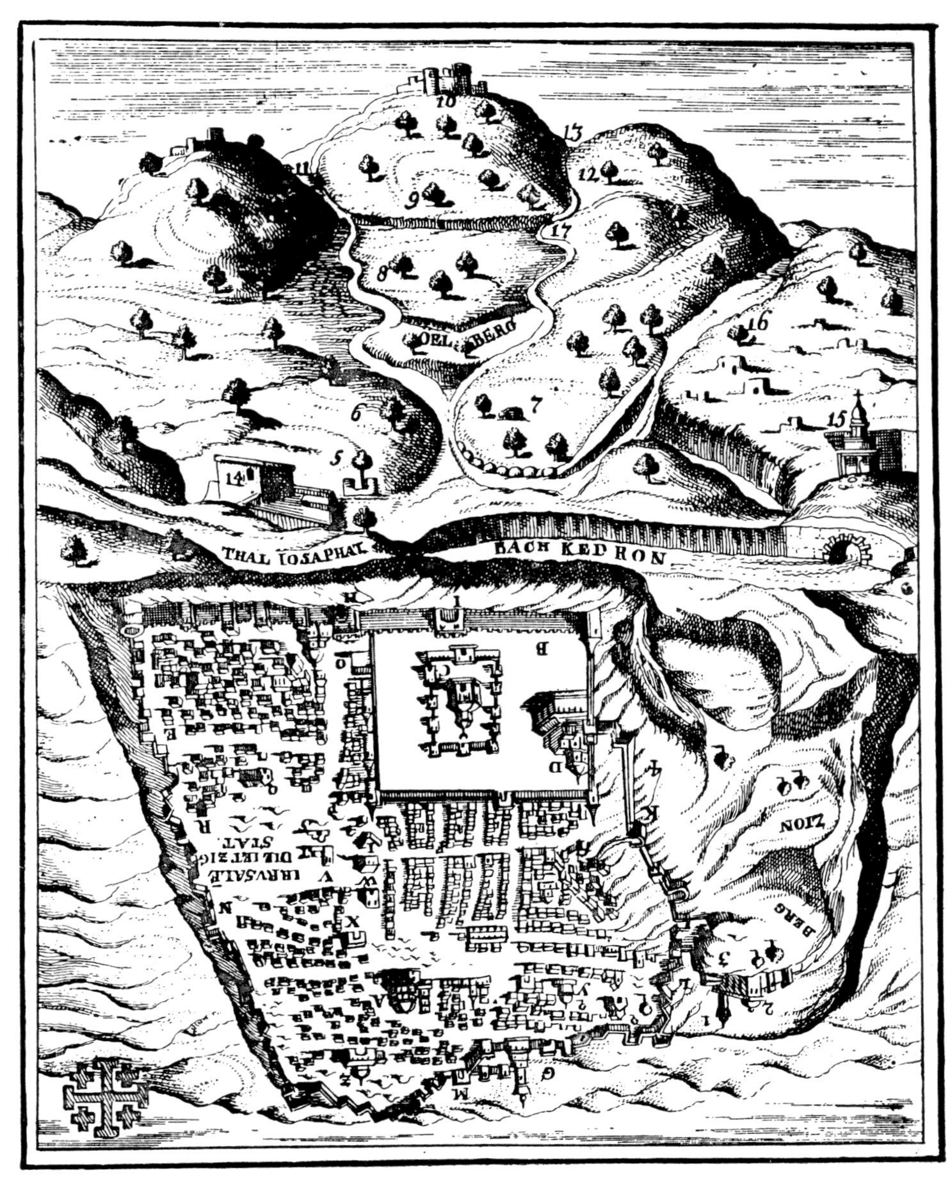

150. The Mount of Olives and Jerusalem 1738

'Jonas Kortens Reise nach dem gelobten Lande', printed in 1741.

The Mount of Olives, 'Oelberg', is copied from Zuallart (see figure 148). The serial numbers indicate holy sites, like 7 – the Garden of Gethsemane, 10 – the church of Ascension, 13 – the road to Jericho 14 – the tomb of St. Mary, 15 – the 'Hand' of Absalom. At the foot of the hill are the Brook Kidron — Bach Kedron, and the Valley of Jehoshaphat – Thal Josaphat.

151. The Mount of Olives About 1900

A picture found in Hebrew prints of Jerusalem.

At the bottom, the words of the Prophet Zechariah: 'And his feet shall stand in that day upon the Mount of Olives'[1]

At the foot of the mountain stands the wall of Jerusalem with the Gate of Mercy (the Golden Gate) in the centre. Beyond the wall–the 'Hand' of Absalom, and on the right – the 'House of Hofshit' and the tomb of the Prophet Zechariah.

1) Zechariah, 14,4

152. Ein-Karem 1677

O. Dapper, 'Beschryving van gantsch Syrie en Palestyn of Heilige Landt', printed in 1677.

A. – Church of St. John the Baptist. B. – Well of St. Mary. C. – House of Zechariah and Elisabeth, on the site ot today's Church of the Visitation.

153. Ein-Karem About 1880

From the book of P. Lortet, 'La Syrie d'aujourd'hui', printed in 1884.

154. The Valley named Elah (Vallis Therebenti) **in the Middle Ages** 1586

From the book of J. Zuallart, 'Il Devotissimo Viaggio di Gierusalemme', printed in 1587. This valley, mistaken for the biblical Valley of Elah by pilgrims of the Middle Ages, stretches west of Jerusalem. On its sides stand, today, the villages of Motza and Mevasseret-Yerushalaim. The true Valley of Elah, which is situated farther into the Judean Hills, to the southwest, witnessed the famous combat of David the Shepherd and Goliath the Philistine. Above the valley, on a height, lies Calonia, an Arab village. Under the hill, in Latin: 'Hic occisus fuit Goliad'—Here Goliath was slain.

155. The Valley named Elah in the Middle Ages 1677

O. Dapper, 'Beschryving van gantsch Syrie en Palestyn of Heilige Landt', printed in 1677.

156. Abu-Ghosh — S(aint) Hieremia 1586

From the book of J. Zuallart, 'Il devotissimo Viaggio di Gierusalemme', printed in 1587.

157. Abu-Ghosh — S(aint) Ieremias 1666

From the book of A. Gonsales, 'Hierusalemsche Reyse', printed in 1673.

The Christian pilgrims mistook Abu-Ghosh for the biblical Anatoth, the birth-place of the Prophet Jeremiah, and named it after him.

By the side of the Arab village, the Crusader Church dominates the highway from Jerusalem to Jaffa.

158. Abu-Ghosh – S(aint) Hieremia 1677

O. Dapper, 'Beschryving van gantsch Syrie en Palestyn of Heilige Landt', printed in 1677.

159. The Way from Bethlehem to Jerusalem 1586

From the book of J. Zuallart, 'Il devotissimo Viaggio di Gierusalemme', printed in 1587.

On the left: Jerusalem, the Tower of David (A), the Jaffa Gate and, below, the Pool of the Sultan (B). From the Jaffa Gate a road starts south to Bethlehem. By its side is the tree (C) in whose shade, according to popular belief, St. Mary and the infant Jesus rested. West of this road is a building (D) on the site of today's Church of St. Simeon, and next to it a domed house which indicates the Monastery of the Cross. Near the road, a well, holy to the Christians, is marked E. Next to it stands the Monastery of the Prophet Elijah – Mar Elias (see next figure). To the south, a house (I) and a field (K) named after the Patriarch Jacob. In their vicinity, the Tomb of Rachel (L) (see figure 164). To the west, the village of Beit-Jalla (M) named Rama by the Christian pilgrims. At the entrance to Bethlehem, a cistern (N) named after King David. Within the town of Bethlehem, surrounded by a wall, a monastery (O) is built on the site of Jesus' birth. Near it is a house (P) named after Joseph, son of Jacob, and farther up the hill a village (Q) with the 'Shepherds' Field' of the New Testament in its vicinity. To the south, Mount Herodion with biblical Tekoa close by. To the east, the mountains of the Wilderness of Judah.

160. The Monastery of Mar Elias (Monast. S. Heli) 1586

From the book of J. Zuallart mentioned above.

By the side of the monastery (A), there was shown a rock carrying the imprint of a human body (B), according to legend, that of the Prophet Elijah who once rested on it. Near by, a house (C) named after the Patriarch Jacob, and a well (D) sacred to Christians.

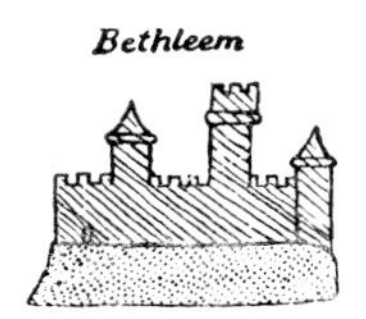

161. Bethlehem and the tomb of Rachel About 1900

'Bethleem – Sepulcrum Rachelis'

From a map preserved in the Florence Library, Italy.

163. Tomb of Rachel 1537

From the Hebrew pamphlet mentioned in figure 64.

162. Tomb of Rachel 1598

From a Hebrew manuscript written in Italy. See figure 91.

The inscription reads: 'Betlehem in Judah, close to it, on the road, is the tomb of Rachel, with a handsome building which is the shrine of Rachel to this day, and this is its shape'.

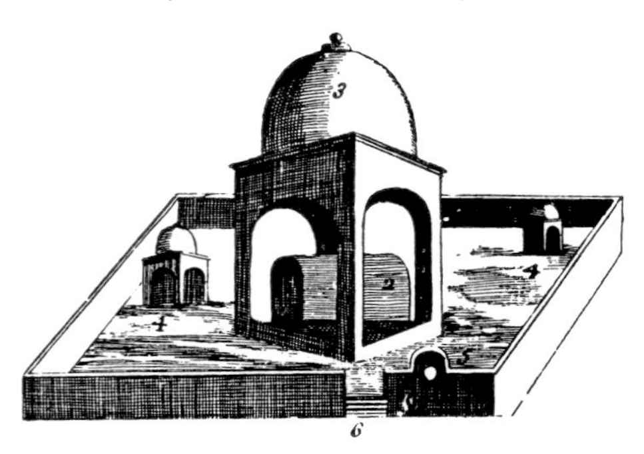

165. Tomb of Rachel 1631

From the book of Eugène Roger, 'La Terre Saincte', printed in 1646.

1. The fence around the tomb.
2. The monument over the tomb.
3. The cupola on four columns.
4. Places of prayer.
5. Drinking water.
6. Entrance and steps.

164. Tomb of Rachel – 'Sepulchrum Rachel' 1586

J. Zuallart, 'Il devotissimo Viaggio di Gierusalemme', 1587.

167. Rachel's Tomb About 1900

On an amulet made in Jerusalem.

Around the edge, in Hebrew: 'May it be Thy wish, O God and God of our fathers, that Thou shouldst keep this child from the Evil Eye and from all disease and harm, from now on and for ever and ever'.

On the reverse there is written: 'May God bless thee and keep thee', and also Jacob's blessing to his son Joseph: 'A fruitful vine by a fountain',[1] and, in abbreviated form, the Psalmist's verse: 'There shall no evil befall thee. Neither shall any plague come nigh thy tent'.[2]

1) Genesis 49,22. 2) Psalms 91, 10.

166. Tomb of Rachel – Rachel's Grafe 1677

←
O. Dapper, 'Beschryving van gantsch Syrie en Palestyn of Heilige Landt', 1677.

THE TOMB OF RACHEL

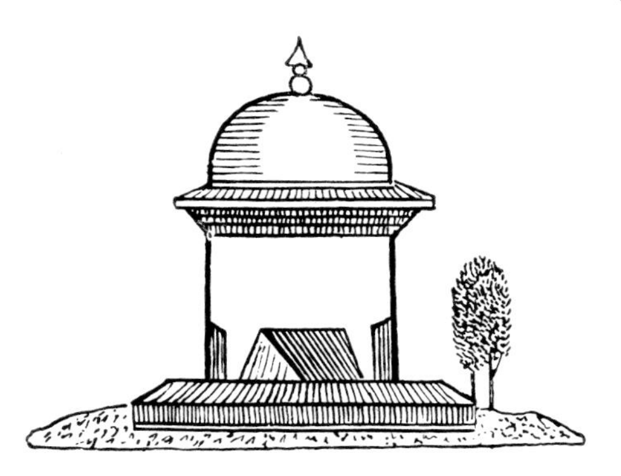

168. Tomb of Rachel 1842

From a German book on the Land of Israel, by J. Gans, printed in 1843.

169. Tomb of Rachel 1840

From the German translation of the book of Rabbi Joseph Schwarz, 'Tevuot Haaretz' – Harvest of the Land, printed in 1852.

170. Tomb of Rachel 1900

Engraved on a brass tablet affixed to the 'Chair of Elijah the Prophet'

(See figure 86, page 46)

171. Tomb of Rachel About 1900

Stained glass window of a synagogue in Szeged (Szegedin), Hungary.

172. Tomb of Rachel 1887

From the book of John Wesseler,

'Reiseerinnerungen aus Palästina', printed in 1888.

173. Tomb of Rachel 1900

Illustration found in Hebrew books printed in Jerusalem, at the end of the nineteenth century.

174. Tomb of Rachel 1930

A stamp from the time of the British Mandate for Palestine.

175. Bethlehem 1845

From the book of O. Georgi, 'Die Heiligen Stätten nach Originalzeichnungen nach der Natur', printed in 1845.

Left: the large church built over the Grotto of the Nativity. In the background, Mount Herodion rising south-east of Bethlehem, on the border of the Wilderness of Judah.

176. **Bethlehem** Fifth Century

A section of the mosaic found in the Cathedral of San Giovanni-in-Laterano, Rome.

(See figure 6, page 4)

177. Bethlehem and the Church of the Nativity 1700

From the book of Pietro Antonio, 'Guida fedele alla Santa Città di Gierusalemme e descrittione di tutta Terra Santa', printed in 1703.

178. The Church of the Nativity – Interior View 1851

J. J. Bourassé, 'La Terre Sainte', 1877.

179. Men of Bethlehem 1830

J. J. S. Taylor, 'La Syrie, l'Égypte, la Palestine et la Judée', 1839.

180. Women of Bethlehem 1863

K. Furrer, 'Wanderungen durch das Heilige Land', 1891.

181. The Monastery of Mar Saba 1631

East of Bethlehem, in the Wilderness of Judah.

Eugène Roger, 'La Terre Sainte', 1646.

182. The Monastery of Mar Saba 1851

J. J. Bourassé, 'La Terre Sainte', 1877.

183. Greek Monks of the Monastery 1880

P. Lortet, 'La Syrie d'aujourd'hui', 1884.

184. Hebron, on the left the structure built over the Cave of Machpelah 1842

A drawing by W. H. Bartlett published in H. Stebbing's, 'The Christian in Palestine', 1847.

185. Hebron, on the right the building over the Cave of Machpelah 1850

From the book of J. P. Newman, 'From Dan to Beersheba', printed in 1864.

186. The Building on the Cave of Machpelah About 1840

S. Munk, 'Palestine, description géographique, historique et archéologique', 1845.

187. The Building on the Cave of Machpelah About 1886

W. L. Gage, 'Palestine – Historical and Descriptive', 1888.

188. Removal of Jacob's bones from Egypt to Hebron About 1400

189. Crusader Seal of Hebron About 1180

Pictures of the Patriarchs: Abraham, Ysaac et Iacob.

From the Haggada of Sarajevo

'His sons carried him into the land of Canaan, and buried him in the cave of the field of Machpelah...'[1]

1) Genesis 50, 13

190. The Tombs of the Patriarchs in the Cave of Machpelah 1593

From a Hebrew illustrated manuscript written in Casale Monferrato, Northern Italy.

The inscription starting at the top of the picture and continuing at the bottom reads as follows: 'These are the journeyings of the Children of Israel which they journey, from strength to strength, to prostrate themselves upon the sepulchres of the Righteous, until they come with tears and supplication to pray for the welfare of their brethern which are in the Diaspora, may the Lord hasten our deliverance, Amen. Hebron, there the four Patriarchs and their wives are buried in the Cave of Machpelah. Over the cave there is a beauteous and wondrous building constructed by David the King, upon whom be peace!'.

191. The building over the Cave of Machpelah About 1700

From the book of Pietro Antonio, 'Guide fedele alla Santa Citta di Gierusalemme e descrittione di tutta Terra Sancta', printed in 1703.

192. The building over the Cave of Machpelah About 1862

From the anonymous Hebrew book 'Shivhei Ha'Ari – Praises of Ha'Ari, printed in 1862.

Ha'Ari – in Hebrew 'The Lion' – is the honoured title by which is known Rabbi Itshak Lurie, the great mystic master of Safed, the capital of Galilee, in the sixteenth century.

193. The building over the Cave of Machpelah About 1900

Engraved on a brass tablet affixed to the 'Chair' of the prophet Elijah (see figure 86, page 46).

Legend tells: When Adam passed the Cave of Machpelah, he saw a faint light streaming from it and understood that this light came from the Garden of Eden. For that reason he chose to be buried there.

The Cave of Machpelah is famed as the bridgehead to Eden. Every one that lives in Hebron knows for certain that when he dies and is buried there, his soul merits an immediate ascent to Eden, without any distress or pangs of passage whatsoever.

194. The Cave of Machpelah on a seal About 1868

The seal belonged to the Jewish community of Hebron.

The inscription mentions the other name of Hebron, also known as Kiryat-Arba – City of the Four, according to legend after the patriarchal couples buried there: Adam and Eve, Abraham and Sarah, Isaac and Rebecca, Jacob and Leah.

195. The Cave of Machpelah About 1900

Pictured on a paper sheet used for the decoration of Succot (Feast of Tabernacles) booths.

196. The Cave of Machpelah About 1900

Engraved on an amulet reputed to secure good health.

197. In the Market of Hebron About 1880

THE TREE OF ABRAHAM IN HEBRON

198. The Tree of Abraham About 1300

Section of an ancient map of Palestine written in Latin.

The fortified castle indicates Hebron — Ebron. Next to it is a tree marked Oak of Mamre — Ilex Mambre, where Abraham 'moved his tent, and came and dwelt by the terebinths of Mamre which are in Hebron, and built an altar unto the Lord'.[1]

1) Genesis 13, 18

199. The Tree of Abraham, About 1900

As a symbol of the Tree of Life on the Hebrew seal of a Jerusalem Yeshiva named after the Patriarch Abraham.

The Seal is preserved in the collection of Dr. H. Feuchtwanger, Jerusalem.

In the centre, the tree of the patriarch with the praise of the Torah written around its crest: 'She is a tree of life, to them that lay hold upon her, and happy is anyone that holdeth her fast'.[1]

Around the edge: 'Seal of the Yeshivah of 'Ohel (Tent of) Abraham, in the Synagogue 'Tiferet (Glory of) Israel', of the sacred community of Hassidim in the Holy City of Jerusalem, may it be rebuilt and restored soon, in our days, Amen'.

1) Proverbs ,3 18.

200. The Tree of Abraham 1482

('the dry tree')

From the German translation by M. Velser of the 'Travels' of the Englishman Sir John Maundeville in the countries of the East.

201. Abraham's Tree About 1860

From an illustrated book of travels.

202. The descent from Jerusalem to Jericho. From J. Zuallart's book mentioned in no. 164. 1586
On top of the mountains the village known to the Christians as Bethany and to the Arabs as Al-'Azariah. It commands the highway from Jerusalem to Jericho and the River Jordan – Jordanus flu., which is seen emptying its waters into the Dead Sea – Mare Mortuum.

203. From Jerusalem to the Wilderness of Jericho 1819
From the book of R. Wilson, 'Travels in the Holy Land', printed in 1824.
A caravan of pilgrims rides down the precipitous slope of the Mountains of Judah to Jericho, showing in the plain. In its vicinity the Jordan flows into the Dead Sea. Beyond, rise the Mountains of Gilead and Moab, in Transjordan.

204. The Conquest of Jericho by the Tribes of Israel About 435

Mosaic set in the wall of the Church of Santa Maria Maggiore, Rome.

In the centre: the town of Jericho surrounded by a fortified wall with towers. Rahab, the harlot, stands above, the only inhabitant who was saved with 'her father's household, and all that she had... because she hid the messengers whom Joshua sent to spy out Jericho'.[1]

One of the walls is about to fall. The Israelites, carrying shields and spears, surround the city.

1) Joshua 6, 25.

See figure 8 for another section of the same mosaic picturing Jerusalem

205. Jericho and its Surroundings Sixth Century

A section of the pictorial Map of Madaba, a mosaic preserved in the floor of the Church of Madaba, in Transjordan. Jericho, its name written in Greek, is surrounded by a wall with towers and gate. Around the city grow date-trees, wherefore the name 'City of Palms'. Left, a building 'of Saint Elisha' stands near the fountain named after him. On top, another building indicates the site of ancient Gilgal with the twelve stones which the tribes of Israel put up after crossing the Jordan: 'And those twelve stones, which they took out of the Jordan, did Joshua set up in Gilgal. And he spoke unto the children of Israel, saying: what mean these stones?—then ye shall let your children know, saying: Israel came over this Jordan on dry land...'[1]

1) Joshua 4, 20 – 22.

The picture of Jerusalem in the Map of Madaba appears on pages 2 – 4.

206. The Conquest of Jericho by the Israelites Fifth Century

From the Scroll of Joshua, a Greek manuscript preserved in the Library of the Vatican, Rome.

207. Joshua and the Angel in front of Jericho, From the manuscript mentioned above. Fifth Century

The Angel of the Lord is pictured with his sword drawn, in accordance with the biblical story;[1] Joshua appears in two postures: first challenging the armed stranger, then falling on his face in low obeisance when the visitor's divine nature is revealed to him.

1) Joshua, 5, 13 — 14.

208. The Conquest of Jericho About 1743

From 'Yosifon', a Yiddish version of Josephus.

209. The Israelites' War in Jericho and its Surroundings From a Passover Haggadah. 1629

Left: the Israelites encompass the town of Jericho standing on the bank of the River Jordan. Right: the Israelites defeat the Amorites. On top: the victory in the town of Gibeon and the Valley of Ayalon (Aijalon), with the sun motionless in the sky in obedience to Joshua's famous behest: "Sun, stand thou still upon Gibeon and thou, Moon, in the Valley of Aijalon..."[1]

1) Joshua 10, 12.

210. Jericho Surrounded by Seven Walls 1366

From the 'Farhi Bible', a manuscript preserved in the Sassoon Library, England.

On top, in Hebrew: 'The town of Jericho is here drawn, its one and only gate bolted and barred against the Children of Israel'. At the bottom: 'This is the gate of the town and it leads into its centre'.

211. Jericho and its Walls From the manuscript mentioned in figure 91 1598

On the right the unfurled parchment carries the following words written in Hebrew: 'The town Jericho in the Land of Israel. Whoever entered it had to encompass it seven times for it had seven walls'. Left: 'the house of Rahab, the harlot'.

עם ישרא' הביטו וראו את הנ"ס הכתוב בס' הישר חומת יריחו שנבקעה תחתיה:

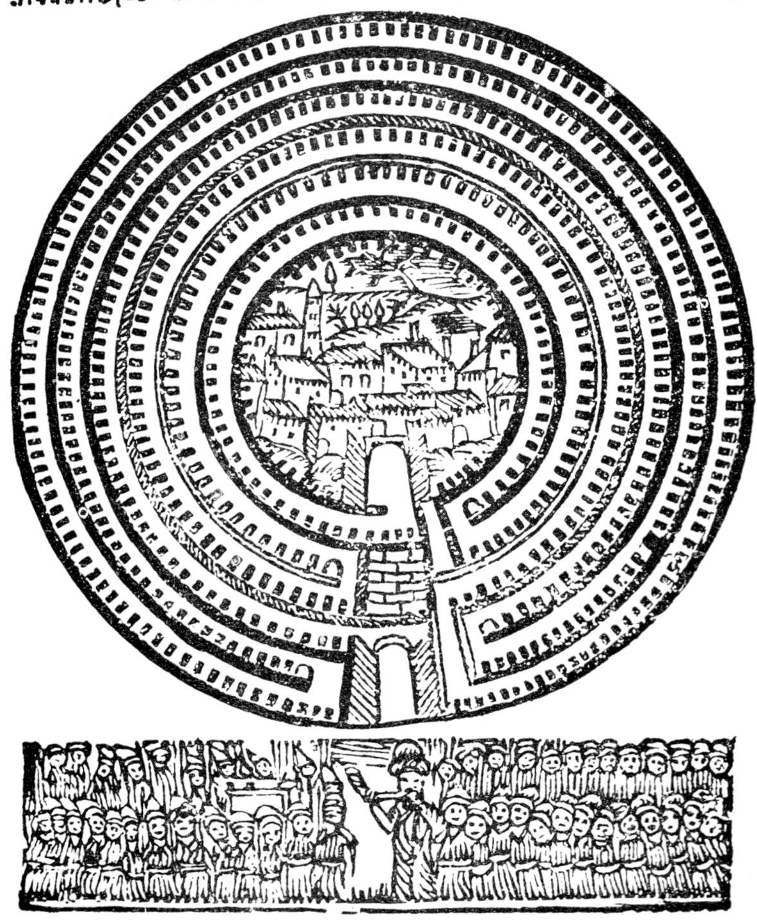

212. Jericho is Surrounded by Seven Walls 1733

From the Hebrew book: 'Zikaron Be Yerushalaim' – Memory in Jerusalem, printed in 1743, in Constantinople.

Below: the Israelites fully armed are led by their commander blowing the horn. The inscription above reads: 'People of Israel, look and behold the miracle that is written in the "Book of Ha-Yashar", the wall of Jericho that crumbled down'.

213. Jericho, City of Palms About 1900

A picture often used for the decoration of books printed in Jerusalem in the late nineteenth century.

214. Jericho About 1700

Engraved on a brass plate affixed to the 'Chair' of the Prophet Elijah.

see figure 86, page 46.

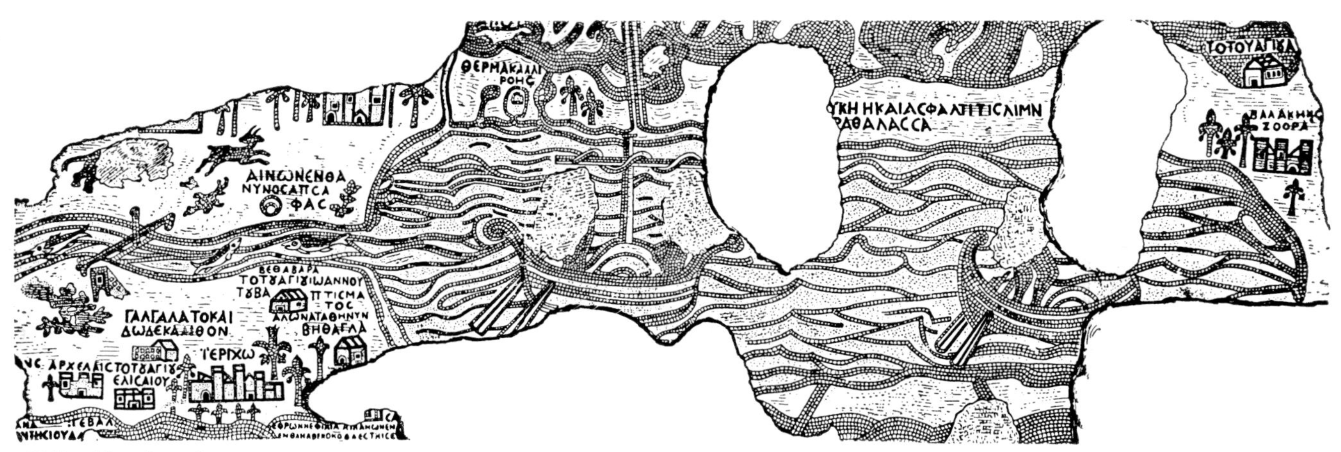

215. The Dead Sea on the Map of Madaba Sixth Century

Part of the extant mosaic floor of the Greek Church of Madaba, in Transjordan.

The names are written in Greek. Contrary to modern usage the west is at the bottom of the map. On the eastern bank of the Sea its various names are written: 'Salt Sea, that is the Sea of Asphalt (Asphaltitis), that is the Dead Sea'. On the southern bank the town Zoar and its palm-trees are drawn (see figure 230); on the eastern side, the Hot Spring are indicated by their Greek name: Callirrhoe; on the left, the River Jordan falls into the Sea (see figure 217). Above the Jordan a lion (partly effaced) chases a deer. Below the deer is the following inscription: 'Aenon now (called) Sapsaphas' and its vicinity where Jesus Christ immersed himself in the Jordan. The name Sapsaphas, the graecized form of the Hebrew word Saphsapha – meaning willow, is a reminder of the many trees which grow on the banks of the Jordan.

On the western bank of the Jordan appear Jericho and Gilgal with its twelve stones (see figure 205), 'Bethabara of Saint John the Baptist', and the 'Floor of Atad now Bethagla', mentioned in the Torah as the 'threshing-floor of Atad...' where 'they wailed with a very great and sore wailing',[1] on the death of Jacob the Patriarch.[1]

Two boats sail on the Sea. (For an enlargement of the boat on the left-hand side see following figure.)

1) Genesis 50, 10.

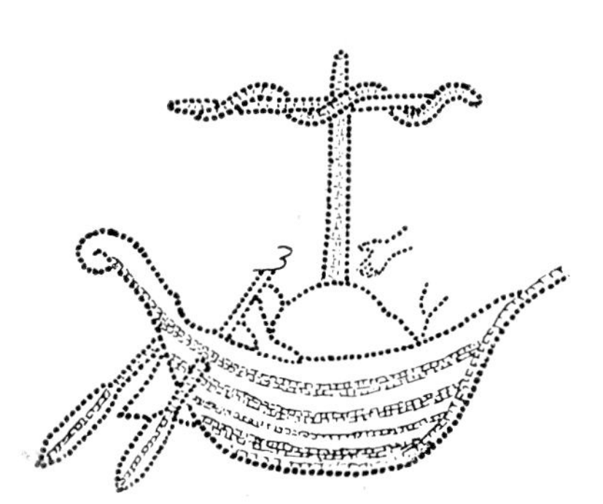

216. A sail-boat on the Dead Sea

The yards are furled over the yard-arm.
See the figure above.

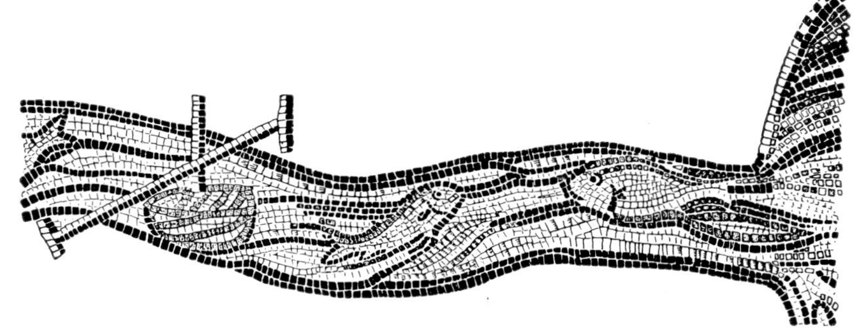

217. The outlet of the Jordan into the Dead Sea Sixth Century

A section of the Madaba Map. See picture on top.

Fish swim in the Jordan. One, which has reached the Sea and tasted its deadly saline waters, turns back, swimming against the current.

A bridge spans the river at the site of today's Allenby Bridge, over which crosses the highway between Jerusalem and Amman, the capital of Jordan.

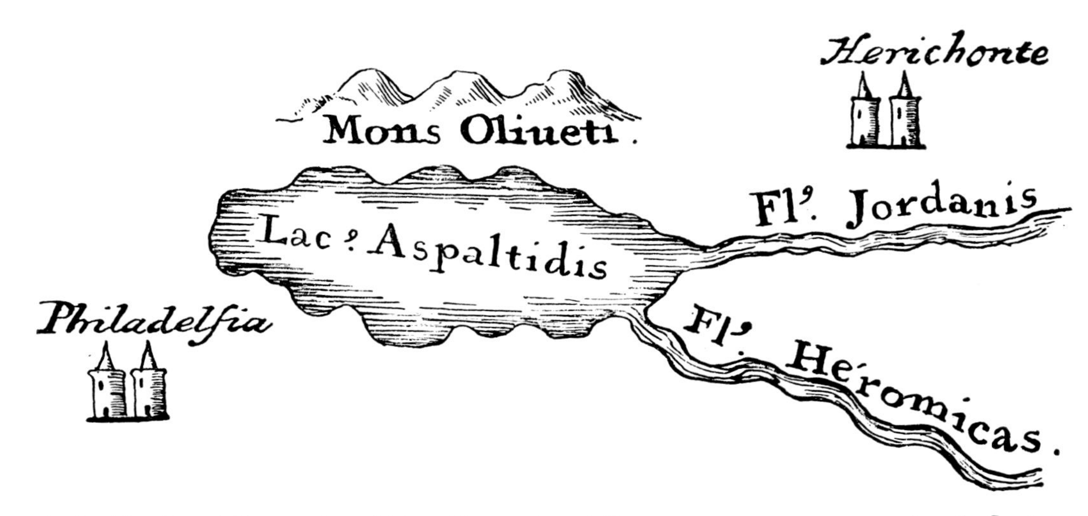

218. The Dead Sea in the Oldest Known Road Map Fourth Century

This map, the copy of an ancient Roman map, is known as 'Tabula Peutingeriana', after its owner and commentator in the sixteenth century, the Austrian scholar C. Peutinger.

The manuscript is preserved in the National Library of Vienna.

The Dead Sea is designated by its Greek-Latin name — Lac(us) Aspaltidis. It is pictured as fed by the Jordan — Fl. Jordanis, and also, mistakenly, by the River Yarmuk — Fl. Heromicas, which in reality joins the Jordan a short distance south of Lake Kinneret (Sea of Galilee). The Mount of Olives — Mons Oliveti, which is close to Jerusalem, is indicated near the western bank of the Sea, and the town Jericho — Herichonte, near the Jordan. On the eastern side of the Sea appears Philadelphia — Philadelfia, the Roman name of biblical Rabbat-Ammon, today Amman, the capital of the Hashemite Kingdom of Jordan.

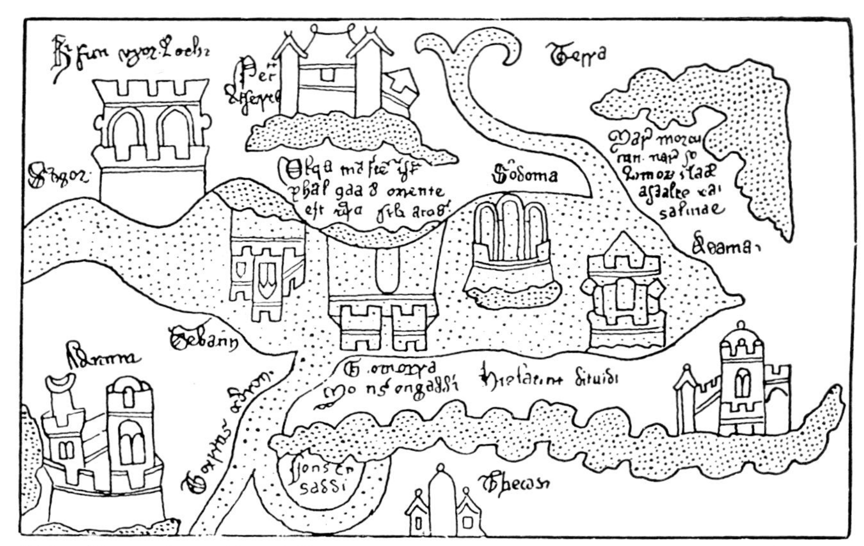

219. Map of the Dead Sea Fifteenth Century

From the map attached to The Itineraries of William Wey', in which he describes his travels in the Holy Land.

At the top right-hand corner, all the Latin names of the sea appear: Dead Sea — Mare Mortuum, Sea of Sodom — Mare Sodomorum, Lake of Asphalt — Lacus Asbalti, Valley of Salt — Vallis Salinae.

In accordance with the biblical tale, five towns are shown sunk in its waters: Sodoma, Adama, Gomorra, Sebaim and Sagor (Zo'ar).

Above Zo'ar there is written: 'Here was Lot's wife' — Hic fuit uxor Loth. The Sea is fed by the Brook Kidron — Torrens Cedron, which is joined by a tributary streaming from the Spring of Ein-Gedi — Fons Engaddi, and starting at the mountain of the same name — Mons Engaddi, where David hid from King Saul — Hic latuit David.

West of the Dead Sea, the town Tekoa is indicated — Thecua. On the eastern bank appears Petra — Petra deserta, under which an inscription reads: 'Behind this mountain is Baal-Gad(?), to the east the Land of the sons of Ammon'. — Vetra montem iste Phalgaad(?) at orientem est terra filiorum Amon.

220. Map of the Dead Sea 1532

From the Latin map of J. Ziegler, the author of the first atlas of the Holy Land, entitled: 'Quae intus continentur'.

The Dead Sea is indicated by its Greek-Latin name — Asphaltis. The Jordan flows into it and a little to the right — the Arnon. Around the Sea all the famous sites are indicated: Jericho — Jerichous, Jerusalem, under its Roman name of Aelia, Mezada — Masada, Ein-Gedi — Henghedi, Zo'ar — Sohar, Ma'alé Akrabim — Akrabbim.

In Transjordan too, biblical places are marked: Minnith, Haroer — 'Aro'er, Dibon.

The map also records the tribes that settled in this area: Benjamin — Biniamin, Reuben — Ruben, and Gad — Ghad, in Transjordan.

The Dead Sea carries its Greek-Latin name: Asphaltis. The Jordan flows into it — Iorda(nus) Fl. On the left hand of the Sea appears Jericho — Iericho, Ephrem and Betphage, a famous Christian site near Jerusalem. In the east rise the Mountains of Moab — Moabi. Between the Jordan and an elongated arm of the Dead Sea appears the name Beihabara, a name mentioned in the New Testament in the life of St. John the Baptist.

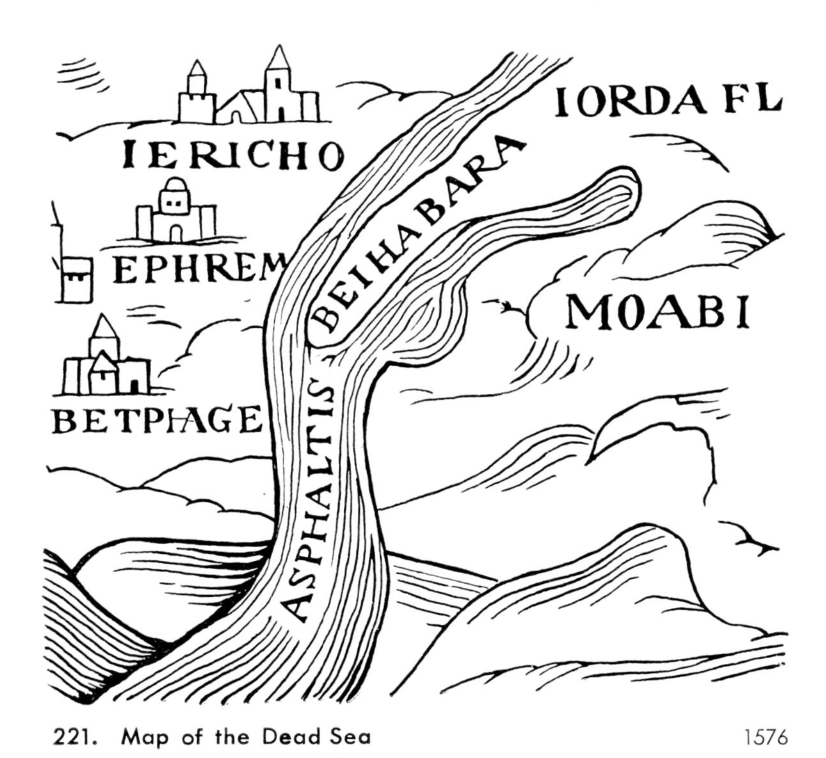

221. Map of the Dead Sea 1576

A section of a map of the Holy Land.

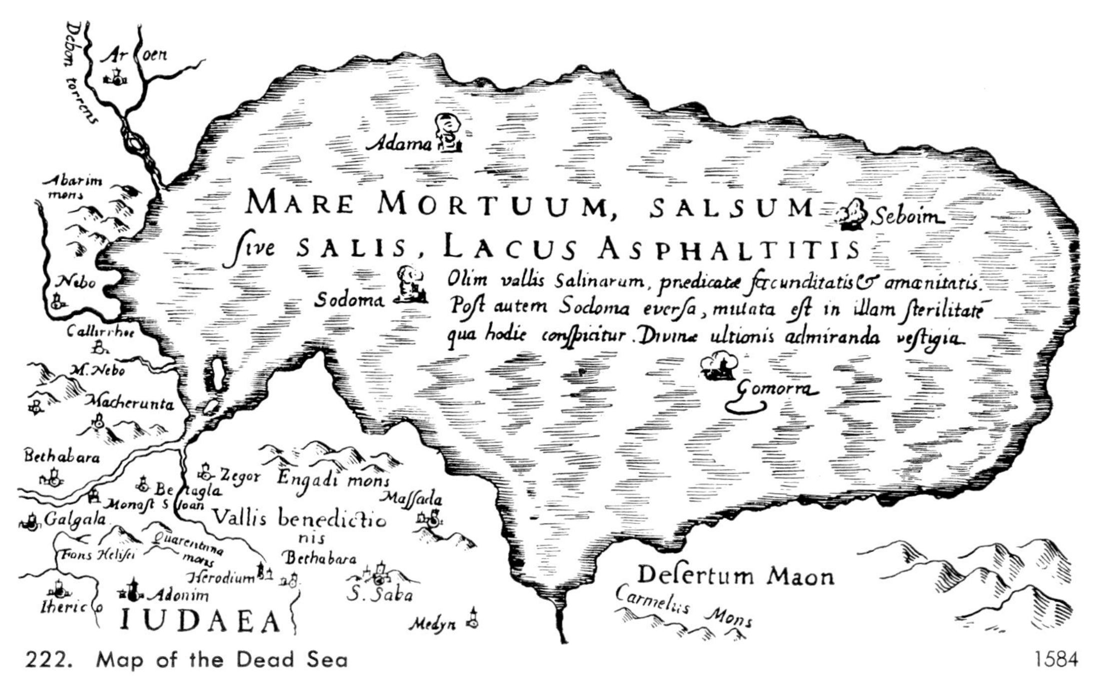

222. Map of the Dead Sea 1584

From a Latin map printed in the book of A. Ortelius, 'Theatrum Orbis Terrarum', 1584.

The Sea is designated by its various Latin names: Dead Sea – Mare Mortuum, Salt Sea – Mare Salis, Asphalt Lake – Lacus Asphaltitis. Within its waters appear four out of the five wicked cities that sank in biblical times: Adama, Seboim, Sodoma and Gomorra. On the bank appear the Desert of Maon – Desertum Maon, and Mount Carmel – Carmelus Mons, two places well-known from the record of David's flight from King Saul. Also indicated are: Mezada – Massada, the Mount of Ein-Gedi – Engadi Mons, the Monastery of Mar Saba – S. Saba, and the Valley of the Benediction – Vallis benedictionis, recorded in the chronicles of the war waged by Jehoshaphat, King of Judah, against Moab and Ammon.

The Latin in the middle of the Sea reads as follows: 'Once upon a time this was the Valley of Salt of famous fertility and pleasantness. But when Sodom was destroyed, it was transformed into that barrenness which is seen today. The signs of divine vengeance are to be wondered at'.

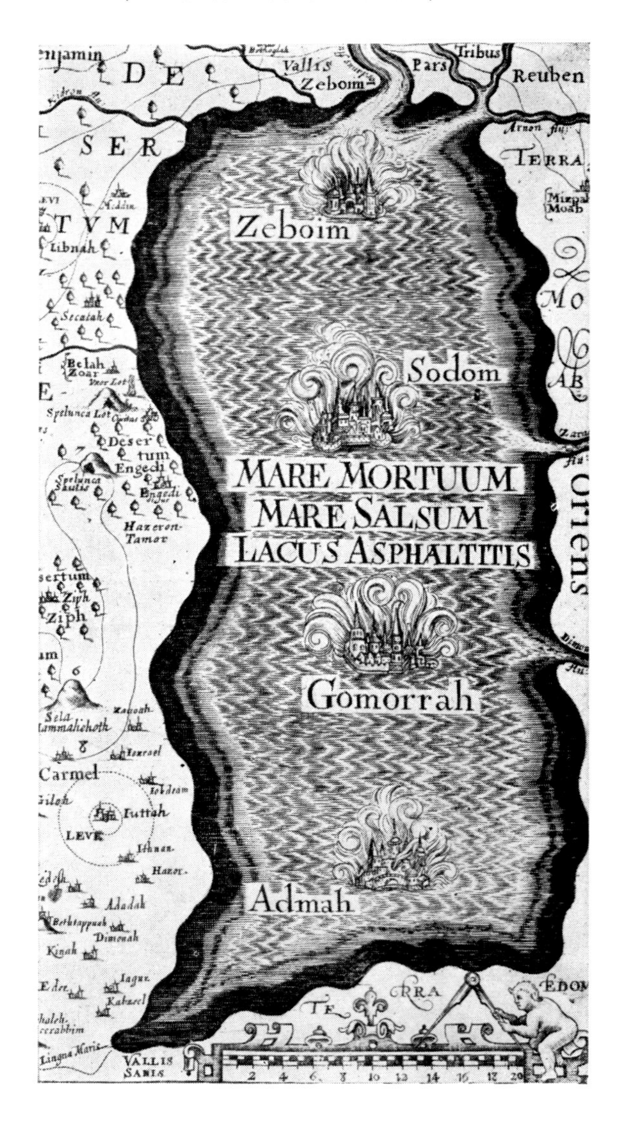

223. Map of the Dead Sea 1650

From the book of Thomas Fuller, 'A Pisgah-Sight of Palestine', printed in 1650.

The three Latin names of the Sea are inscribed: Mare Mortuum, Mare Salsum, Lacus Asphaltitis. Within the Sea four of the destroyed cities are pictured plunging down in flames: Zeboim, Sodom, Gomorrah, Admah.

From a map of the Land of Israel attached to a Passover Haggadah, printed in Amsterdam.

In the Sea, designated by its Hebrew name — the Sea of Salt — appear the four towns that were engulfed by its waters according to Holy Writ: Sodom, Gomorrah, Adama and Zeboim.

224. Map of the Dead Sea 1695

On the left bank of the Dead Sea appear the towns belonging to Judah, as mentioned in the Book of Joshua: Jericho, Ein-Gedi, Tekoa, and others. On the right bank of the Sea are drawn two tributaries of the Dead Sea: the rivers Arnon and Zered.

225. Map of the Dead Sea 1816

From a map of the Land of Israel printed in 1816.

226. The Sea of Salt, the Jordan and Jericho 1875

The houses of 'Overturned Sodom' appear within the waters, resting at the bottom of the Sea. Between the bank of the Sea and 'Jericho — City of Palms', a large rock is drawn with the following legend: 'The Wife of Lot', and next to it the biblical reference: 'But his wife looked back from behind him, and she became a pillar of salt'.[1]

The Jordan's outlet into the Dead Sea is marked by the legend: 'Here the Jordan falls into the Salt Sea'.

1) Genesis 19, 26.

227. The Town Sodom Fifteenth Century

From a Passover Haggadah preserved in the Bezalel Museum, Jerusalem, Israel.

The angel spreading 'fire and brimstone' hovers above the city.[1]

1) Genesis 19, 24.

228. Sodom and the Wife of Lot Thirteenth Century

From a Passover Haggadah, manuscript of Sarajevo, Yugoslavia. On the left: Lot's wife leading her two daughters away from Sodom. Centre: Lot's wife changed into a pillar of salt when she turned round to look at the 'brimstone and fire' falling from heaven on the wicked city. 'The sun was risen upon the earth when Lot came unto Zoar'.[1]

1) Genesis 19, 23.

230. The Town Zoar
Sixth Century

From the Madaba Map.

Above the building situated on the shore of the Dead Sea and representing the town surrounded by palm-trees, appears the following inscription: 'Bela also Segor now Zoora'. Above it a gabled house indicates the sanctuary 'of Saint L(ot)'. Below, the four Greek letters written vertically 'EPHM...' form the word 'desert' without mentioning its name.

229. Sodom 1278

Below is written: 'This is Sodom when the angels overturned her'.

From a Hebrew manuscript preserved in the British Museum. (Add. 11, 639).

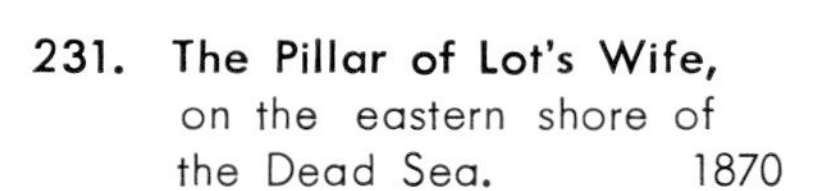

231. The Pillar of Lot's Wife, on the eastern shore of the Dead Sea. 1870

E. H. Palmer, 'The Desert of the Exodus', 1871.

232. Mezada (Massada) — the last fortress of the Jews 1842

From a drawing of the English artist W. Tipping.

233. Ein-Gedi 1848

The camp of the American expedition led by Captain W. F. Lynch.

From the book of W. F. Lynch, 'Narrative of the United States Expedition to the River Jordan and the Dead Sea', 1849.

234. Beduin Guard of the American Expedition 1848

From the book mentioned in figure 233.

235. Beersheba — an ancient well and a Beduin camp About 1880

W. M. Thomson, 'The Land and the Book', 1880.

This ancient well, extant in Beersheba to this day, is named after the Patriarch Abraham. The stones at the mouth are deeply grooved from the centuries of rubbing by the ropes of those who came to draw water.

236. Tourists' Tents in Beersheba 1864

H. B. Tristram, 'The Land of Israel', 1865.

237. One of the Seven Wells of Beersheba About 1880

P. Lortet, 'La Syrie d'aujourd'hui', 1884.

238. Gaza in the Map of Madaba Sixth Century

The two last letters of the name Gaza appear at the top. A large building with a colonaded porch stands out from among the houses; it is indicated as 'of Holy Victor', a local saint also mentioned by a pilgrim of the year 570. On the left appears the last part of the name Nea(po)lis, apparently the new suburb built, at the time, near the harbour of Gaza.

239. Gaza 1598

From the Hebrew manuscript mentioned in fig. 91.
Above: 'The village Gaza is the town of Samson, a beautiful city'.

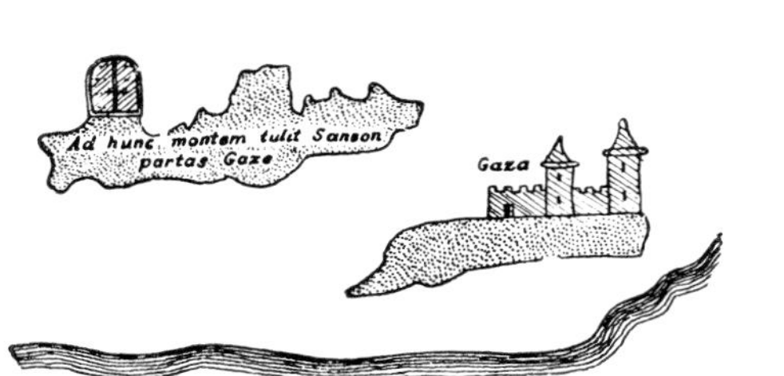

240. Gaza and its Vicinity About 1300

From a Latin map of the Holy Land preserved in Florence, Italy.

Right: picture of Gaza. Left: a mountain, as the Latin says, with the portals of Gaza that were carried to this spot by Samson.

241. Samson Carrying the Gates of Gaza 1766

From a book entitled by the Hebrew name 'Tsena u-Rena', a Yiddish translation of the Pentateuch.

242. Gaza K. Furrer, 'Wanderungen durch Palästina', 1865. 1863

243. Gaza A drawing of the English artist W. Tipping. 1842

244. Gaza — a medieaval Moslem house 1830

I. J. S. Taylor, 'La Syrie, l'Egypte, la Palestine et la Judée', 1839.

ASHKELON

245. The Conquest of Ashkelon by the Egyptians 1280 B. C.

In the time of Ramses II, Pharaoh of Egypt.

This bas-relief is carved on the walls of the Hypostyle Hall, in the ruins of Karnak, Upper Egypt.

Ashkelon, built on a hill, is surrounded by a wall in which there are two gates with jutting buttresses. Egyptian soldiers storm the city: one line of shield and swordsmen. A soldier armed with a hatchet attempts to break the gate, while another climbs a ladder to the top of the wall. The besieged raise their arms despairingly in sign of submission. One is seen holding a candlestick, a gift to the victor. At the top right-hand corner a hieroglyphic inscription, in vertical lines, says:

'The wretched town which his majesty captured when it was wicked, Ashkelon. It says: "Happy is he who acts in fidelity to thee, (but) woe (to) him who transgresses thy frontier; Leave over a heritage, so that we may relate thy strength to every ignorant foreign country!"'.

247. Ashkelon
Sixth Century

From the Madaba Map.

Left of the name Ackalon, fragments of an inscription meaning 'of the Egyptians', a group of martyrs who were put to death in 310. They are also mentioned by a Christian pilgrim of the year 570.

246. Ashkelon – Ackalon in Greek
Sixth Century

From a mosaic floor discovered in the Arab village Main, the biblical Baal-Maon, in the mountains of Transjordan.

248. Engagement between Crusader Knights and Moslem Warriors, near Ashkelon 1250

Pictured in a stained-glass window of the Church of St. Denis, near Paris.

249. The Ruins of Ashkelon 1818

L. N. Comte de Forbin, 'Voyage dans le Levant', 1819.

250. The Ruins of Ashkelon 1840

D. Roberts, 'The Holy Land from Drawings Made on the Spot', 1842.

View from the north. In the distance relics of the Crusader wall of the city and, underneath, remains of a large church, apparently from the Byzantine period.

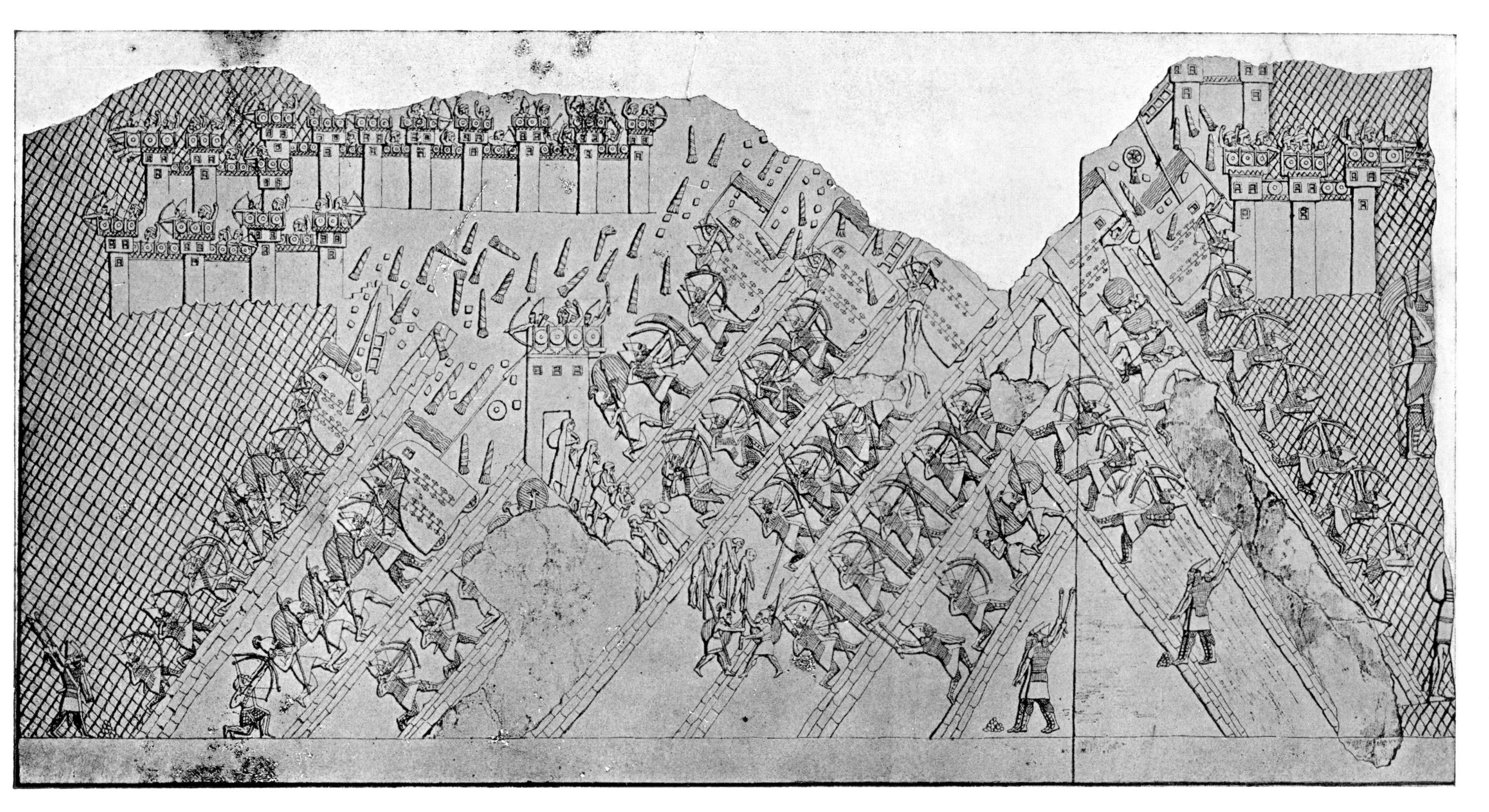

251. Lachish besieged by Assyrian forces 701 B.C.

Portion of a relief from the Palace of Sennacherib, king of Assyria, discovered in the ruins of his capital, Nineveh, northern Iraq, and preserved in the British Museum, London.

The town is surrounded by a fortified wall manned by soldiers armed with bows and slings. Some of the defenders hurl stones and burning torches on the attackers. Assyrian soldiers rush to the assault along the ramps they have built against the wall. They carry bows and arrows, lances and circular shields. Some of the bowmen are protected by large shields carried in front of them. In between the attackers are seen the battering rams with which they hammer down the fortifications. Soldiers using slings have small heaps of stone-pellets at their feet. From the gate captives walk forth carrying bundles on their backs. Near the gate, to the right, two Assyrians impale three prisoners, probably notables of the conquered city, on wooden poles struck through their bellies (next figures).

252. Assyrian soldiers attacking Lachish with slings, lances, bows and arrows.

253. The defeated inhabitants are brought before Sennacherib (see next fig.)

254. Sennacherib, King of Assyria, sits on his glorious throne, in front of the city of Lachish, receiving the prisoners and the spoil of the pillaged town. The cuneiform inscription above reads: "Sennacherib, king of the world, king of Assyria, sat upon a throne and passed in review the booty (taken) from Lachish". Facing the king are an officer, soldiers and kneeling inhabitants of Lachish.

SIEGE OF LACHISH – Details of the Assyrian Relief

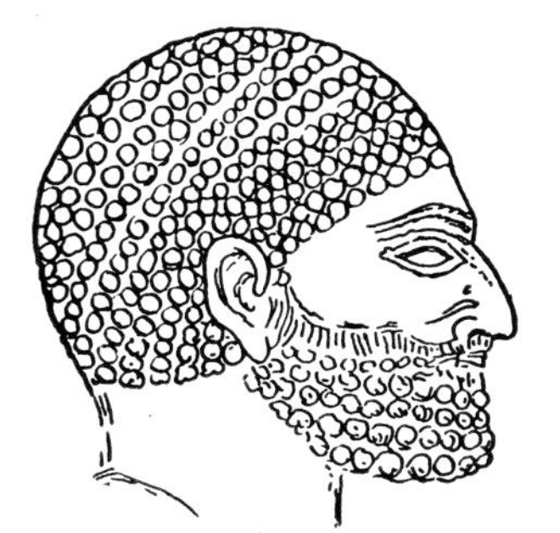

255. An inhabitant of Lachish

On the left:
257. Two Assyrians impale three prisoners

256. The warriors on the wall shoot arrows

258. The Lachish people go into exile

259. The agriculture of Lachish
Date-palms, fig-trees and vines.

260. Detail of a vine laden with clusters of grapes

261. Jaffa on a Crusader Seal
About 1200

Right: the citadel with its name written around the edge: City of Jaffa – Civitas Jope.

Left: the Governor in Crusader armour on horseback. His name is written around the margin: Comes Hugo.

262. Jaffa and its port 1483

Part of a pictorial map attached to the book of the German pilgrim B. von Breidenbach, 'Peregrinationes', 1486.

On top of the hill of Jaffa, a fortress, and in its vicinity a second fortress. Facing the port – caves, in the port – a few pilgrims. One is led away by a coastguard because he cannot afford to pay the toll levied on each pilgrim entering the Holy Land. On the left, the bow of the pilgrims' vessel (fig. 282) The Latin inscription in the body of the picture reads: Jaffa also Joppe the port to which pilgrims come to the Holy Land from the side of the sea – Jaffa sive Joppe portus ubi peregrini applicant ad terram sanctam de mari.

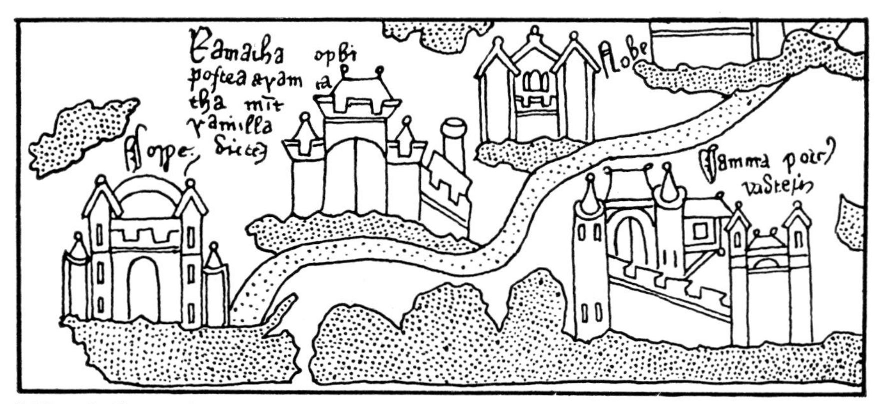

263. Jaffa and its vicinity Fifteenth Century

A section of the pictorial map of Palestine attached to 'The Itineraries of William Wey', printed in 1857.

Left: Jaffa – Joppe. Right: Yavne, the port of the Jews – Jamnia portus Judeorum. Near by, the town of Ramla which Christian pilgrims mistakenly believed to be Arimathea and formerly biblical Ramathaim-Zophim – Ramatha Sophin postea Aramatha nunc Ramilla dicitur. Right of Ramla is indicated Nobe, the Arab village of Beit-Nuba, on the ancient way from Jaffa to Jerusalem. A river is shown flowing between Jaffa and Yavne. Its name is not mentioned, but it undoubtedly is the Brook Sorek, which runs down from the Mountains of Judah to the Mediterranean Sea.

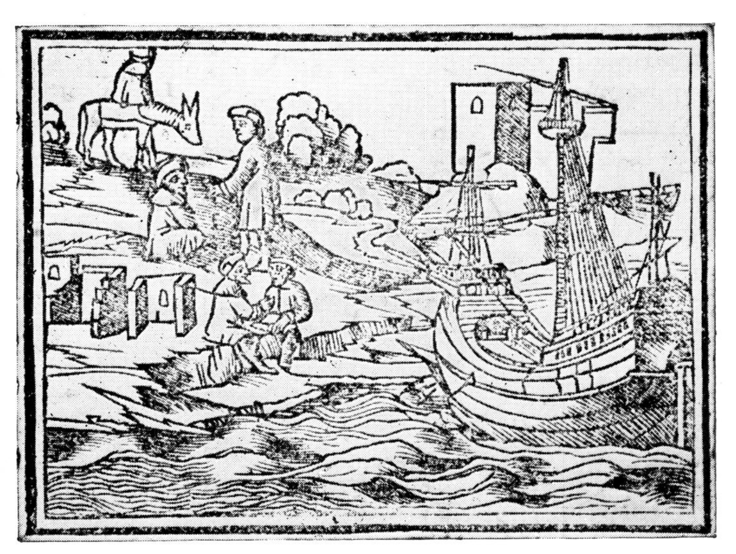

264. Jaffa and its port About 1500

B. Noé, 'Viazo da Venesia al sancto Jherusalem', 1519.

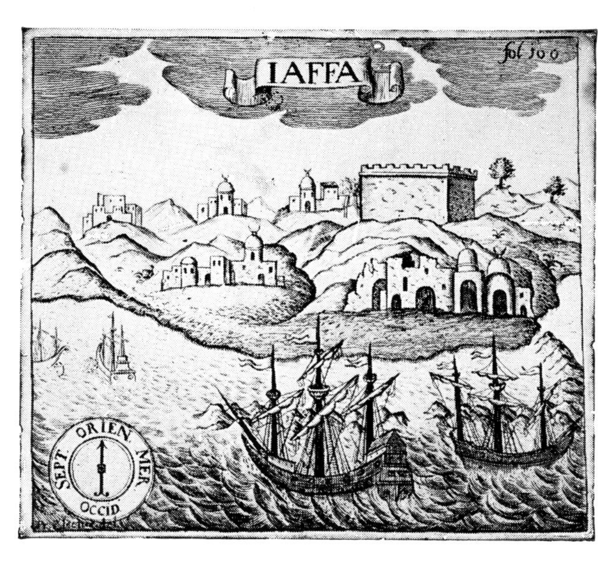

265. Jaffa and its port 1658

E. Zwinner, 'Blumen-Buch dess Heiligen Landes Palestina..., 1661.

266. Pilgrims at the entrance of a port, presumably Jaffa Fifteenth Century

From a manuscript preserved in the Library of the British Museum, London (Add. 24,189, fol. 8).

Christian pilgrims pay toll to Moslem guards on disembarking in the Holy Land.

A typical example of attributing to the Near East the appearance of the designer's own western environment. Both the style of the town with its red-roofed houses and the costumes of the guards are completely foreign to the Holy Land of those times.

267. Jaffa, view from the sea 1677

O. Dapper, 'Beschryving van gantsch Syrie en Palestyn of Heilige Landt', 1677.

Vessels at anchor, on shore various buildings. On the side of the hill, a mosque, and on the top a fortress flying the Turkish flag. A caravan leaves the port on its way to Jerusalem.

268. Jaffa and its port P. Angelicus Myller, 'Peregrinus in Jerusalem', 1729. 1726

Among the rocks pictured in the foreground is the one to which, says legend, beautiful Andromeda was chained, offered as a sacrifice to the Monster of the Sea.

269. Jaffa, a view from its northern shore 1830

From the book 'Itinéraire de Paris à Jérusalem' in which the French writer Chateaubriand describes his travels to the Holy Land, printed in 1871.
A similar picture by W. H. Bcrtlett, appears in J. Carne's, 'Syria'... 1835.

270. Jaffa, a view from its southern shore 1834

A picture by W. H. Bartlett, which appears in the book of Carne, 'Syria, the Holy Land', printed in 1845.
The army of the Egyptian Ibrahim Pasha encamps on the hills rising south of Jaffa, on the site now covered by the new quarter of the town named Givat-Aliya.

271. Jaffa, a view from the south 1853

From the book of the Swiss traveller, Titus Tobler, 'Topographie von Jerusalem', 1854.

272. Jaffa and its harbour About 1830

J. J. S. Taylor, 'La Syrie, l'Egypte, la Palestine et la Judée', 1839.

273. A Turkish guard on Jaffa's harbour 1860

A drawing by W. H. Bartlett.

274. Jaffa seen from the sea About 1850

275. Jaffa viewed from the north 1852

G. D(arboy), 'Jérusalem et la Terre Sainte', 1852.

276. Jaffa – Vendors of women's trinkets – beads, bracelets and rings. 1880

P. Lortet, 'La Syrie d'aujourd'hui', 1884.

277. Jaffa – shop of kerosene lamps 1880

P. Lortet, 'La Syrie d'aujourd'hui', 1884.

278. Jaffa and its northern shore 1856

H. B. Tristram, 'Scenes in the East', printed in 1870.

View to the north-east, over the area of sands now occupied by the city of Tel-Aviv.

279. Seal of the Jewish Community of Jaffa About 1892

Above are the words of the Bible: "And unto the Great Sea... shall be your border".[1]

In German: 'Jsraelitische Gemeinde (Israeli Community), Jaffa, Palestine'.

[1]) Joshua 1, 4.

280. Fountain at the entrance to Jaffa About 1880

Ch. W. Wilson, 'Picturesque Palestine', 1880.

It was named in Arabic Sebil (Drinking-place of) Abu-Nabut, after the Governor of Jaffa who erected it at the beginning of the nineteenth century, when Turkey ruled the country.

281. A caravan at the Jaffa fountain, on the highway to Jerusalem — 1862

F. E. Pâris, 'Souvenirs de Jérusalem', 1862.

282. A sailing boat in the port of Jaffa 1483

From a pictorial map attached to the 'Peregrinationes' of Bernhard von Breidenbach, printed in 1486.

See figures 25, and 262.

283. Three vessels nearing the Jaffa coast 1587

Salomon Schweigger 'Reyssbeschreibung ... nach... Jerusalem', 1608.

A passenger boat, a freighter and a small guard-ship. Flying-fish add an exotic note to the picture.

284. John Maundeville
Fourteenth Century
Johannes de montefilla

From a German translation of the 'Travels' of Sir John Maundeville.

The manuscript is kept in the Public Library of New York. According to Maundeville's testimony he visited the Holy Land in the year 1332.

286. Pilgrims landing on the shore of the Holy Land 1855

'Palestine, past and present', by H. S. Osborne, 1858.

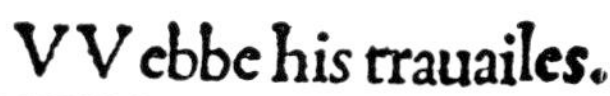

285. Edward Webbe 1590

An English traveller, on his way to the Holy Land.

From his book of travels printed in 1590 and entitled: 'The rare and the most wonderfull things which E. Webbe... hath seene... in his travailes in the cities of Jerusalem, Damasko, Bethlehem and Galely and in the Landes of Jewrie'.

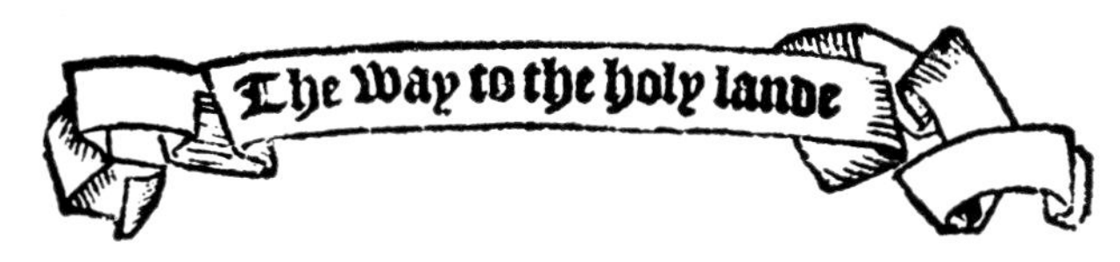

287. 'The Way to the Holy Lande'

A manuscript from the fifteenth century. The pilgrim sets out, carrying the staff of the traveller and the rosary of the pious Christian.

288. A pilgrims' caravan on the way to Jerusalem 1581

Solomon Schweiger, 'Reyssbeschreibung aus Teutschland nach... Jerusalem', 1608.

The Christian pilgrims on horseback travel under the protection of Arab guards, some on foot, some riding. The horsemen carry shields and lances, the footmen, bows and arrows. The baggage goes in front, borne by camels and donkeys.

289. A tourist in the Holy Land 1565

On camel-back, under a canopy.

J. Helfferich, 'Kurtzer und wahrhafftiger Bericht von der Reise... nach Hierusalem... auff den Berg Sinai', 1577.

290. 'Two Journeys to Jerusalem' About 1605

It was a usual practice for the foreign traveller to put on local costume as a measure of precaution.

291. From Jaffa to Jerusalem by night 1883

H. Brugsch, 'Prinz Friedrich Karl im Morgenlande', 1884.

292. A station for the night by the side of the road 1806

From the book of travels 'Voyage en Orient', by the French writer Chateaubriand, printed in 1851.

The baggage is collected on a straw mat, in the foreground. Some Arab servants put up tents for the use of the travellers, others brew coffee.

293. A public vehicle 1875

The first public carriage to ply on the road between Jaffa and Jerusalem.

294. The coach of Sir Moses Montefiore 1875

In which he travelled to Jerusalem on his last visit to the Holy Land.

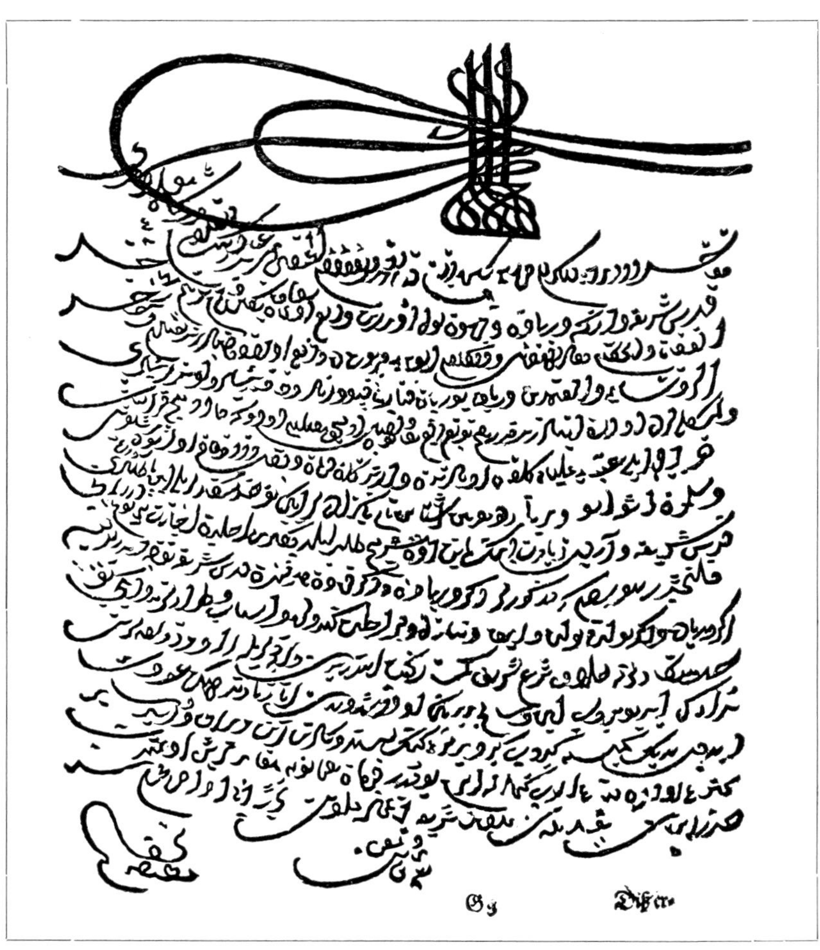

295. Turkish 'passport' delivered to a Christian pilgrim 1581

Solomon Schweigger, 'Reyssbeschreibung... nach... Jerusalem', 1608.

On top, the royal cipher of the Turkish Sultan.

296. Seal of Crusader Ramla About 1250

Right: the crenellated wall, the main gate, its defence tower, and the domes of the public buildings. Around, the Crusader name of the city – civitas Rama – city of Rama. Left: the Governor on horseback with mention of his name: Seal of Baldwin – Sigillum Balduini.

297. Ramla 1483

From a pictorial map attached to the book of B. von Breidenbach, 'Peregrinationes', printed in 1486.

(See figures 25, 262, and 282)

To the extreme right, the square tower of the White Mosque, and to the left, the minaret of the Great Mosque which originally was a Crusader church in the thirteenth century. Both buildings still exist.

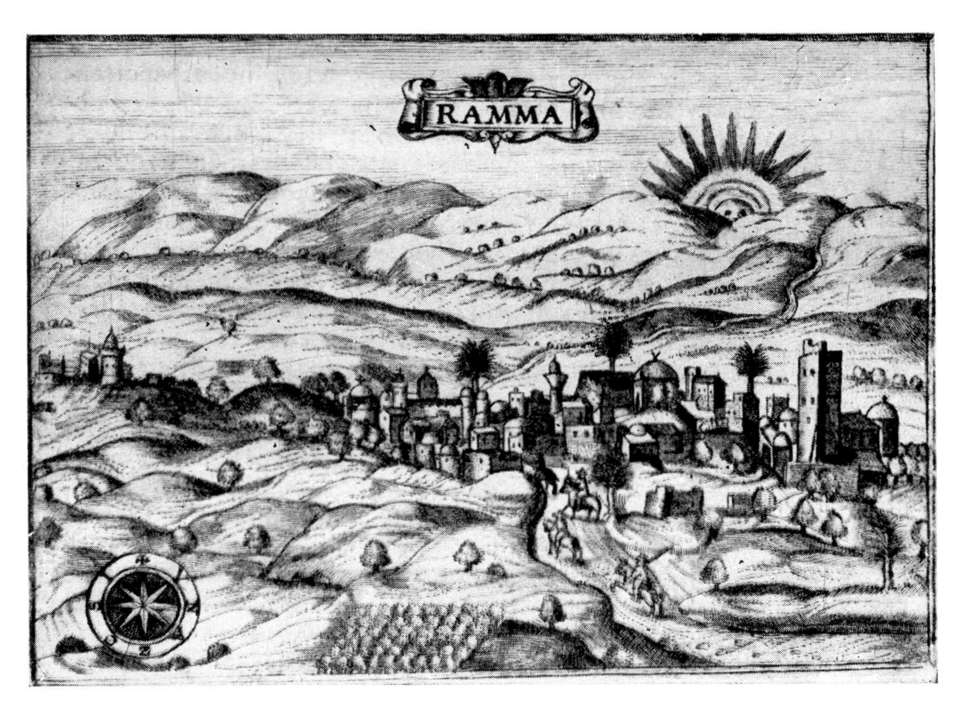

298. Ramla, called Ramma by the Christian pilgrims 1586

J. Zuallart, 'Il devotissimo Viaggio di Gierusalemme,...', 1587.

To the right, the White Tower stands out clearly near the highway to Jerusalem.

299. Ramla 1667

A. Gonsales, 'Hierusalemsche Reyse', 1673.

This drawing gives prominence to the famous fenced orchards of Ramla.

300. Ramla, by the name of 'Ramma' used by Christian pilgrims 1677

O. Dapper, 'Beschryving van gantsch Syrie en Palestyn of Heilige Landt', 1677.

On the road, a caravan making its way to Jerusalem. To the right, the White Tower.

301. Ramla 'Reyzen van Cornelis de Bruyn', 1688. 1681

302. The Tower of Ramla
About 1880

Ch. Wilson, 'Picturesque Palestine', 1882.

In the foreground a pair of oxen draw a primitive plough.

303. The ancient water cistern in Ramla 1681

'Reyzen van Cornelis de Bruyn', 1688.

304. Lydda 1483

From a map attached to B. von Breidenbach's 'Peregrinationes', printed in 1488.

To the right, the minaret of a mosque built on part of the Crusader Church of St. George. The Latin inscription reads: 'Church, now ruined, on the site where St. George was beheaded' – Ecclesia hodie desolata ubi Sanctus Georgius quondam fuit decollatus.

305. Lydda, view from the east P. Lortet, 'La Syrie d'aujourd'hui', 1884. 1880

306. Lydda, a view from the west 1880

From the book of the American missionary W. M. Thompson, 'The Land and the Bible', printed in 1881. On the left, the Great Mosque, next to the ruins of the Church of St. George.

307. Latrun — Domus Boni Latronis 1586

J. Zuallart, 'Il devotissimo Viaggio di Gierusalemme', 1587.

Latrun is built on top of a hill (A), its name Domus Boni Latronis — the House of the Good Thief, for, according to the legend, it was the home of the thief who was crucified with Jesus. Beyond the village (B) Arabs gallop on horseback. At a small widening of the road stands a well (C) named after Job. Left of the village and across the road are the ruins of a fort (D). At the foot of the hill, travellers are climbing on horseback to Jerusalem (E). At the bottom to the left, a building with a cupola (F) was believed to contain the tombs of the Maccabees.

308. Latrun— Domus Boni Latroni(s) 1677

O. Dapper, 'Beschryving van gantsch Syrie en Palestyn of Heilige Landt', 1677.

309. Mount Gerizim on a Roman coin Second Century

At the foot of Mount Gerizim is a street lined with pillars from which two ways lead up the mount. The street to the left is made of steps. A Roman temple stands on the top of the hill. Around the edge the Greek inscription reads: Of Neapolis, Syria-Pal(estina): year 87. The era of Neapolis started in 72 A. D. The year 87 corresponds to 159 A. D.

310. Shechem and its vicinity in the Madaba Map Sixth Century

Left: Shechem is indicated by its Roman name, Neapolis – New Town, which the Arabs corrupted into Nablus. On top: Mount Ebal – Tur Gobel, and below: Mount Gerizim – Tur Garizin. Between them: '(Sy)char which is now (Sy)chora', today the Arab village Askar. At its right, 'Here is Jacob's Well', and below, ancient Shechem: 'Sichem also Sicima and Salim'. Nearby is the tomb 'of Joseph', and at the bottom, the blessing said by Jacob his father: 'Joseph, God shall bless thee with the blessing of the deep that coucheth beneath'[1], and also the words of Moses to the House of Joseph: 'Blessed of the Lord be his land'[2].

1) Genesis 49, 25. 2) Deuteronomy 33, 13.

311. Shechem and Joseph's Tomb 1889

A drawing by Sh. Horenstein, Vienna, author of the Hebrew book 'Givat-Shaul', a description of the Holy Land.

312 – 313. Shechem and Mount Gerizim About 1900

Pictures illustrating Hebrew books printed in Jerusalem.

To the right: Mount Gerizim with the tombs of Joseph and his sister Dinah at its foot. On the top of the mount – the tomb of Hamor, the father of the founder of Shechem, whose name is mentioned in the Bible: 'And Hamor and Shechem his son came unto the gate of their city'...[1]

1) Genesis 34, 20.

314. Shechem and Mount Gerizim 1863

'Pictorial Journey through the Holy Land', 1863.

315. Shechem – Nablus About 1905

A drawing by E. M. Lilien.

316. Samaria – colonnade of the ancient street 1835

A drawing by W. H. Bartlett, which appeared in J. Carne's 'Syria...', 1835.

317. Samaria – remains of the colonnade About 1851

J. J. Bourassé, 'La Terre Sainte', 1877.

CAESAREA

318. Medallion (enlarged) First-Second Century.

Found in 1959 in the waters of Caesarea by the Link expedition for submarine archaeology.

Corresponding closely with the description of Flavius Josephus, it depicts a breakwater with towers protecting a narrow harbour entrance. In the foreground two ships sail on the sea.

On the reverse of the medallion a Triton is pictured.

319. Caesarea on a Crusader seal About 1200

On the right: the fortified gate and the inscription: Civitas Cesaree – Town of Caesarea. Left: the Governor on horseback, carrying shield and lance. Around the edge the inscription reads: Seal of Ugo Graneri – Sigillum Ugonis Granerii.

320. The seal of the Archbishop of Caesarea About 1120

On the left: the archbishop 'E(bremarius) Cesariensis Archiepiscopu(s)'. On the right: Saint Peter baptizes Cornelius: 'Petrus Baptizans Cornelium'.
'Now there was a certain man in Caesarea, Cornelius by name, a centurion of the band called the Italian band, a devout man, and one that feared God, with all his house... and he (Peter) commanded them to be baptized in the name of the Lord'.[1]

1) Acts, x, 1. 48.

321. Caesarea – remains of an ancient sea tower 1830

J. J. S. Taylor, 'La Syrie, l'Egypte, la Palestine et la Judée', 1839.

322. Caesarea – remnants of its ancient port 1840

W. H. Bartlett, 'Walks in and about the city and environs of Jerusalem', 1844.

In the foreground, numerous Roman columns half submerged; in the background, ruins of a Crusader tower which can be seen to this day.

323. Caesarea – general view from the south 1850

A drawing by the English artist W. Tipping.

324. Caesarea – ruins of the ancient harbour 1887

F. et E. Thévoz, 'La Palestine illustrée', 1888–1891.

325. Caesarea – ruins of an ancient building 1887

F. et E. Thévoz, 'La Palestine illustrée', 1888–1891.

326. The village of Tantura, near historical Dor About 1887

F. and E. Thévoz, 'La Palestine illustrée', 1888 – 1891.

327. Ruins of Dor, with the vestiges of the Crusader fortress 1873

'The Survey of Western Palestine' of the Palestine Exploration Fund, printed in 1882.

In the thirteenth century, under Crusader rule, Dor had a small fort – Castellum Merle – for the protection of the coast.

328. Atlit – a view from the south 1880

Ch. W. Wilson, 'Picturesque Palestine', 1882.

329. Atlit – Crusader ruins 1880

Ch. W. Wilson, 'Picturesque Palestine', 1882.

Atlit was called by the Crusaders Castrum Peregrinorum or Chastiau Pelerin – Castle of the Pilgrims.

Right: two fortified towers, one carrying a banner and a cross. Around the edge the inscription reads: Fortress of Haifa — Castrum Caife. Left: the Governor, brandishing a sword, rides at a gallop. His name is written around: S. Garsie Alvarez D(omi)ni Cayphe.

330. Crusader seal of Haifa About 1250

A section of the map of the world named after the Monastery of Abstorf, Germany.

Haifa, as it was called by the Crusaders — Cayphas, and Acco — Accaron.
This map clearly shows the supremacy of Acco, the main port of the Crusaders, over Haifa, then a small village.

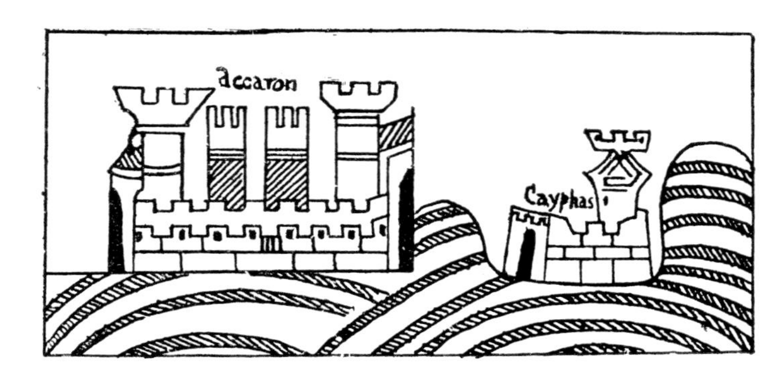

331. Haifa and Acco About 1224

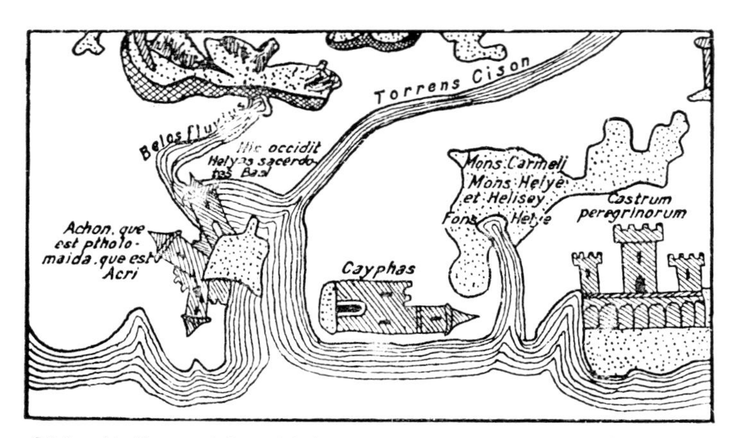

332. Haifa and its vicinity About 1300

From a Latin map of Palestine preserved in Florence.

On the right: Atlit, indicated by its Crusader name: Castle of the Pilgrims — Castrum peregrinorum. In the centre: Haifa — Cayphas, at the foot of Mount Carmel, the Mount of Elijah and Elisha — Mons Carmelj, Mons Helye et Helisey. On Mount Carmel flows the spring of Elijah — Fons Helye. The brook Kishon — Torrens Cison, flows eastwards with the following inscription on its bank: Here Elijah slaughtered the priests of Baal — Hic occidit Helyas sacerdotes Baal. On the left stands Acco, indicated by its various Crusader names: Achon que est ptholomaida, que est Acri. Next to the town flows the River Naaman, indicated by its ancient name of Belus — Belos fluvius, Belos being a Greek rendering of the name of the Canaanite god Baal.

333. Haifa and its vicinity 1483

From a pictorial map of Palestine attached to B. von Breidenbach's, 'Peregrinationes', printed in 1486.
(See figures 25, 262, 282 and 297)

Haifa — Caypha, is pictured on the seashore, at the foot of Mount Carmel —Mons Carmeli, topped by a building marked with a cross. The River Kishon — its name unmentioned, is shown rising in the heart of Carmel, a mistake often found in mediaeval maps. To the right stands Atlit, indicated by its Crusader name, Castle of the Pilgrims — Castrum peregrinorum.

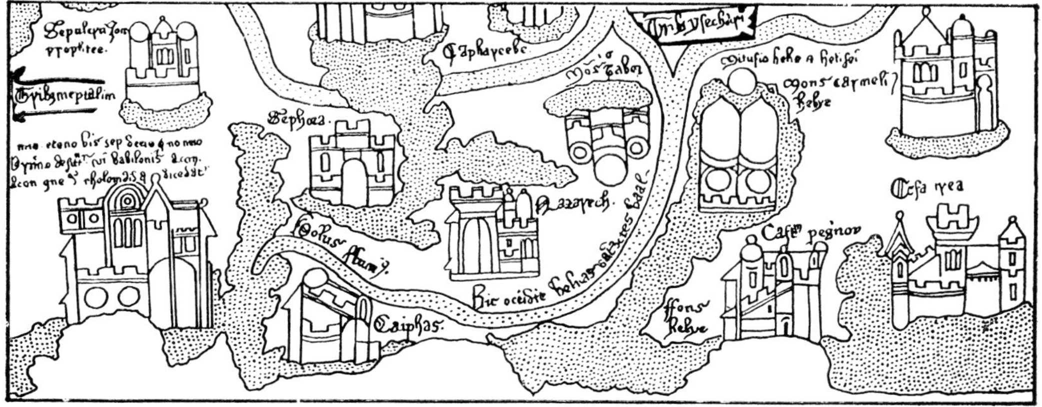

334. Haifa and its vicinity Fifteenth Century

From a pictorial map of Palestine attached to the 'Itineraries of William Wey'.

At the bottom of the picture, on the seashore, appears Haifa – Caiphas. To its left is Acco, designated by its Greek name in the corrupted form of Tholomaida: Anno centeno bis sex decimo que noueno Primo destruitur vi Babilonis Acon. Acon que etiam Tholomaida dicebatur.

Above Acco the Tribe of Naphtali is mentioned — Tribus mepthalim, and the tomb of the Prophet Jonah—Sepulcru(m) Jone proph(e)tee, is pictured. Today this tomb is shown in the Arab village of Mashad, ancient Gat-Hepher, between Nazareth and Tiberias. On the right: Sepphoris – Sephora, appears near Nazareth. The River Belus, today the Naaman, runs into the sea between Haifa and Acco. Along its northern bank an inscription reads: Here Eiljah slew the priests of Baal – Hic occidit Helyas sacerdotes Baal, thus mistakenly transposing here a scene truly enacted on the banks of the River Kishon. A little above is Mount Tabor – Mons Tabor, and beyond, on a branch of the Belus, the name Caphartebe is inscribed. On the top right, the tribe of Issachar is mentioned – Tribus Ysechar, and a little below, Mount Carmel — Mons Carmeli Helye, with the House of Elijah and Elisha — Mansio Helie et Helisei, represented as a large fortified castle, in the top right hand corner. Near the shore is the Fountain of Elijah—Fons Helye. Atlit — Castrum peregrinorum and C(a)esarea appear on the right.

Explanation to figures on page 130

335. This picture was drawn by a Spanish monk — Prospero dello Spirito Santo, who lived on Mount Carmel. The view is from Acco facing south-west. On the top of Mount Carmel stands the Carmelite Monastery and at its foot—the Cave of the Prophet Elijah. Haifa is on the seashore. To its left the River Kishon flows into the sea, and at the bottom of the picture is Acco with a sailing vessel in its bay, opposite the outlet of the River Naaman, Belus of the Greeks.

336. From the book of the French traveller, Laurens d'Arvieux, 'Voyage... dans la Palestine', 1717. Haifa is built on the sea-shore, over an area now situated next to Bat-Galim, a suburb of the modern city. On the incline of the mount a large Beduin camp is portrayed.

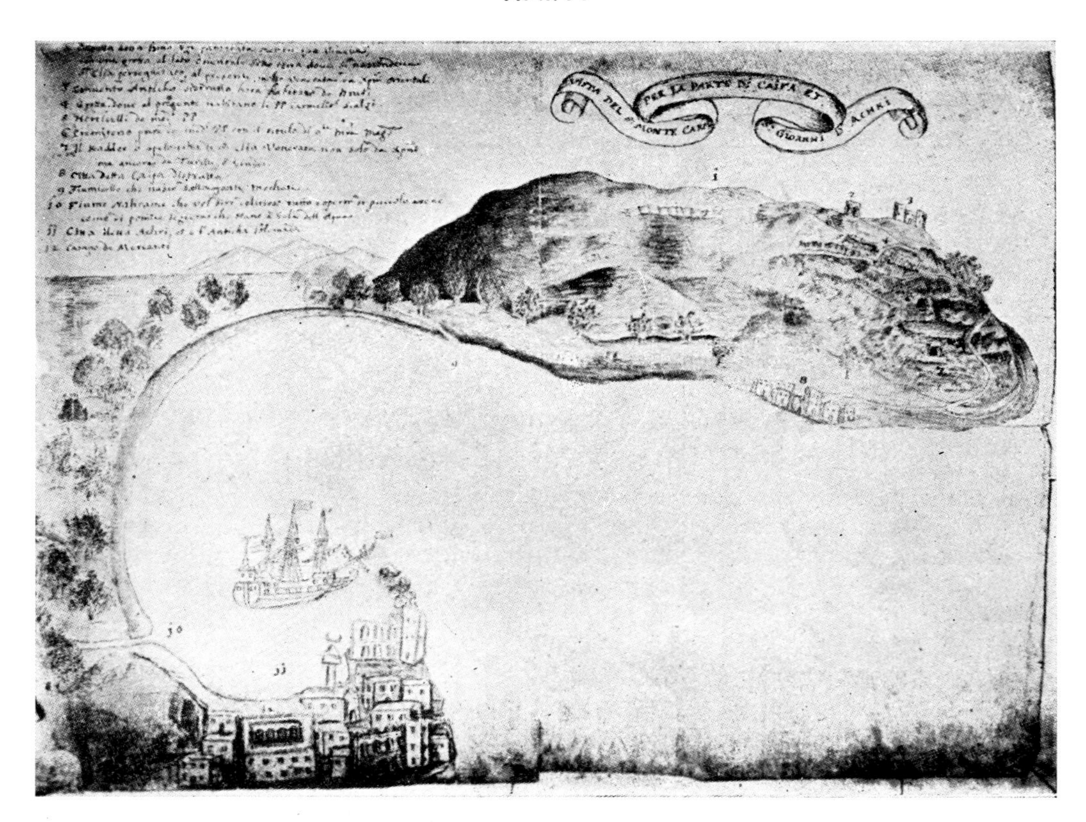

335. Haifa and its Bay, view from the north 1632

Explanation at bottom of previous page

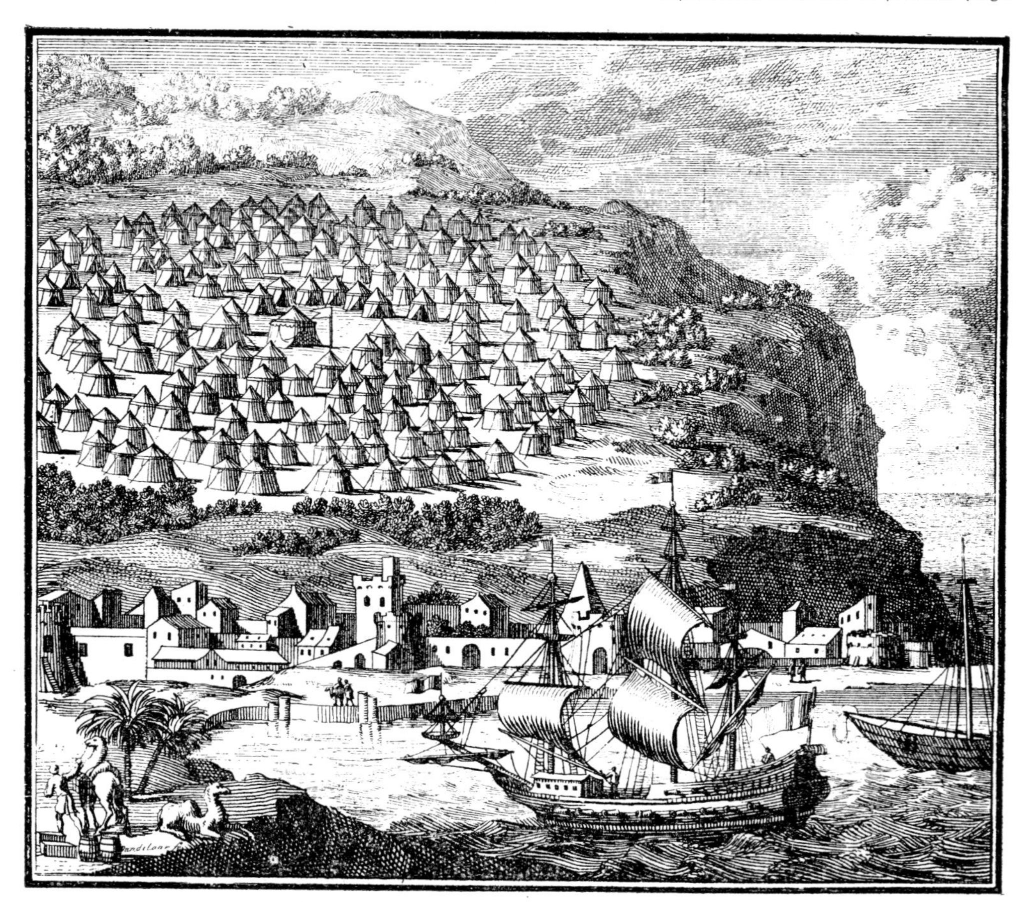

336. Haifa and Mount Carmel, view from the sea 1662

Explanation at bottom of previous page

337. Haifa, Mount Carmel and the Bay, viewed from the sea 1652

From the book of the French pilgrim, J. Doubdan, 'Le Voyage de la Terre Sainte', 1657.

At the foot of Mount Carmel, drawn out of all proportion to the bay, a few houses and a tower represent Haifa. On the left, at the northern end of the bay stands the town of Acco. Between the two, in the plain, the Rivers Kishon and Naaman make their way into the sea. The Carmelite Monastery appears on the top of Mount Carmel.

338. Haifa, Mount Carmel and the Bay, Abcut 1697
viewed from the sea

From the book of the English traveller, H. Maundrell, 'Journey from Aleppo to Jerusalem', 1697.

Similar to the previous picture, with the same disproportion of sizes.

339. Haifa and Mount Carmel 1681

'Reyzen van Cornelis de Bruyn door de... Syrien en Palestina', 1688.

On top of the Cape, the Carmelite Monastery.

340. Haifa and Mount Carmel, 1800
viewed from the shore of the bay

341. Haifa and its Bay, 1800
viewed from the heights of Carmel

From the book of the Englishman, Willyams Cooper, 'A Selection of Views in Egypt, Palestine...', 1822.

In the foreground, the artist drawing the picture. On the seashore, soldiers from the British Forces sent to resist Napoleon's siege of near-by Acco. On the hill, half-way up the Carmel, the fortress El-Burj, which had guarded the town since the middle of the eighteenth century.

342. Haifa and Mount Carmel, seen from the bay 1816

J. S. Buckingham, 'Travels in Palestine through the countries of Bashan and Gilead', 1821.

343. Haifa and Mount Carmel, viewed from the east 1834

An illustration by the painter W. H. Bartlett, published in the book of J. Carne, 'Syria, the Holy Land', printed in 1836.

El-Burj stands out clearly on the hill.

344. Haifa and the Carmel Cape About 1830

From the book of T. H. Horne, 'The Biblical Keepsake', printed in 1835.

The sun lights up the mountains of Galilee. Midway between the Cape and the city, on a hill, the small fort – El-Burj. Far away, beyond the bay, is Acco – St. Jean d'Acre.

345. Haifa and its bay, seen from the Cape of Carmel 1834

A picture of W. H. Bartlett, published in J. Carne's, 'Syria, the Holy Land', 1836.

The Carmelite Monastery, represented incommensurately large, tops Mount Carmel, at whose foot a diminutive Haifa is surrounded by a fortified wall. Beyond the bay stands Acco, with white sails on its waters.

346. Haifa, viewed from the north-west 1852

C. W. M. van de Velde, 'Reis door Syrie en Palestine', 1854.

347. Haifa and Mount Carmel, seen from the east 1880

W. M. Thompson, 'The Land and the Bible', 1883.

El-Burj, the small fortress of Haifa, is on the height rising at the back of the town. On top of the promontory stands the Carmelite Monastery and, a little below, the conspicuous building of Stella Maris — Star of the Sea.

348. Haifa, Mount Carmel and Acco About 1875

From a pictorial map of Palestine, drawn by Rabbi Haim Solomon Pinie of Tsefat (Safad), Upper Galilee. (See figure 54, page 36)

Haifa, on the right, and Acco, on the left, appear as two fortified cities along the shore of the Mediterranean, in Hebrew – Yam Hagadol – the Great Sea. Above Haifa is Mount Carmel with the altar of the Prophet Elijah, made of large stones, on its top, and a little below the cave opens where he hid from his pursuers, at a site still venerated. Next to the cave stands a large domed building which, according to Jewish tradition, covers the tomb now unknown, of Elisha, Elijah's disciple. Between Haifa and Acco flows the River Kishon, its name shown in large characters.

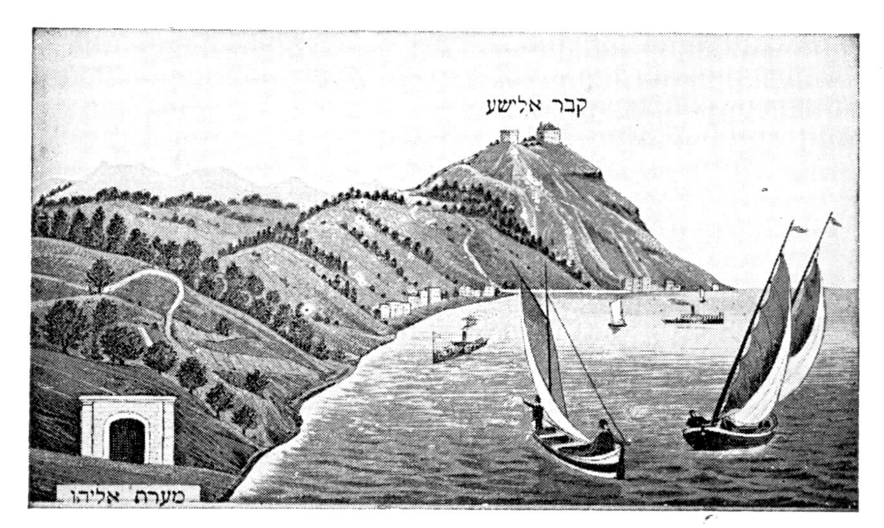

349. Haifa and Mount Carmel, viewed from the east About 1900

An imaginary drawing. At the foot of the mountain, in the bottom left-hand corner of the picture, an arch represents the Cave of Elijah and, at the highest peak of the range, on the Cape of Carmel, stands the tomb of the Prophet Elisha, according to Jewish tradition.

350. The Cave where Elijah dwelt

Pictures printed on the flags used in the celebration of Simhat Torah – The Rejoicing of the Law, the last day of the Feast of Tabernacles (Succoth). They also appear on napkins used for the blessing of the Sabbath loaf.

351. The Tomb of the Prophet Elisha

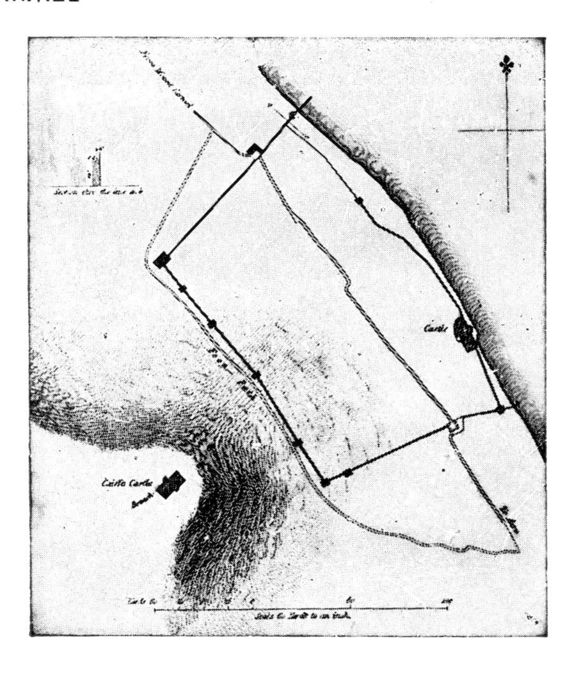

352. The first plan of Haifa About 1840

Drawn by engineers of the British Army.

'Papers of the Corps of Royal Engineers', VI, 1843.

The wall of Haifa is clearly drawn with its two gates: the eastern gate where the way 'to Acre' starts, and the western gate where the way 'from Mount Carmel' ends. The large building on the sea-shore marked 'Castle' was recently demolished. On a small promontory overlooking the city stands El-Burj – 'Caiffa Castle', whose site, today, is occupied by a public garden, Gan-Hazikaron, near the town hall.

353. Haifa and Mount Carmel — Mons Carmelus 1663

Latin map from the book of the pilgrim Antonius Gonsales, 'Hierusalemsche Reyse', printed in 1673.

As in many mediaeval maps, the west is at the bottom of the page and the east at the top. In the bottom left-hand corner, on the shore of the Mediterranean — Mare Mediterraneum, Haifa – Caiphae, is indicated. The Cave of Saint Elijah–Grotta S(aint) Eliae, is on Mount Carmel, and next to it, on a height, a convent–Conuentus, on the site of today's Carmelite monastery, with, a little above it, the inscription: The Holy Place of the Blessed Virgin – Sacellum B. V. (Beatae Virginis). By the side of this inscription a building is marked: The place where the fire came down — ubi ignis descendit. At the bottom of the picture, above a row of stylised pine-trees, flows the Fountain of Elijah — Elizei fons. Next to it is a convent – Conuentus; it was dedicated to St. Margaret, and its ruins, known by the Arabic name of ed-Deir – the Convent, are still extant. In the bottom right-hand corner, Tyri, today, a suburb of Haifa named Tirat-Hacarmel, is shown, with a fountain — Fons, a little above it. Farther inland, on a hill, is the town of Carmel – ciuitas Carmeli, on the site of today's Arab village of Kababir. Still higher, two rows of caverns, one long, one short, are marked: the 400 caves where formerly were the sons of the Prophets — 400 Grotta(e) ubi olim Filij Prophetarum; apparently these are the caves known in Arabic as Arak er-Rahib — the Caves of the Monks.

In the centre of the map, a settlement indicated by the name Rosaria marks the area now occupied by a ruin named Rushmia, while, above it, Asphia exists to this day as Isfiya – a Druze village. To the right, a cluster of trees represents the Forest of Carmel – Saltus Carmeli, and slightly higher up, more in the middle of the picture, another group of lighter, slimmer trees is marked: Grove of laurel trees — Silua Laurorum. At the top of the picture, on the edge of the Valley of Esdraelon – Campus Esdrelon, stands another village — Mansura, which no longer exists. On the summit of Mount Carmel appears the altar of Elijah with his sacrifice – Sacrificium Eliae, sending heavy clouds of smoke into the sky. At the foot of the mountain, the place where the 450 false prophets were slaughtered – Ubi 450 Falsi Prophaetae Occisi, is marked on the bank of the River Kishon — Torrens Cison, also indicated by its Arabic name for both river and source, Al-Mokara – Fl. (fons) mocata, in use to this day among the Arab population.

354. Map of the Bay of Haifa 1770

From a collection of maps preserved in the British Museum, London (Add. 13, 959).

The map is written in Italian. The north is at the bottom of the picture and the south on top. The map indicates: Ancient Haifa – Chaifa Vecchio, and New Haifa – Chaifa Nova, down the sea-shore. At the top of the picture, the Cape of Carmel – C(apo) di monte Carmelo, thrusts into the sea, while at the other end of the bay Acco is marked – S. Gio(vanni) d'achiri. Following the coast down north we meet the white cliffs of Rosh-Hanikra – C(apo) Bianco, the equivalent of the Arabic name – Ras al-Abiad, today the border between Israel and Lebanon, and still farther north the town Tyre – the biblical Zor – Sur, in Arabic. The numbers marked on the surface of the bay indicate sea-depths for the use of navigators.

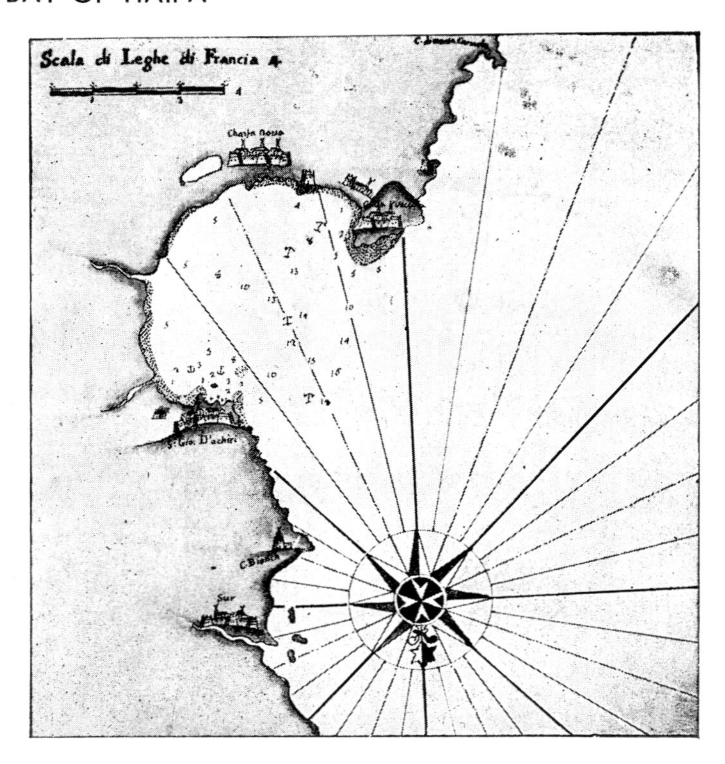

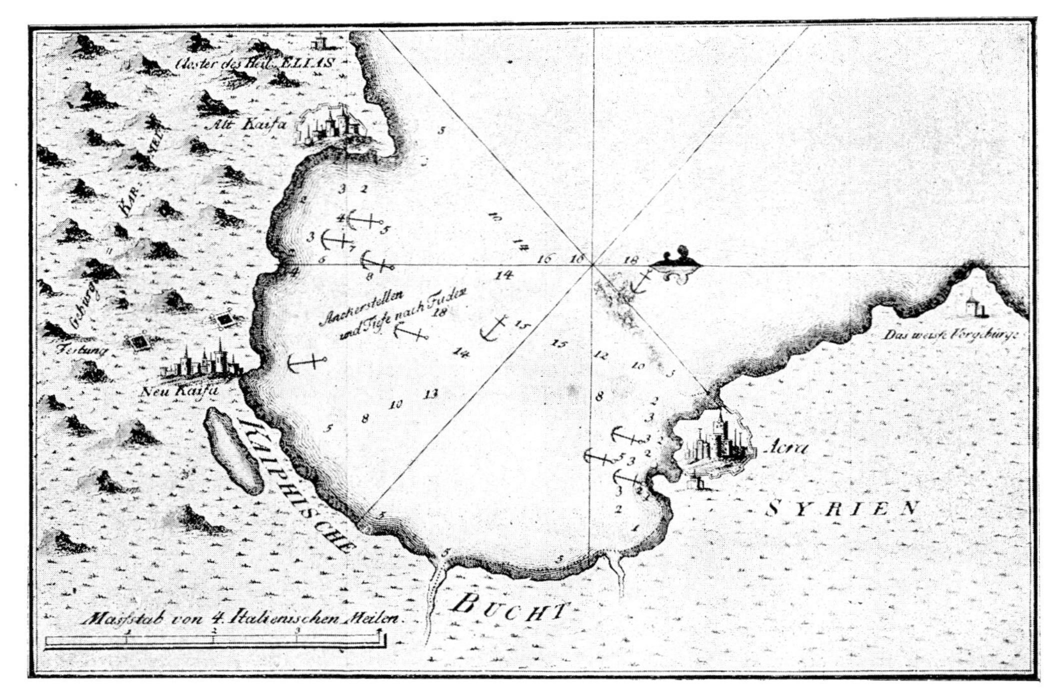

355. Map of the Bay of Haifa 1773

From a German translation of the Russian original written by S. Plestschejew, 'Von Insel Paros... nach Syrien und Palästina', 1774.

The map is written in German. The north is to the right and the south to the left. At the top of the picture, on the left, stands the monastery dedicated to the Prophet Elijah – Closter des Heil(igen) Elias. Underneath, within the bend of the bay, is Ancient Haifa – Alt Kaifa, and farther below, along the sea-shore, New Haifa – Neu Kaifa. Next to it is the Fort – Festung, on the site of today's Gan-Hazikaron. The mountains of Carmel – Gebürge Karmel, run parallel to the sea-shore. In the Bay of Haifa, Kaiphische Bucht, appears a wide swamp, which was drained about 35 years ago. At the other end of the bay is the town Acco – Acra, and, farther right, the promontory known in Arabic as Ras al-Abiad – the White Head, in German – Das weisse Vorgebürge.

MAP OF CRUSADER ACCO

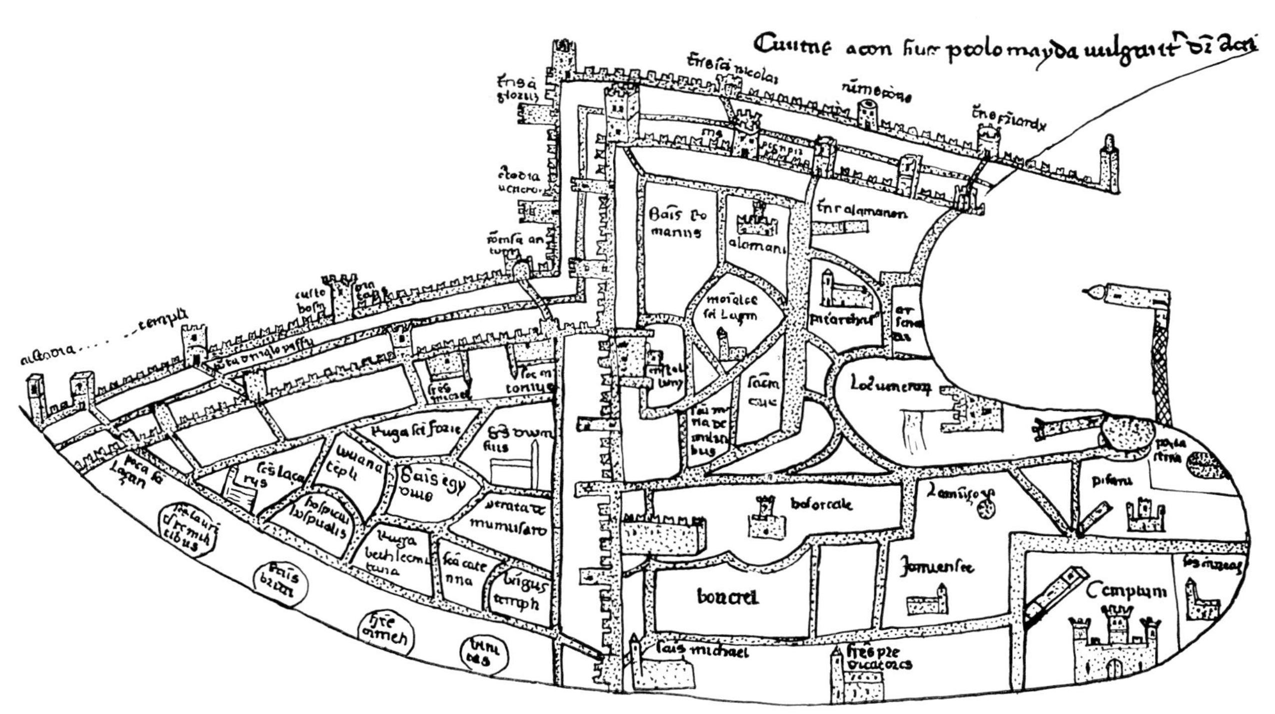

356. Map of Crusader Acco, by the Italian traveller, Marino Sanuto — About 1310

A copy of the manuscript is preserved in the Bodleian Library, Oxford (Tanner 190, fol. 207).

The map shows Crusader Acco, on the eve of its fall into the hands of the Moslems. The text on top reads: The Town Acco or Ptolomaida vulgarly named Acre — Civitas acon sive ptolomayda vulgarit(er) d(icitu)r Acri. The town is surrounded by a double rampart and an inner wall divides it into two: the old section built on the bay, and the new section spreading to the north along the sea-shore. The rampart is fortified along all its length by many towers.

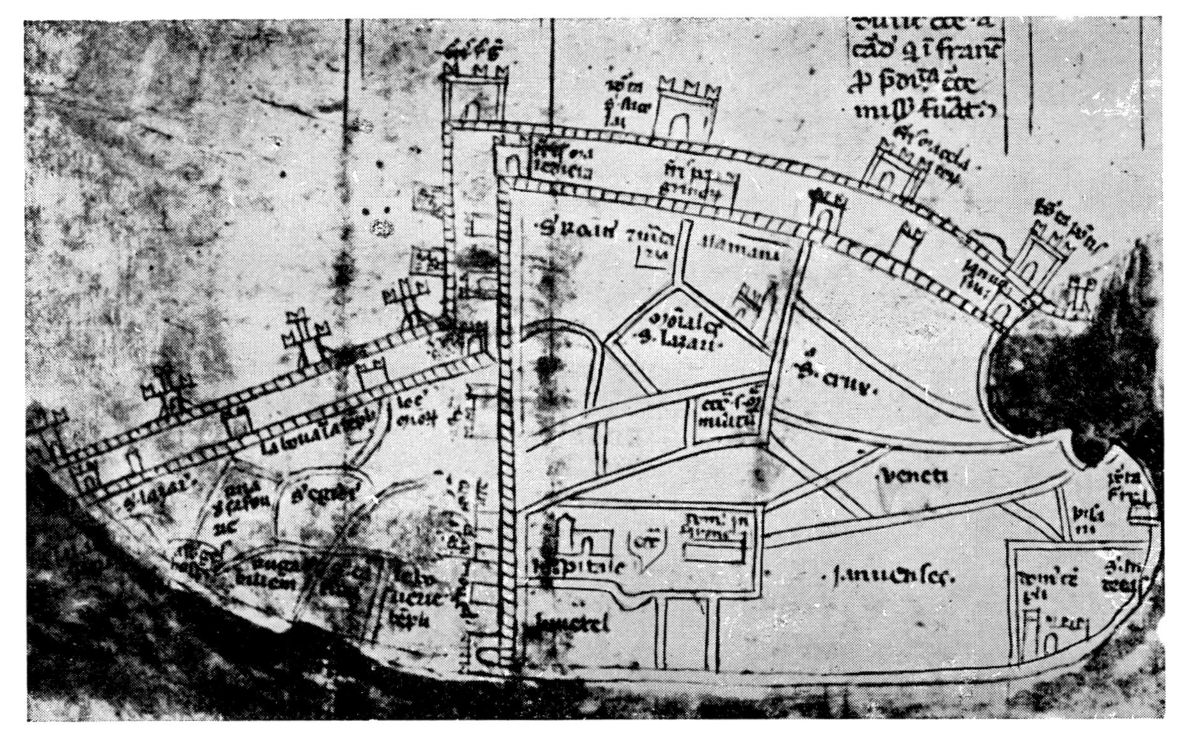

357. Map of Crusader Acco — About 1330

Attached to the account made by Paulinus Puteolanus under the title 'Chronologia Magna de passagiis in Terram Sanctam', and preserved in the Library of St. Mark, Venice.
Similar in all its details to the previous figure.

358. Map of Crusader Acco About 1250

From a manuscript of the English historian Matheus Paris. Preserved in the Library of Corpus Christi College in Cambridge.

(see next page)

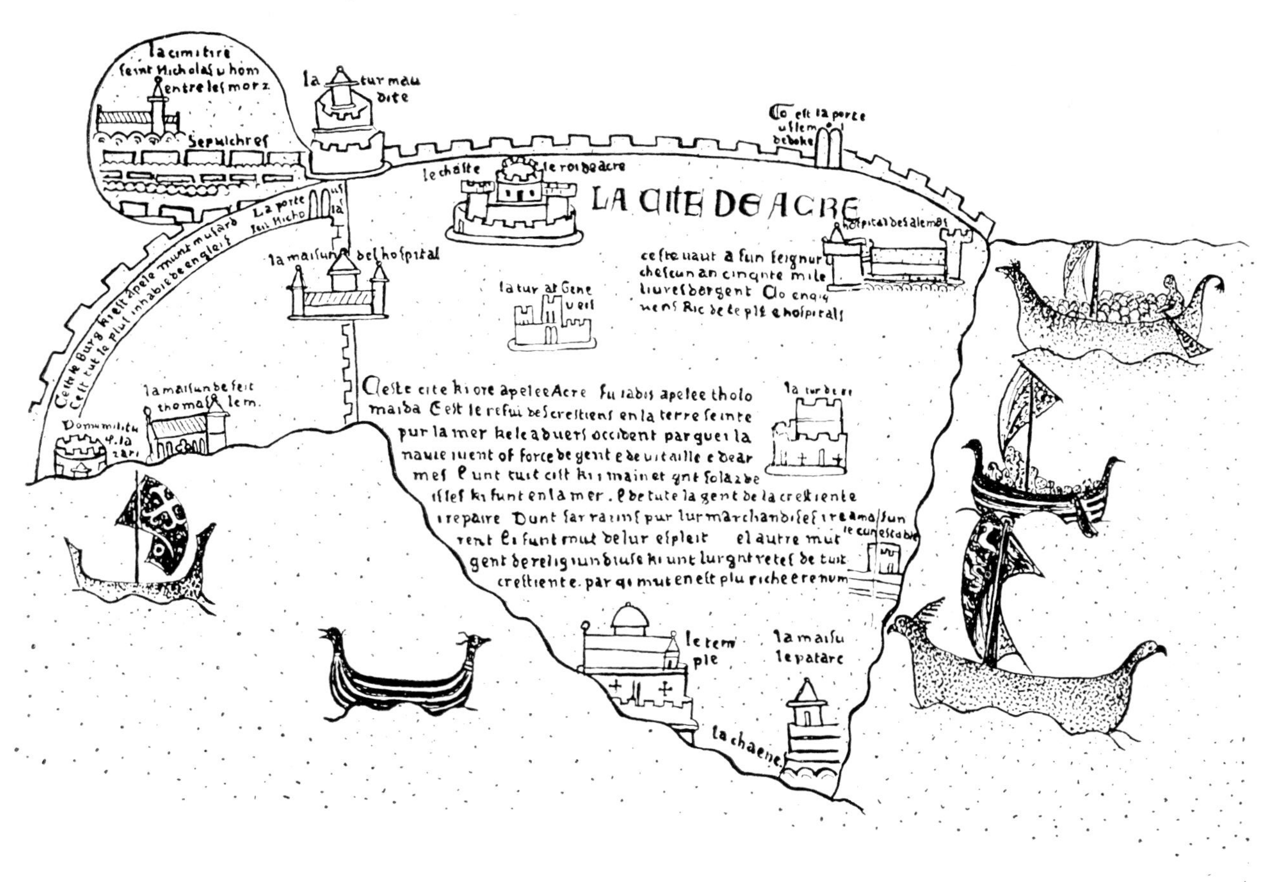

359. Crusader Acco, a copy of the map on the preceding page. Written in medieval French About 1250

The Town of Acco – La Cité de Acre, is built on a promontory jutting out into the sea. The lengthy inscription in the body of the map reads: 'This town today named Acco was, of old, named Ptolemaida. It is the haven of the Christians on the western shore of the Holy Land. And since boats arrive here its population has greatly increased and also its victuals and arms. And the islands of the sea are a great support to those who live there (in Acco). People from all the countries of Christendom gather there as well as Sarrazins (Moslems) who come in connection with their trade and conclude there many of their affairs. Also many people of various religious orders (come) who enjoy great revenues from all Christendom. Thus the town has gained much riches and renown. It brings in to its lord fifty thousands pounds of silver every year. This is the sum that Count Richard requested from the Templars and the Hospitallers'.

At the tip of the city projecting into the sea, the inscription – 'la chaene', indicates the chain that was drawn across the port to close it at night and in war-time. Above it stands 'the House of the Patriarch' – la maisu(n) le pat(ri)arc(he), and next to it, a large domed building with two crosses marks 'the Seat of the Order of the Templars' – le temple. Above, along the sea shore is the House of the Constable' – (l)a maisun (l)e cunestable, and farther up' the Hospital of the Germans' – hospital des clema(n)s. To its left, near the crenellated wall of the city, stands the large 'castle of the King of Acre' – le chaste le roi de acre, above 'the Tower of the Genoans' – la tur as Geneveis. Further left, 'the House of the Hospitallers' – la maisun del hospital, straddles the inner wall separating the old from the new city of Acre. On the sea-shore, on the left, stands 'the House of St. Thomas the martyr' (from Canterbury) – la maisum de sei(n)t thomas le m(artyr), and next to it a crenellated tower indicates the 'House of the Order of St. Lazare' – domu(s) militu(m) S(ancti) lazari. Along the outer wall of the city, the inscription reads: 'This is the quarter named Mount Musard. It is the most inhabited by the English' – Ceste le Burg ki est apele munt musard. Cest tut le plus inhabie de engleis. On the right a gate carries the legend: 'This is the gate where is the mill of doke[1] – Co est la port u(er)s le mol(in) de doke. Left of the gate a fortified tower is indicated as 'the Cursed Tower' – la tur maudite, and below it a smaller gate is marked, 'The Gate where is St. Nicholas' – la porte u(er)s sei(n)t Nichola(s). Beyond the wall and within a circular enclosure is the 'Cemetery of St. Nicholas where the dead are buried' – le cimetire seint Nicholas u hom ent(er)re les morz, with the further indication, 'Sepulchres' – Tombs.

1) This mill was built on the banks of the near-by River Belus (Naaman). Under the corrupted form of Da'ck its memory has remained among the Arabs, who still call by this name a ruin situated in the area.

360. Crusader boat in the port of Acco Twelfth Century

A model in the Maritime Museum of Haifa

361. Crusader vessel Thirteenth Century

From a Latin manuscript of the Crusader period.
(For pictures of other boats plying on the routes to the Holy Land see page 110)

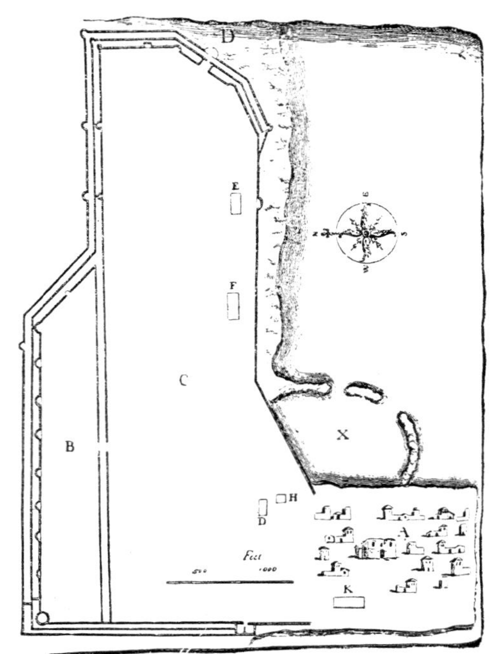

R. Pococke, 'Description of the East', 1743–45.

A – the old town. B – the new town. C – area of the Crusader town. D – site of the castle of the Great Master of the Order of St. John. E – abode of the knights and Church of St. John. F – convent of nuns. H – church. K – Cathedral of St. Andrews I – remains of the Iron Fortress. X – remains of the ancient harbour (see figures 386 — 387).

362. Map of Acco 1738

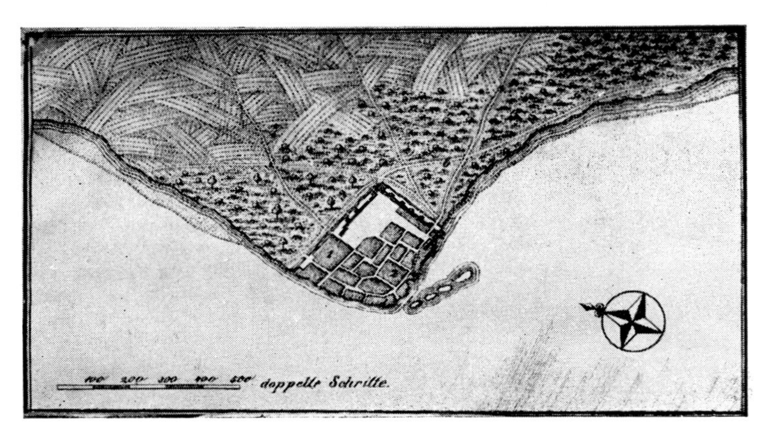

363. Map of Acco and its vicinity 1766

From the book of C. Niebuhr, 'Reisebeschreibung', printed in 1837.

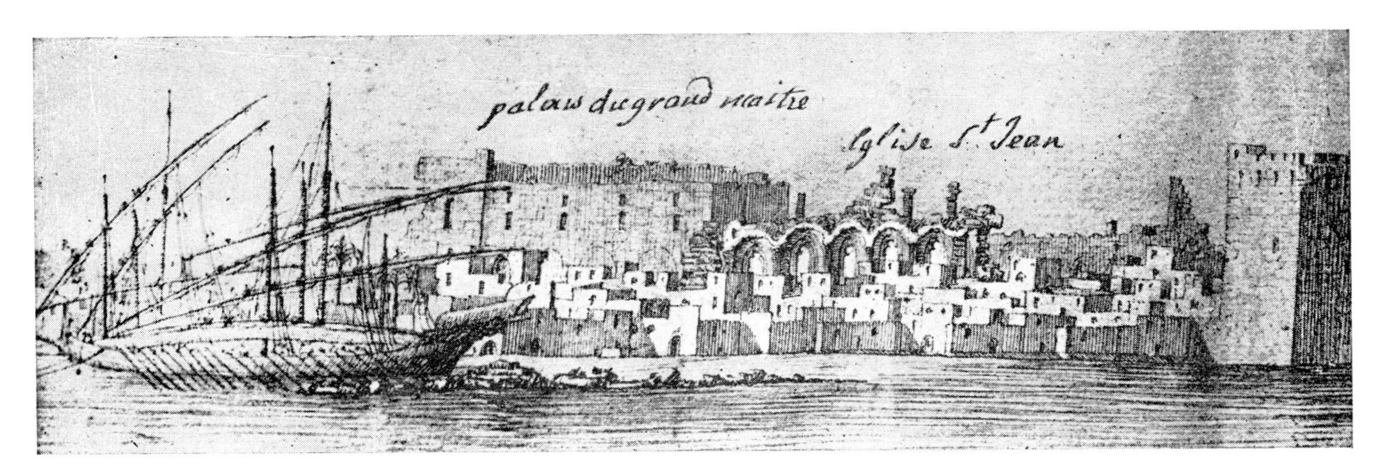

364. Acco – general view from the sea 1686

A picture preserved in the Bibliothèque Nationale, Paris.

Right: remains of the large Crusader church named by the French for St. John – Eglise St. Jean. It gave its name to Acre, which the Crusaders knew as St. Jean d'Acre. To the left appears the palace of the Great Master (of the Order of St. John) – Palais du grand maitre, where the large fortress stands today.

365. Acco – St. Andrew's Cathedral 1681

'Reyzen van Cornelius de Bruyn door de... Syrien en Palestine', 1688.

On the right, in the distance, Mount Carmel appears, the village of Haifa nestling at its foot.

J. Yanosky – J. David, 'Syrie ancienne – Syrie moderne', 1848.

It is named for its many columns the Jnn of the Columns – Khan al-Umdan in Arabic.

366. A Khan (caravanserai) in Acco About 1845

367. Acco – a view from the mainland 1799

A drawing by Vivent Denon. Printed in H. Deherain's, 'L'Egypte Turque', 1931.

In the centre, the Great Mosque. On the right, in the waters, is seen the lighthouse, whose remains are still visible. (see figure 368)

368. Acco – the Governor Ahmad Jazzar Pasha 1799

Barthelemy and Méry, 'Napoléon en Egypte', 1824.

Standing on the rampart of the town, the Turkish governor, Ahmad Jazzar, leads the defence against the army of Napoleon Bonaparte investing the city.

J. B. Spilsbury, 'Picturesque scenery in the Holy Land', 1804.

The defendant kneels low in front of his judge who holds the rod of punishment, while an axe for quick execution lies by his side. The executioner hovers in the background.

369. Acco – The Governor Jazzar Pasha on the seat of Justice 1800

370. Acco – the French Army storming the city 1799

A drawing in the British Museum, London. 'The Geographical Magazine', 29, 1956 – 7.

371. The British Admiral Sidney Smith in Acco 1799

A drawing by John Eckstein, in the National Gallery of Portraits, London.

372. Acco on a medallion 1799

Commemorating the victory of Sidney Smith.

'Repulsed Buonaparte in 11 attacks made by him on Acre 1799'.

(see figure 338)

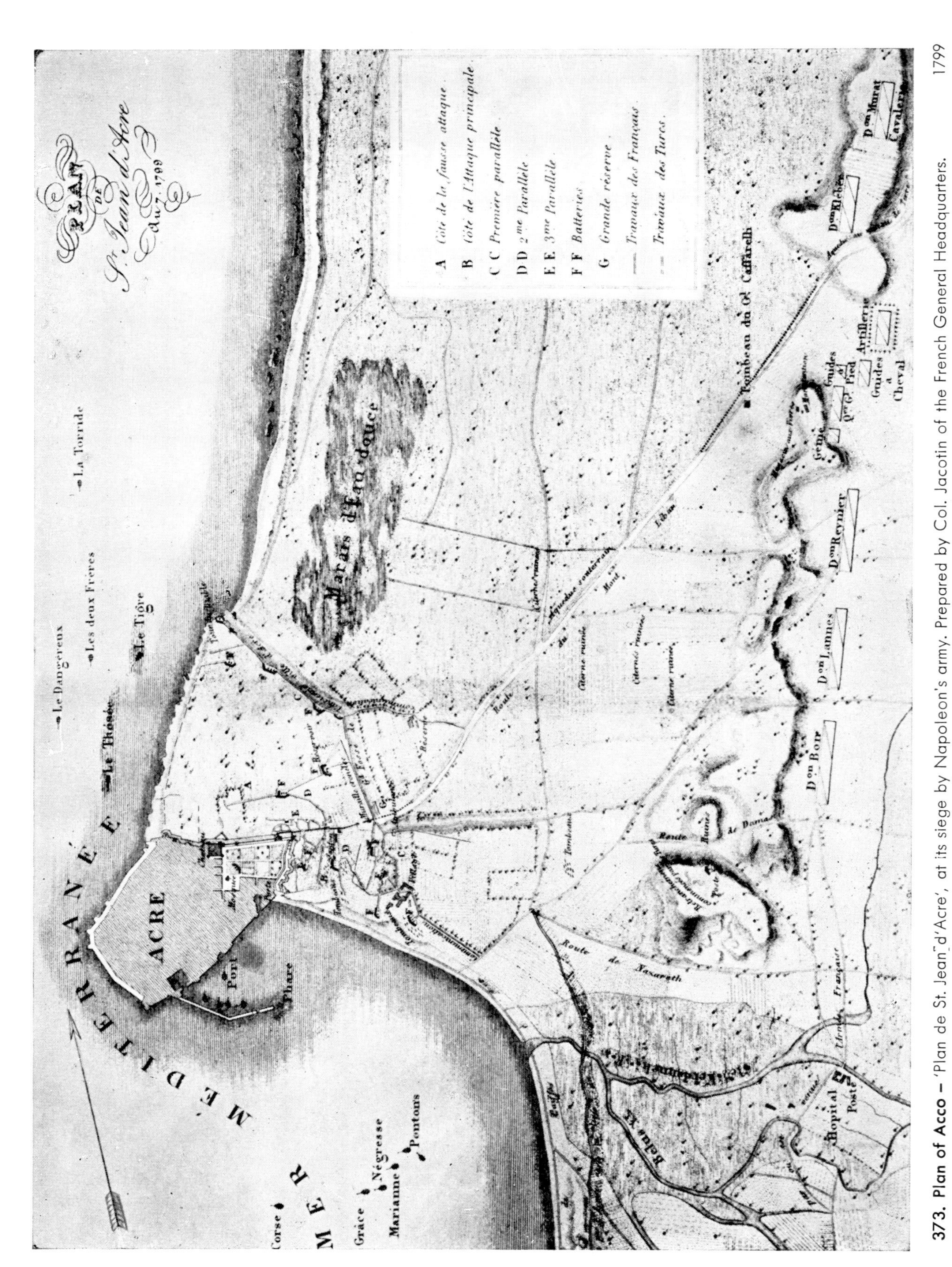

373. Plan of Acco – 'Plan de St. Jean d'Acre', at its siege by Napoleon's army. Prepared by Col. Jacotin of the French General Headquarters. 1799

An English version of the plan was published in 'The Papers of the Corps of Royal Engineers', VI, 1843.

Explanation on next page.

Acco, under its French name of St. Jean d'Acre, which dates from the time of the Crusades, is built on a promontory jutting into the Mediterranean — Mer Méditerranée. The town is completely surrounded by a rampart through which access is gained by a single gate – Porte, extant to this day. The harbour is protected by a breakwater starting on the mainland, at a square basin which served as an anchorage for small vessels in rough weather, and ending with the lighthouse – Phare. Remains of the breakwater and the foundations of the lighthouse can still be seen. The position of the warships of the French fleet supporting the land forces and completing the investment of Acco from the side of the sea is indicated.

374. The Army of Napoleon Bonaparte at the siege of Acco 1799

From the book of Barthélémy and Méry, 'Napoleon en Egypte', printed 1814.

Outside the city wall, by the side of the bay, a Moslem cemetery marked by the word Tombs – Tombeaux, twice repeated, is set next to a grave sacred to Moslems — Santon, known to this day by the name of en-Nebi (the Prophet) Saleh. At the southern end of the cemetery stands a large building next to a village whose name is not mentioned. Further south-east, by the side of the height known today as Napoleon's Hill, is the cemetery — Tombeaux, of the Christians. North-east, outside the fortified wall, a shaded line marks the place of the moat of the Crusader city of Acco — Grand fossé de l'ancienne ville d'Acre, with, at its northern end, on the sea-shore, the remains of a fort, the Tower of the Devil — Tour du Diable, and on its southern side, the relics of a fortified, crenellated wall — Muraille crénellée. Next to the wall is a reservoir. Beyond the moat stretches a wide marsh of sweet water — Marais d'eau douce. On the expanse between the rampart of Turkish Acco and the remains of the Crusader wall, a few capital letters appear; they indicate the French positions and give some information of the strategy used by Napoleon: A. Direction of the false attack — Côté de la fausse attaque. B. Direction of the main attack — Côté de l'attaque principale. CC. First parallel (of trenches) – Première parallèle. DD. Second parallel – 2me. Parallèle. EE. Third parallel – 3m. Parallèle. FF. Gun Batteries – Batteries. G. Main Reserve – Grande réserve. French works – Travaux des Francais. Turkish works — Travaux des Turcs. The medical aid is marked – Ambulance, and the reserves – Réserves.

From Acco a road proceeds to the north-east, to Lebanon – Route du Mont Liban; parallel to it runs the Turkish aqueduct, part of it underground – Aqueduc souterrain, which can still be seen next to the Acco — Nahariya highway. All this area is dotted with ruined wells — Citernes ruinées. On the eastern side of the town, the conspicuous height named today after Napoleon is marked Military Station — Poste, next to a trench started by the Turks – Retranchement commencé par les Turcs. Not far are ruins — Ruines. On the right-hand side of the height runs the road to Damascus — Route de Damas, in the direction of today's highway to Tsefat (Safed) in Upper Galilee; on the left is the road to Nazareth – Route de Nazareth.

Behind Napoleon's Hill is the hospital – Hôpital, and the military mail post — Poste, by the side of a branch of the River Belus which flows into the bay, crossing the route to Haifa — Caiffa, on its way. A line drawn in the southern section of the map indicates the direction followed by the French forces advancing from Haifa to Acco — Par où est venue l'Armée Francaise. Northwards from Napoleon's Hill, along the range, spread the French divisions, indicated by the names of their commanders – D(ivisi)on Bon, Don Lannes, Don Reynier, Don Kéber, Don Murat, and the Cavalry – Cavalerie, which occupied the area of what today is the Acco agricultural school. Between the divisions of Kléber and Reynier are the General Headquarters – Q(artier) G(énéral), next to the Engineers' Corps – Génie, the guides on foot — Guides à Pied, and on horseback — Guides à Cheval. Nearby are a gun-post – Artillerie, the provision store — Magasin aux Vivres, and the bakehouse — Manutention. The tomb of G(énéral) Caffarelli is indicated in the same vicinity. Caffarelli, of Italian extraction, one of Napoleon's most distinguished generals, was killed during the siege.

375. Plan of the Siege of Acco J. Grant, 'British Battles on Land and Sea', 1875. 1799

1—4. Warships: Corride. Deux Frères. Dangereux. Theseus. 5. Fortress. 6. Sea Gate. 7—8. Harbour. 9. Lighthouse. 10—12 Gun-boats. 13—17 Warships: Marianne, Négresse, Dame de France, Alliance, Tigre. 18. Bay of Acco. 19. Mediterranean Sea. 20. Cultivated valley. 21—22. Ruined cisterns. 23. Subterranean aqueduct. 24. Old Turkish entrenchment. 25. French hospital. 26. River Belus (Naaman). 27. Road to Haifa. 28. French Army Headquarters. 29. Lannes Division. 30. Reynier Division. 31. Fresh water lake. 32. French reserve. 33. Arab village Manshiye. 34. French camp. 35—36. Richard's Hill. 36. Trenches.

376. Acco seen from the east Paul Lortet, 'La Syrie d'aujourd'hui', 1884. 1880

On the right, the minaret and large cupola of the Great Mosque, named after Ahmed Jazzar Pasha, which is still the largest mosque in Acco. The line of arches indicates the roof of the 'White Market', the main commercial centre of the town in the time of the Turks. On the rampart, a row of guns.

377. Acco, the fortified wall along the sea-shore 1830

A drawing by W. H. Bartlett which appeared in J. Carne's 'Syria, the Holy Land', 1845.

The western wall of Acco built on the rocks of the sea-shore. In the distance appears the Mount of Carmel, at the southern end of the bay.

378. Acco and its vicinity, seen from the south 1839

From the book of the English artist, David Roberts, 'The Holy Land from drawings made on the spot', 1842.

379. Acco seen from the sea F. C. Roux, 'Les Echelles de Syrie et de Palestine', 1928. About 1820

The Great Mosque and its slender minaret appear to the right of the massive citadel. Small craft are anchored in the port.

380. The British fleet attacks Acco 'A hundred pictures of famous historical events'. 1840

When Muhammed Ali, Viceroy of Egypt, rebelled against the Turkish Sultan, he conquered Palestine and Lebanon, making Acco the capital of this area, The British fleet came to the help of the Sublime Porte, in 1840, and forced him to retreat from Palestine.

381. Acco on a Turkish medal 1840

Awarded to the soldiers who took part in the battle of Acco. At the top of the citadel, the Turkish flag, and underneath, in Turkish: Palestine and Syria (esh-Sham), the Fortress of Acco (Acca).

382. Acco – the Great Mosque and the Turkish Citadel 1830
J. J. S. Taylor, 'La Syrie, l'Egypte, la Palestine et la Judée', 1839.

383. Acco – entrance to the market 1830
J. J. S. Taylor, 'La Syrie, l'Egypte, la Palestine et la Judée', 1839.

384. Acco – the Great Mosque 1814
H. Light, 'Travels in Egypt, Nubia, Holy Land', 1818.

385. Acco J. J. S. Taylor, 'La Syrie, l'Egypte, la Palestine et la Judée', 1839. 1830

386. Acco – the ancient lighthouse 1814

Its remains are still visible in front of the small fishermen's harbour.

H. Light, 'Travels in Egypt... Holy Land' 1818.

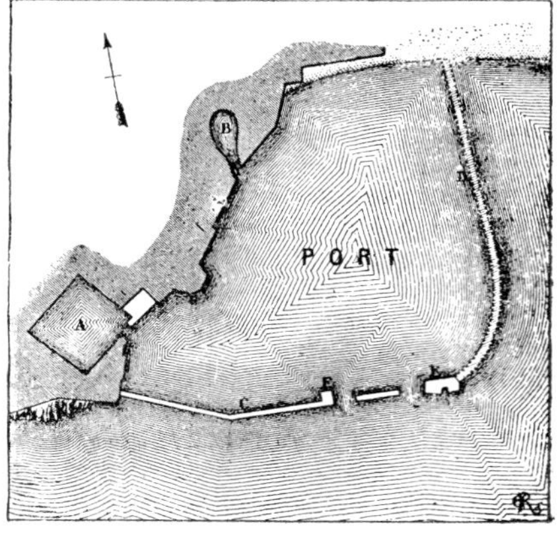

387. Acco – the Crusader port. Restoration

G. Rey, 'Études sur les monuments... en Syrie', 1871.

A – anchorage. K – lighthouse.

388. Acco – a private house 1880

389. Acco – a Moslem couple 1880

P. Lortet, 'La Syrie d'aujourd'hui', 1884.

390. Achziv – 1887
from the sea

F. & E. Thévoz, 'La Palestine Jllustrée', 1888–91.

Beyond Achziv, a Galilean mount and its cape, in Hebrew: Rosh-Hanikra.

391. Acco – Achziv – Tyre
About 1300

Section of a Latin map of Palestine preserved in Florence.

Achziv is indicated by its Crusader name — Casalimberd.

On the left, the city Tyre – ancient Tyrus. On the right – Acco.
(see figure 332).

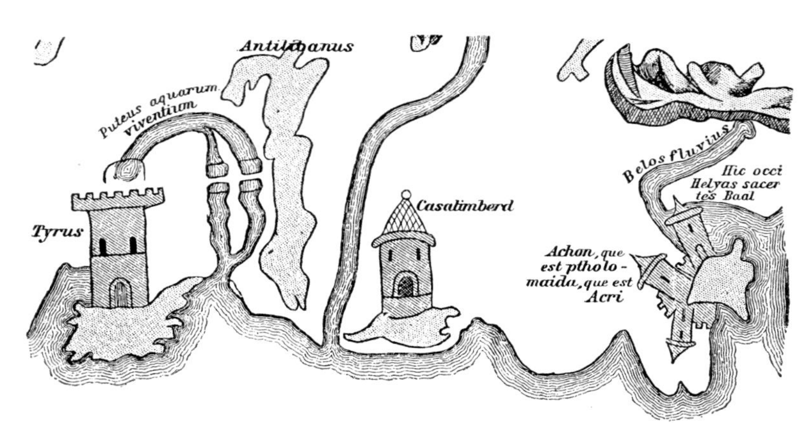

392. Rosh-Hanikra – 1880
Head of the Grotto

Ch. W. Wilson, 'Picturesque Palestine', 1882.

This spot, which marks the beginning of the Ladders of Tyre, is also the border between Israel and Lebanon.

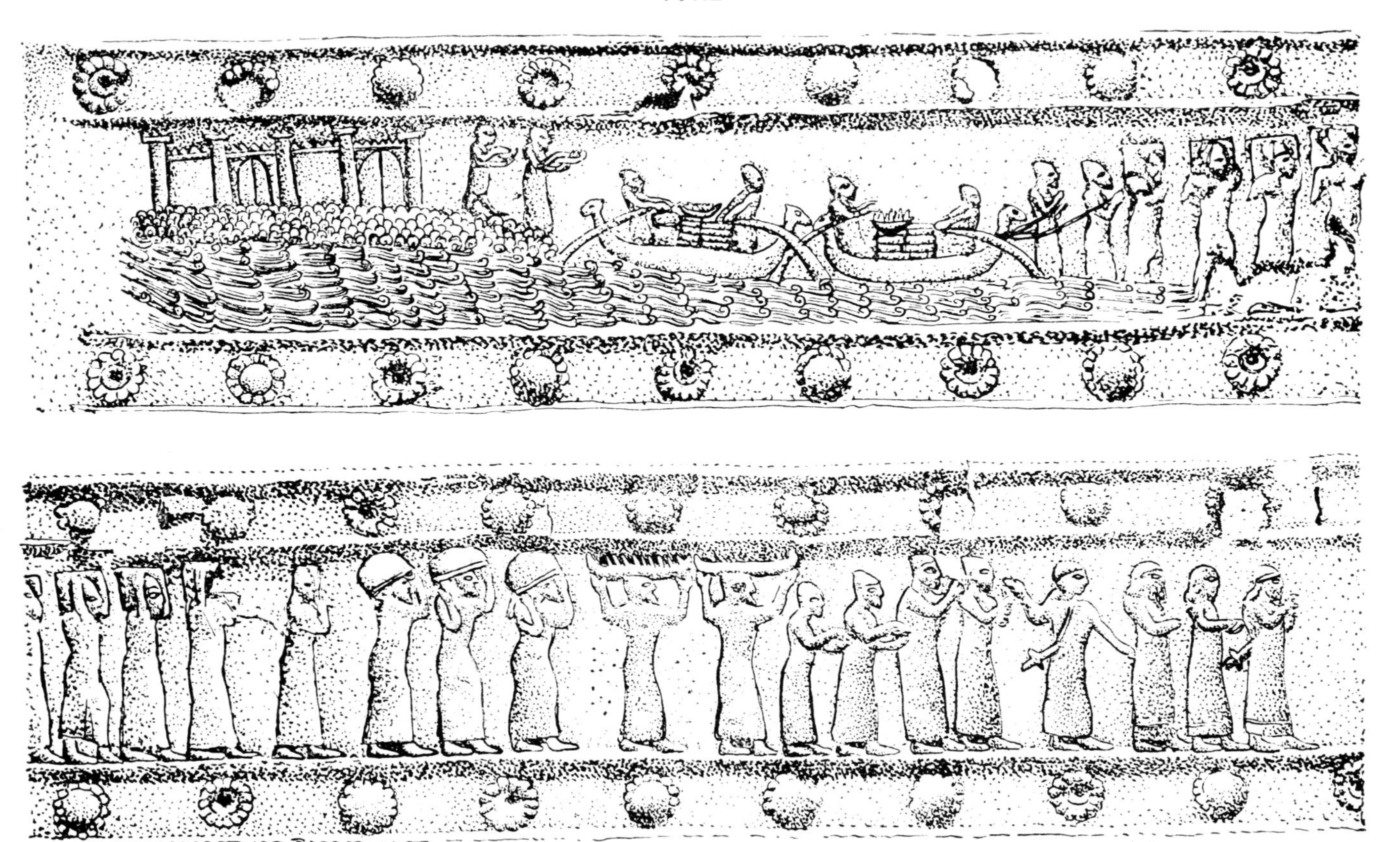

393. Tyre is built on an island Assyrian soldiers on barges carry away the booty of the town. About 859 B.C.

A scene carved on one of the bronze plates which covered the portals of the palace of Shalmaneser III, King of Assyria. The plates were discovered at Tel Balawat, in Northern Iraq, and are exhibited in the British Museum, London.

394. Tyre – seen from the mainland Paul Lortet, 'La Syrie d'aujourd'hui', 1884. About 1880

The gap separating the town from the mainland was filled up by Alexander the Great, in 333 B.C.

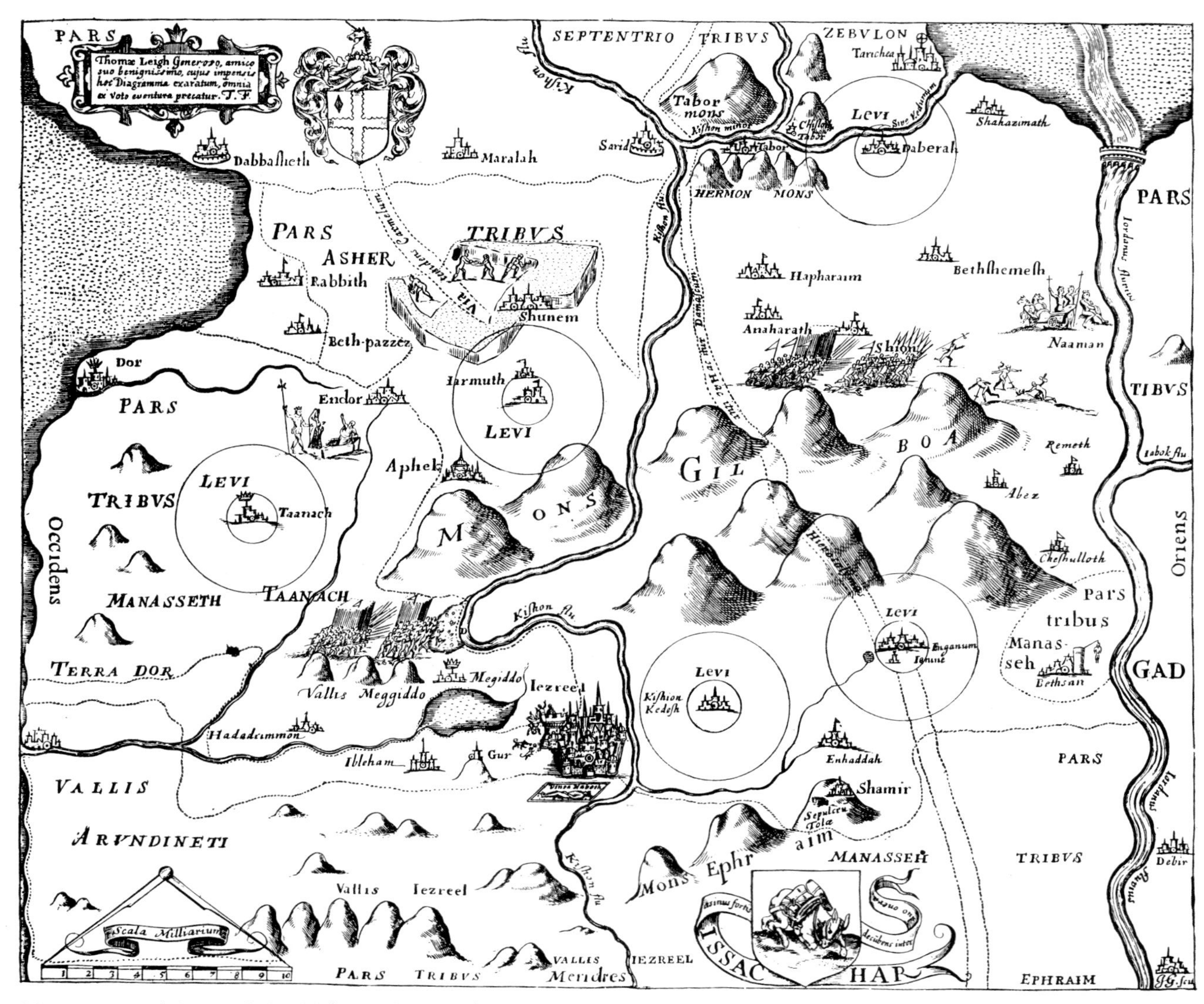

395. Pictorial Map of the Valley of Jezreel Thomas Fuller, 'A Pisgah-Sight of Palestine'. 1650

The main purpose of this map is to locate biblical sites and illustrate the events attached to their names. It contains the usual mistakes typical of similar works of the period. The most striking is the origin of the River Kishon which is shown issuing from the Sea of Galilee (Kinneret), in the top right-hand corner. The River Jordan — Jordanus fluvius — is pictured as a separate body of water that flows through the sea and out of it under a bridge, then runs southwards and receives the waters of the Yabbok — Iabok flu(vius). The River Kishon, dividing into several branches, irrigates a large area both northwards and southwards. It is indicated successively by the names Kishon, Kishon minor or Kedumim (the ancient), as written in the song of the Prophetess Deborah.[1] At the top of the picture, Mount Tabor — Tabor mons, rises between two branches of the River Kishon while, facing it across Kishon minor, stands Hermon Mons, that is, Little Hermon, a name often used by Christian pilgrims for the Hill of Moréh of the Bible, which stands in the Valley of Jezreel.

The town of Jezreel, represented as a fortified city, occupies the middle lower section of the map, and next to it is marked the vineyard of Naboth of biblical memory — Vinea Naboth, with Naboth himself reclining in it.[2] The town of Megiddo, topped by a crown, is not far from Jezreel in the Valley of Megiddo, where a small lake feeds a stream that flows westwards to the Mediterranean. Between Megiddo and Taanach, the Israelites are seen pursuing the Canaanites who are sinking in the mire of the River Kishon, as told in the song of Deborah.[3] A little farther up is Endor, with another pictorial representation of a biblical scene: King Saul, crowned and holding a halberd, consults the witch of Endor, and the ghost of the Prophet Samuel rises out of the grave.[4]

Higher, is the town of Shunem with the reapers working in the fields as when the Prophet Elisha visited the town.[5] Eastwards, between the rivers Kishon and Jordan, at the foot of Mons (Mount) Gilboa, the Israelites, after their victory in the Valley of Jezreel, are pursuing the fleeing Midianites.[6] On the bank of the Jordan, the chariot of Naaman, the officer of the King of Aram, is watched by two attendants, while he himself washes in the waters of the river, according to the advice of the Prophet Elisha.[7] Continued on next page

1) Judges 5, 21. 2) I Kings 21. 3) Judges 5, 19. 4) I Samuel 28, 7-19. 5) II Kings 4. 6) Judges 7, 19. 7) II Kings 5.

396. Napoleon's army encamped in the Valley of Jezreel, at the foot of Mount Tabor 1799

J. B. Spilsbury, 'Picturesque Scenery in the Holy Land', 1804.

397. The Battle of Jezreel, 1799

Barthélémy and Méry, 'Napoléon en Egypte', 1824.

The French routed a large force of Turks sent by the Sublime Porte to relieve Napoleon's siege of Acco.

Continued from previous page

On the top right-hand side of the map are indicated the towns conquered by the tribe of Issachar, as recorded in the book of Joshua:[8] Daberah, Bethshemesh, Hapharaim, Anaharath and Enganim which appears under the Arabic name of Jenin. On the top left-hand side and in the middle are some of the towns of Zebulun: Dabbasheth, Maralah, Sarid, Chisloth-Tabor. In the south is one half of the tribe of Manasseh and its main town, Dor, on the shore of the Mediterranean amidst the Land of Dor—Terra Dor. South of Dor is the Valley of the Reeds, Vallis Arundineti, in Hebrew Brook of Kanah, named after the river running through it which marks the border between the territories of Manasseh and Ephraim.[10] The town of Shamir appears in the mountains of Ephraim next to the Tomb of Tola – Spulcru(m) Tolae, one of the judges mentioned in the Bible: 'Tola the son of Puah... and he dwelt in Shamir in the hill-country of Ephraim'.[11] In the east is Beit-She'an, Betshan, from whose high tower hangs the corpse of King Saul.[12]

All the names mentioned in the map are Hebrew-Biblical, except one — Tarichea, which is the Greek name of a settlement standing on the shore of the Sea of Galilee. The map is traversed from south to north by the highway leading from Jerusalem to Damascus.

8) Joshua 19, 17-23. 9) Joshua 19, 10-16. 10) Joshua 16, 8. 11) Judges 10, 1. 12) I Samuel 31, 10.

398. Mount Tabor and the Valley of Jezreel 1652

Jean Doubdan, 'Le Voyage de la Terre Sainte', 1657.

Left: a highly imaginary representation of Mount Tabor with a wall surrounding its peak, where appears a picture of Jesus' Transfiguration in a halo resting on clouds. At the bottom right-hand corner – a drawing of the remains of the Byzantine-Crusader church which, to-day, are incorporated in the Franciscan Abbey on top of the mount.

In the Valley of Jezreel enclosed by the mountains of Samaria, Gilboa and Galilee, the River Kishon winds its leisurely way to the Mediterranean. Beduin camps are the only indication of human life in the valley.

399. Mount Tabor – Mount of Transfiguration 1668

Jacques F. Goujon, 'Histoire du Voyage de la Terre Sainte', 1670.

Similar to the previous picture with an identical representation of Jesus' Transfiguration, and the inscription: Plan of the sacred Mount Tabor – Plan du sacré mont de Thabor. The Mountains of Samaria rise to the right, and of Galilee to the left. At their foot emerges the River Kishon flowing to the sea.

400. The Valley of Jezreel and Mount Tabor 1858

A picture preserved in the Library of the British Museum, London.

A Beduin camp in the fields of Jezreel. To the left appears a caravan proceeding from Nazareth to Jenin. The tents cover a site now occupied by the town of Afula, whence a road debouches north to Nazareth, in the direction of the caravan.

401. The Caravanserai at the foot of Mount Tabor 1842

A drawing by W. H. Bartlett which appeared in H. Stebbing's, 'The Christian in Palestine', 1847.

In the seventeenth – nineteenth centuries this caravanserai called in Arabic: Khan et-Tujjar – The Inn of the Merchants, was an important trading centre in Galilee, where, on fixed days of the week, merchants conducted a brisk business. Here, we see the Thursday market – in Arabic: Suk el-Khamis, to which crowds flocked from all around. Today, Khan et-Tujjar is but a forsaken ruin by the side of the Tiberias – Afula highway.

402. The Valley cf Jezreel 1840

F. Egerton, 'Journal of a tour in the Holy Land', 1841.

The festive tents of a night encampment prepared for the use of European travellers.

403. The Arab village Zar'in, on the site of the ancient town of Jezreel 1880

Paul Lortet, 'La Syrie d'aujourd'hui', 1884.

The fellahin houses cluster on the hill in true oriental fashion.

404. A Beduin camp in the Valley of Beit-Shean 1882

From the book of travels of the Austrian Crown Prince Rudolph, printed in 1884.

Beduin, having planted their long spears in the ground, enjoy, in the sunshine, a smoke from their typical long-stemmed pipes.

405. Beit-Shean – the Arab townlet Beisan 1894

From the illustrations of the 'Album de la Terre Sainte', ed. Maison de la Bonne Presse, 1894.

A poor Arab village built of clay and mud bricks. The only stone building is the mosque, with its square minaret rising high above the village. On the horizon, the Mountains of Gilead, in Transjordan.

406. Nazareth – in the mountains of Galilee 1631

Eugène Roger, 'La Terre Saincte', 1646.

A. Entrance to the monastery
B. House of the Orientals
C. House of Mary
D. Refectory of the monks
E. Dormitory
F.—G. Gardens
H. Relics of a tower
I. Minaret of the mosque
L. Housing of Arab pilgrims
M. House of the interpreter
N. Spring of Mary
O. Pool
P. Cavern in the Greek-Orthodox church
Q. Arab place of prayer
S. The way to Mount Tabor

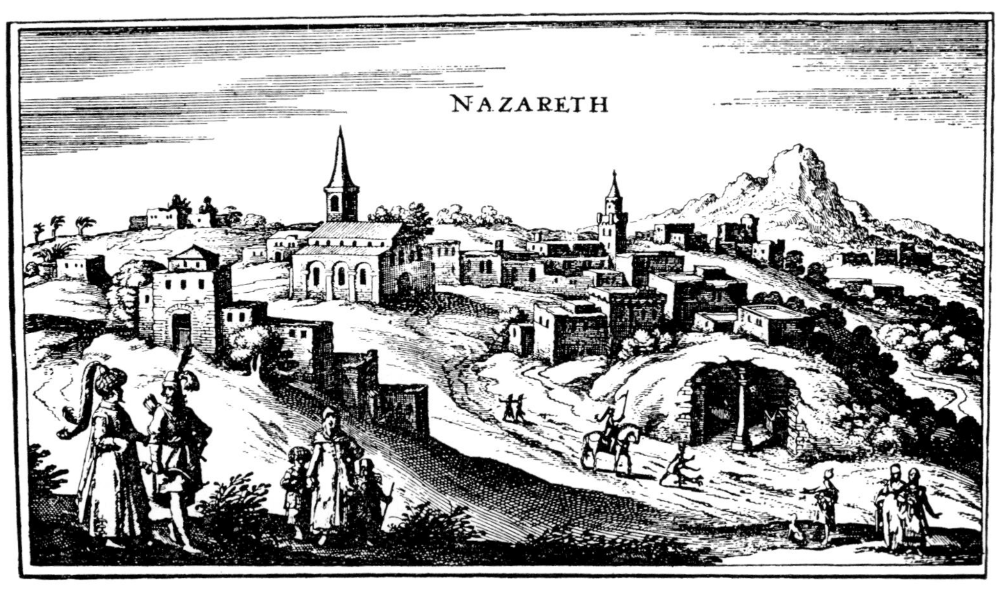

407. Nazareth About 1660

J. Jansonius, 'Illustriorum Hispaniae Urbium', printed in 1660.

Apparently a wholly imaginary illustration of Nazareth and its inhabitants. The cave pictured to the right, whose entrance is supported by a pillar, may be the artist's fanciful conception of the Cave of the Annunciation and the Column of Mary.

448. Nazareth About 1830

From the 'Album of the Holy Land'.

Another imaginary picture of Nazareth with no relation to reality.

409. Nazareth and the Spring of Mary 1845

Otto Georgi, 'Die Heiligen Stätten nach Orginalzeichnungen nach der Natur', 1854.

410. Nazareth About 1851

J. J. Bourassé, 'La Terre Sainte', 1860.

The minaret of the mosque stands out in the middle of the town. On the right lies the large monastery of the Franciscans and the Church of the Annunciation.

411. One of Nazareth's quarters 1851

412. The Franciscan Monastery in Nazareth 1851

From the book of the German traveller, E. W. Schulz, 'Reise in das gelobte Land', 1842.

413. Nazareth, a view from the south 1854

Igino Martorelli, 'Terra Santa, aspirazione religiose', 1854.

1) The Church of the Annunciation. 2) The Church of Saint Joseph. 3) The Synagogue Church. 4) Church of Mensa Christi (Table of Christ). 5) Maronite Church. 6) Church of the Archangel Gabriel. 7) Spring of Mary. 8) Pilgrims' Hostel. 9) Convent of the Dames of Nazareth. 10) The way to Mount Tabor. 11) The way to Tiberias. 12) The Leap of the Lord (Mount of Precipitation). 13) The village Yaffa — biblical Yafa.

414. Nazareth — the Church of the Annunciation 1892

P. W. von Keppler, 'Wanderfahrten und Wallfahrten im Orient', 1899.

415. The Spring of Mary About 1880

Paul Lortet, 'La Syrie d'aujourd'hui', 1884.

416. The Spring of Mary 1848

W. F. Lynch, 'Narrative of the... Expedition to the River Jordan and the Dead Sea', 1849.

426. Tiberias, a view from the south 1850

W. H. Bartlett, 'Footsteps of our Lord', 1851.

On the left, still extant, a main bastion of the town's ancient rampart. Near the shore a felucca, fisherman's boat, its sail half-furled.

427. Tiberias, seen from the south 1839

D. Roberts, 'The Holy Land... from drawings made on the spot', 1842.

In the foreground, ruins of ancient buildings that have subsequently disappeared.

428. Holy Tombs in Tiberias 1598

From an illustrated Hebrew manuscript, written in Casale Monferrato, Northern Italy.

To the right, the Tomb of Rabbi Akiva, a famous first century Sage, and to the left that of his wife within a cave. Between the two the graves of the 24,000 pupils of the learned Rabbi who, as the legend tells, died between Passover and Pentecost of one year. "It was said that Rabbi Akiva had twelve thousand pairs of disciples... and all of them died at the same time, because they did not treat each other with respect".[1]

Below, the tombs of other famous rabbis of the first and second centuries: Rabbi Cahana, Rabbi Yohanan ben Zakkai, Rabbi Hiya and Rabbi Meir Baal-Haness (the Miracle-Worker).

1) The Babylonian Talmud, Yebamot 62b.

429. Tiberias and its Holy Tombs About 1875

Section of a Hebrew pictorial map of the Land of Israel.

Across the map in large Hebrew characters, on the right: 'Sea of Kinnere' (Sea of Galilee), and on the left: 'the holy town of Tiberias, may it be rebuilt and restored soon'.

The River Jordan enters the Sea at the bank facing the town across the water, with Beduin tents drawn up in regular triangles and indicated by the inscription 'Black Tents' – Ohalei Kedar.

Tiberias is surrounded by a fortified wall with only one gate. Outside the wall, famous holy tombs are indicated: the tomb of Harambam (Maimonides), Rabbi Isaiah Horovits, better known by the name of the Holy Shiloh composed of the initials of the title of his main work – Shnei Luhot Haberit (The Two Tablets of the Law), Rabbi Yohanan ben Zakkai, Rabbi Ammi. On the slope of the hill, rising to the right, appear the tombs of Rabbi Akiva and his wife. A small domed building near the shore represents the Hot Springs and next to it, on a height, stands the tomb of Rabbi Meir Baal-Haness (the Miracle-Worker), overlooking the cave of Rabbi Cahana.

430. Jewish women in Tiberias About 1880

Paul Lortet, 'La Syrie d'aujourd'hui', 1884.

431. The Gate of Tiberias, 1893

'Album de la Terre Sainte', published by Maison de la Bonne Presse.

432. The Hot Baths of Tiberias. The town is further up the shore. 1850

A painting by W. Tipping, in 'Jewish Wars' of Josephus, edited by R. Traill, 1851.

433. The Hot Baths of Tiberias 1853

J. R. Brown, 'A Crusade in the East', 1853.

At the bottom, 'The Lake' of Galilee. On the shore, the 'Jews Quarter', surrounded by an additional inner wall. a – the gate. b – the Serail, the Governor's residence. c – gate to the Jewish quarter. f – mosque. g – building with large arches. h – small gate in the town wall. i – the new market.

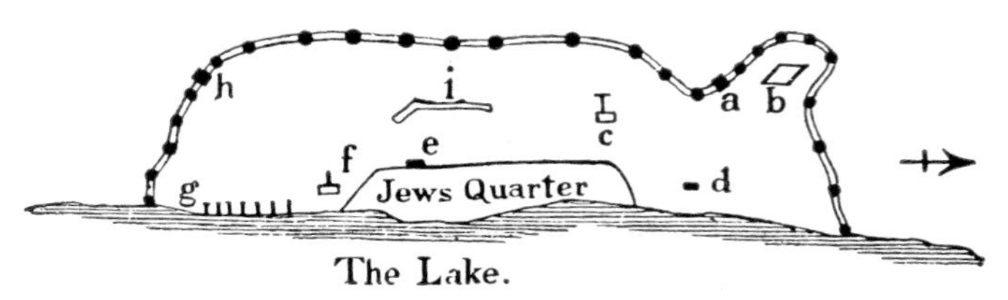

434. Plan of the town of Tiberias 1812

J. L. Burckhardt, 'Travels in Syria and the Holy Land', 1822.

435. Tiberias, a view from the west 1860

F. A. Strauss, 'Die Länder und Stätten der Heiligen Schrift', 1861.

The dark height drawn in the foreground is, today, covered by the houses of the new suburbs of Tiberias.

436. Tiberias, a view from the west 1863

'Pictorial Journey through the Holy Land', 1863.

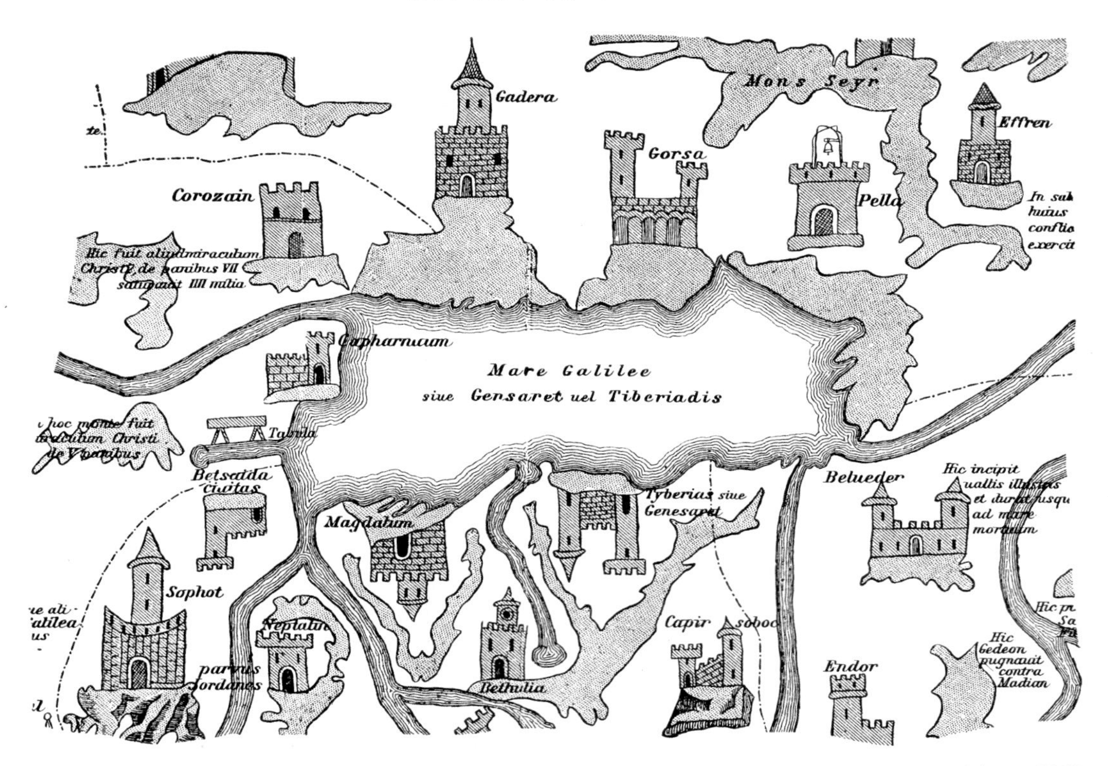

437. Map of the Sea of Galilee About 1300

A section of the map of Palestine preserved in the Library of Florence.

The Sea is indicated by its various names: Sea of Galilee – Mare Galilee, Sea of Gennesareth – Gensaret, and Sea of Tiberias – Tiberiadis. On its shores stand the towns: Tiberias which is Gennesaret – Tyberias siue Genesaret, Migdal – Magdalum, and the town of Bethsaida – Bethsaida civitas. Next to the latter a rough table on trestles, marked Tabula, indicates the site where Jesus multiplied the loaves and fishes to feed the flock of his followers. According to tradition the miracle took place in the Valley of Tabgha at about the site indicated in the map. Next to Bethsaida is Capharnaum. Korazim – Corozain, is placed on the eastern shore although it stood, in reality, near the north-western coast. On the top of the mountains stand Gadara – Gadera, Gerasa – Gorsa and Pehal, under its Greek name of Pella. Encompassing Pella on almost three sides rise the Mountains of Seir – Mons Seyr, which are actually much further south. Belvoir – Belueder, the Crusader fortress, is pictured on the bank of the Jordan and, next to it, Endor, where King Saul consulted the witch. Along Endor flows a stream carrying no name; probably it is meant to represent the River Kishon, which many mediaeval maps mistakenly show starting its course in the Sea of Galilee. Below Tiberias a building is marked Bethulea, the name of a town mentioned in the Book of Judith and which Christian pilgrims placed in the Mountains of Galilee. The site of Tsefat (Safed) – Sephot, is indicated by a fortress and tower, in whose vicinity, according to the map, the Little Jordan flows – Parvus Jordanes, one of the tributaries of the main river. Beyond it, a fortified gate marks the site of the biblical town of Kadesh-Naphtali, in short – Neptalin.

438. Map of the Sea of Galilee 1650

Thomas Fuller, 'A Pisgah-Sight of Palestine', 1650.

Illustrating an ancient legend, the Jordan is shown crossing the Sea of Galilee as a separate body of water.

439. Map of the Sea of Galilee 1681

A section of the Latin map of Palestine attached to the book of O. Dapper, 'Asia, oder genaue und gründliche Beschreibung des gantzen Syrien und Palestinas', printed in 1681.

The lake is indicated by its usual names: 'Sea of Galilee and Tiberias' – Mare Galilaeae et Tiberiades, and 'Lake of Genesareth' – Stagnum Genesareth. On its shores stands the town 'Tiberias previously Kinnereth' – Tiberias olim Cenereth. Next to it are the Hot Springs, marked 'Baths of Hammat' – Balnea Emaus, 'Migdal' – Magdalum, the 'Land of Genesaret' – Terra Genesareth, Bethsaida and Capernaum. On the opposite side of the lake, on top of a mountain, stands 'Gerasa which is also Gergesa' – Gerasa quae et Gergesa, to which Jesus came with his disciples as told in the Gospel: 'And when he went forth to land, there met him out of the city a certain man, which had devils a long time... and there was there an herd of many swine feeding on the mountain... Then went the devils out of the man and entered into the swine, and the herd ran violently down a steep place into the lake, and were choked'.[1] The whole scene is pictured on the map.

To the right of Gerasa appears Mount Sussita by its Latin name of Hippos, and a little above it the words 'Aquae calidae' indicate the Hot Springs of Hamat-Gader (Arabic: el-Hama), which flow into the River Yarmuk and are named after the nearby town of Amatha.

In the vicinity of Tiberias stand Jotapata on top of a hill and Spelunca – the cavern where Josephus Flavius was seized by the Romans. Not far, on a peaked hill, is the 'Town on the Mountain' – Vicus montanus, mentioned in the 'Sermon on the Mount': 'A city that is set on an hill cannot be hid'.[2]

According to another interpretation the reference is to the city of Zefat (Safed) which stands on a high peak and overlooks all its surroundings. The River Jordan flows out of the Sea of Galilee. Next to its outlet, the name Tarichea, marked twice, indicates a town famous at the time of the Jewish rebellion against Rome.[3] Next to it is Bellifort, probably a corruption of the name Belvoir, a main Crusader fortress against the Moslems. Below Bellifort is Keshion – Cesion, a town of Issachar, next to which, repeating a mistake often found in mediaeval maps, the River Kishon is shown starting its course from the Sea of Galilee to the Mediterranean Sea.

1) Luke 8, 27—33. 2) Matthew 5, 14. 3) Wars II, 21, 4. III, 10, 1.

440. Remains of a bridge on the River Jordan, at its outlet from the Sea of Galilee 1848

W. F. Lynch, 'Narrative of the United States Expedition to the River Jordan and the Dead Sea', 1849.

Near this spot there stands today the modern bridge over which the highway passes from the new settlement Degania — on the right, to Tiberias — on the left. At the back, the tents of the American expedition led by Captain W. F. Lynch, for the exploration of the River Jordan and the Dead Sea. One of the two small boats flies the United States flag. At the time it was possible to ford the river at this spot on foot and on horseback.

441. The Arab village of Majdal, ancient Magdala, the home of Mary Magdalene About 1880

Paul Lortet, 'La Syrie d'aujourd'hui', 1884.

442. The Caravanserai called in Arabic Jub Yusef – Joseph's Pit 1839

J. J. S. Taylor, 'La Syrie, l'Egypte, la Palestine et la Judée', 1839.

443. Zefat (Safed) with its citadel on the top of the mount 1837

J. M. Bernatz, 'Palästina', 1868.

444. Zefat, seen from the north 1850

W. H. Bartlett, 'Footsteps of our Lord' ,1851.

On the mountain peak, relics of the ancient fortress towering over the houses of the town. In the distance, on the shore of the Sea of Galilee, the town of Tiberias. In the foreground an Arab shepherd and his flock.

445. Zefat, the fortress on the hill crest 1851

E. W. Schultz, 'Reise in das Gelobte Land', 1852.

On the slope of the mountain, the olive trees typical of Galilee; at its foot, the tents of the visitors.

ZEFAT AND ITS VICINITY

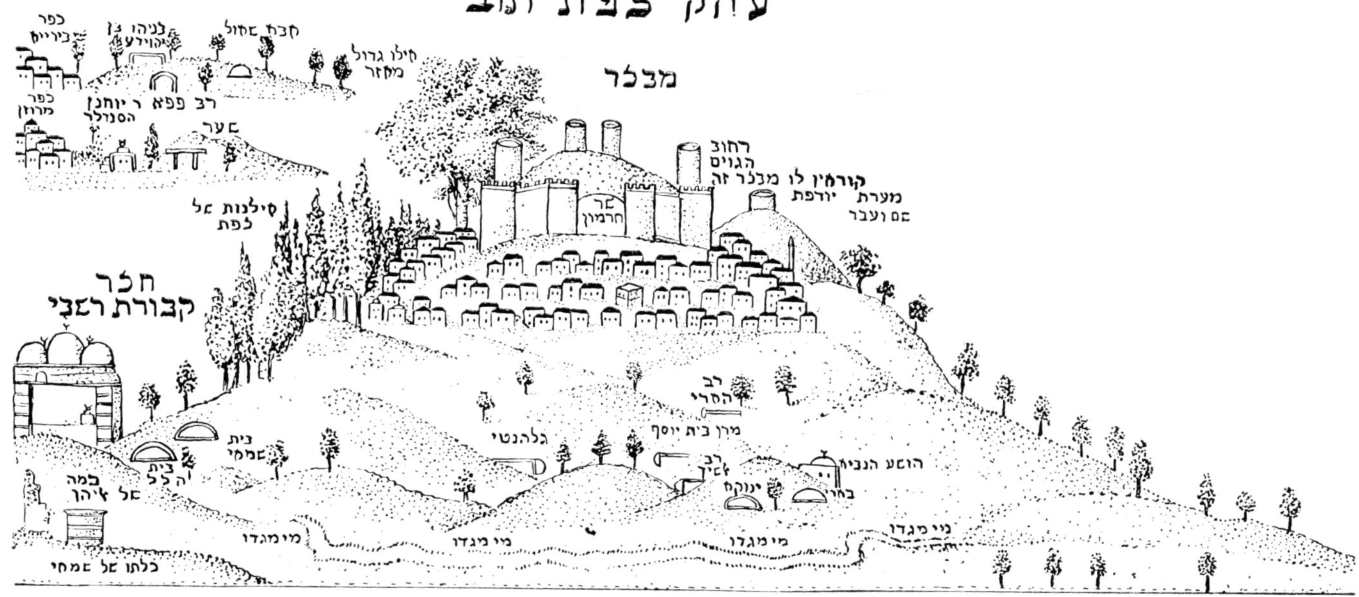

446. Zefat and its vicinity 1875

Section of a Hebrew pictorial map entitled 'The Image of the Holy Land and its Borders' by Haim Pinie of Zefat.
In large characters on top: T(he) H(oly) T(own) Zefat M(ay it be) S(oon) R(ebuilt).

On the top of the hill, a castle with the inscription: 'This fortress is called Yodfat', which points to a confusion with the central Galilean stronghold of the Jews during the revolt against Rome. The small houses of the town are spread in orderly fashion at the foot of the hill. On the right, another inscription, reading, 'the street of the Gentiles', defines the non-Jewish quarter. A little lower, the place of the 'Cave of Shem and Ever' is marked. Legend holds that on this site, Shem, Noah's son, and his great – grand-son Ever, taught the religious commandments. The cypress-trees on the left are entitled 'the Trees of Zefat'. The side of the mountain is covered by a cemetery where tombs of famous scholars and sages are portrayed: Rabbi Yizhak Lurie, the principal exponent of the Kabbala (mysticism) in the sixteenth century, named by his pupils Ha-Ari Hakadosh – the Holy Lion. Below is the grave of Rabbi Joseph Caro, author of 'Shulhan Arukh', a code of Jewish law. Also marked are the tombs of Rabbi Galanti, Rabbi Alsheikh, the compiler of a well-known commentary on the Torah, the Prophet Hosea and his father Beeri, next to the cave of the 'Yanuka', the child prodigy of kabbalist folklore.

On the left-hand side appears Meiron, and, in large characters, the words: 'the Courtyard of Rashbi's Tomb'. 'Rashbi' stands for the initials of Rabbi Shimon bar Yokhai, the famous talmudic sage of the second century. Below it appear the tombs of other renowned scholars of the 'House of Shammai' and the 'House of Hillel', and the grave attributed to the 'daughter-in-law of Shammai'. Hillel and Shammai, in the first century A. D., were the heads of two famous schools of religious law which upheld opposite principles. A rock nearby is marked the 'High Place of Elijah', known today as the 'Chair of Elijah', on which, says legend, the Prophet will sit at the end of days and blow the trumpet announcing the coming of the Messiah.

Between Meiron and Zefat flows a stream, the 'Waters of Megiddo', which runs down to the Sea of Galilee.

The village Meiron appears on the top left-hand side with the tomb of Rabbi Yohanan Hasandlar – the Shoemaker, and the gate of an ancient synagogue marked 'Gate' – Shaar. On top is the village Biria and the holy tombs of its vicinity: 'Abba Shaul' and 'Benayahu son of Yehoyada' the commander of King Solomon's army.

447. Zefat and its Holy Tombs 1889

A drawing by Sh. Horenstein, author of the Hebrew book, 'Givat Shaul', a description of the Holy Land.

448. Zefat and Meiron About 1900

From a paper sheet covered with coloured pictures of the sacred cities and sites of the Holy Land, which was used for the decoration of booths at the Feast of Tabernacles.

On the right: Zefat ('Saffed') built on the side of a steep mountain. A large house in the front row carries the Hebrew inscription: 'Yeshiva (House of Study) of Hatam Sofer', in memory of a famous Hungarian Rabbi, Moshé Sofer.

On the left: the shrine of Meiron, which contains the graves of Rabbi Shimon bar Yokhai and his son Elazar. On the roof are the stone basins in which clothes are thrown and oil is poured to kindle the traditional bonfire each year, on Lag Ba'omer, the anniversary of Rabbi Shimon's death.

ספר

לבושי שרד

על

יורה דעה

ציון התנא האלקי רשב"י ור"א בנו

צפת

449. Meiron on the frontispiece of a book 1863

From the book 'Levoushei Serad' (Garbed in Glory), printed in Zefat.

The picture represents the shrine of Rabbi Shimon bar Yokhai with the following words in Hebrew underneath: 'Tomb of the divine sage, Shimon bar Yokhai, and Rabbi Elazar, his son.

449*. Tombs of Rabbi Shimon and Elazar, his son 1537

See figure 64.

450. Zefat and Meiron About 1900

On the right — Zefat and on the left — Meiron, the building over the tomb of second century Rabbi Shimon bar Yokhai marked with the initials of the blessing: '(May his) virtues protect us. Amen'.

Below Zefat, on the right, a wind-mill marks the sources of the 'River of the Mills' (Nahal Hatahanot), a deep gorge filled, during the rainy season, with a powerful stream which sets water-mills revolving.

451. Meiron – the holy shrines About 1880

Ch. W. Wilson, 'Picturesque Palestine', 1882.

On the left, the domed building on the tombs of Rabbi Shimon bar Yokhai and his son Elazar. On the right, the tomb of Rabbi Yohanan Hasandlar — the Shoemaker. Between them, a few trees on the slope of the mount conceal the entrance to the cave of Rabbi Hillel and his disciples. The town of Zefat appears on the mountain top beyond, and on the right there is a glimpse of the Sea of Galilee.

452. Meiron – the shrine of Rabbi Shimon ond Elazar 1889.

A drawing by Sh. Horenstein, Vienna, author of the Hebrew book, 'Givat Shaul', a description of the Holy Land.

Bonfires in memory of the two saintly men are lit on the roof.

453. The Egyptian conquest of Merom 1285 B. C.

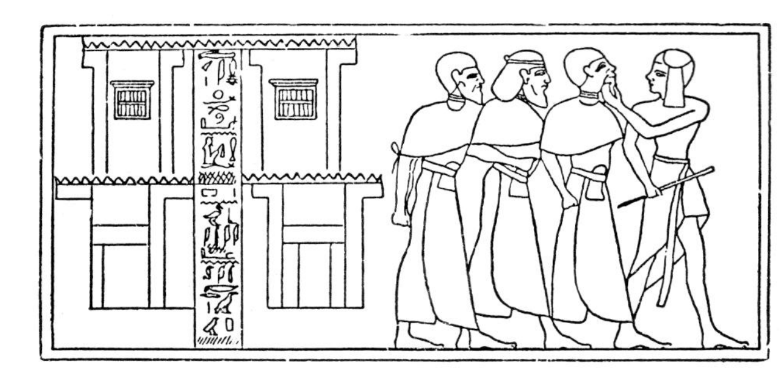

454. The Egyptian conquest of Beit-Anat 1285 B. C.

In both pictures the captured city is represented in stylized form and its name is carved vertically in hieroglyphics over its rampart. Three bound inhabitants are taken into captivity by an Egyptian soldier.

The Merom of this relief is probably the same Merom where Joshua the son of Nun struck a major blow on the Canaanites, as related in the Bible: 'And all these kings met together and they came and pitched together at the waters of Merom, to fight with Israel... So Joshua came and all the people of war with him against them by the waters of Merom suddenly, and fell upon them. And the Lord delivered them into the hand of Israel, and they smote them, and chased them'.[1]

Beit-Anat – House of Anat, is named after a Canaanite deity. When the Land was divided among the Tribes of Israel Beit-Anat (Beth-Anath) became a town in the territory of Naphtali, in the mountains of Upper Galilee.[2]

1) Joshua II, 5–8. 2) Joshua 19, 38.

455. The town Kedesh besieged by the Egyptians 1310 B. C.

During the reign of Pharaoh Seti I.

The town, built on the top of the hill, is well fortified. Of its two gates, the one on the right is clearly drawn. At the bottom right-hand side, an Egyptian soldier drives off captured cattle. In the middle of the picture, the name of the town is carved vertically in hieroglyphic characters over the city's rampart.

This bas-relief is carved on the wall of the ancient Egyptian temple known today by the Arabic name of Medinet-Habu, in the ruins of Karnak, Upper Egypt.

Kedesh was a well-known town in the territory of Naphtali and one of the cities of refuge: 'And they set apart Kedesh in Galilee in the hill-country of Naphtali'.[3]

3) Joshua 20, 7.

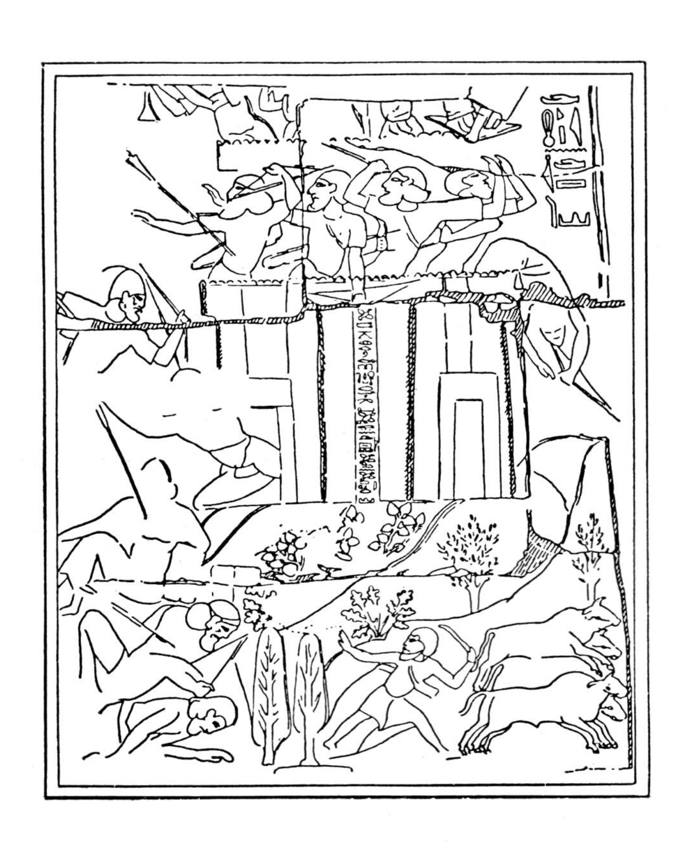

456. The Valley of Hula, seen from the village of Hunin — About 1880

Paul Lortet, 'La Syrie d'aujourd'hui', 1884.

Hunin is today a deserted site next to the village of Margaliot in Upper Galilee. In the desolate valley, enclosed by the mountains, vast swamps deepen and widen into Lake Hula, seen on the right. Today all this area has been drained, reclaimed for agriculture and settled.

457. The Swamps of the Hula Valley — About 1900

In the valley, the black tents of Beduin nomads and buffaloes wallowing in the mud of the swamps. To the left, the mountains of Upper Galilee at whose base, today, runs the Rosh-Pinna — Metulla highway.

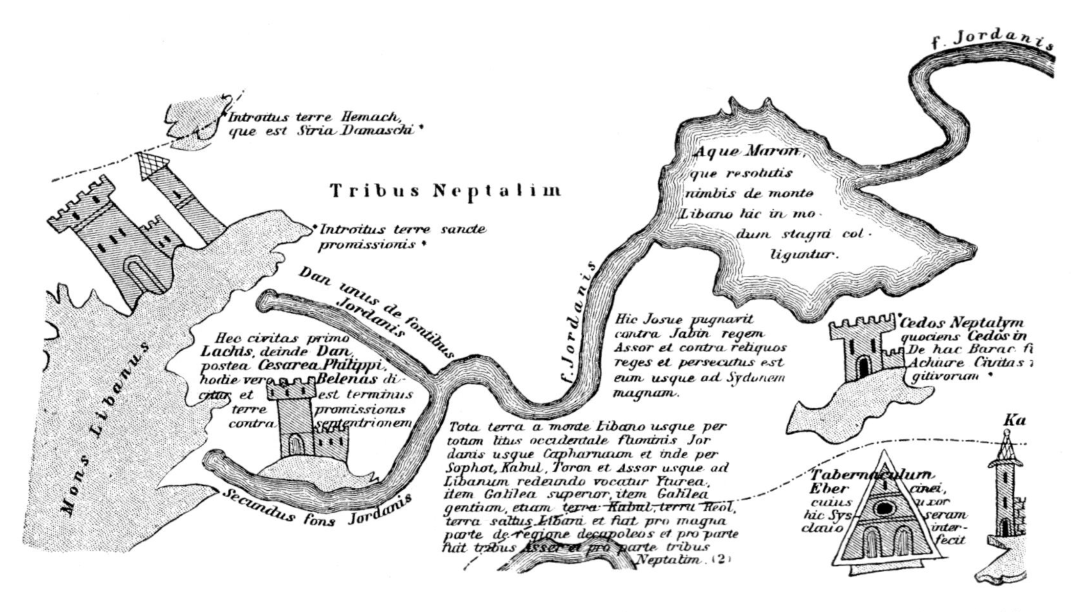

458. Map of the Lake of Hula and the Sources of the Jordan About 1300

Section of a Latin map preserved in the Library of Florence.

The Lake of Hula is designated by the biblical name: Waters of Maron (Merom), also used by Christian pilgrims of the Middle Ages. The legend inscribed within the lake reads: 'The Waters of Maron, after the clouds resolve into rain on Mount Lebanon, collect together here in the form of a swamp' — Aque Maron, que resolutis nimbis de monte Libano hic in modum stagni colliguntur. On the western shore of the lake there is written: 'Here Joshua fought Jabin King of Hazor and the other kings and pursued him until Greater Sidon' — Hic Josue pugnavit contra Jabin regem Assor et contra reliquos reges et persecutus est eum usque ad Sydon magnam. The Jordan — f(lumen) Jordanis—is fed by the 'Dan, one of the sources of the Jordan'— Dan unus de fontibus Jordanis, and by the 'Second source of the Jordan' – Secundus fons Jordanis, both emerging, according to the map, on Mount Lebanon — Mons Libanus. Within the territory embraced by these two arms stands a town: 'This is the town which was formerly named Lachis (Laish), then Dan and later Cesarea Philippi, today it is called Belenas (Banias), and it is the border of the Promised Land in the north'— Hec civitas primo Lachis, deinde Dan, postea Cesarea Philippi, hodie vero Belenas dicitur et est terminus terre promissionis contra septentrionem.

Beyond the Jordan is the territory of Naphtali – Tribus Neptalim, indicated between the 'Entrance to the promised Holy Land' — Introitus terre sancte promissionis, and the 'Entrance to the Land of Hamat which is Syria of Damascus' – Introitus terre Hemach que est Siria Damaschi.

On the western shore of the lake stands: 'Kedesh Naphtali which is Kedesh in Galilee wherefrom came Barak son of Abinoam, a city of refuge' — Cedos Neptalym que aliquociens Cedos in Galilea De hac Barac filius Achiure(?), Civitas fugitivorum.

Immediately under Kedesh is 'The tent of Heber the Kenite, whose wife slew Sisera with a tent-peg' — Tabernaculum Eber cinei, cuius uxor hic Sysseram clauo interfecit. Left of this, the long inscription at the bottom of the picture reads: 'All this land from Mount Lebanon along all the western bank of the River Jordan until Capernaum and then by way of Zefat, Kabul, Toron and Hazor, and back to Lebanon, is named Iturea and also Upper Galilee, and also Galilee of the Gentiles, the Land of Kabul, the Land of Reol(?), the Land of the forest of Lebanon and became the major part of the region of the Decapolis and part was the Tribe of Asher and part the Tribe of Naphtali' — Tota terra a monte Libano usque per totum litus occidentale fluminis Jordanis usque Capharnaum et inde per Saphot, Kabul, Toron et Assor usque ad Libanum redeundo vocatur Yturea, item Galilea superior, item Galilea gentium, etiam terra Kabul' terra Reol(?), terra saltus Libani et fiat pro magna parte de regione decapoleos et pro parte fuit tribus Asser et pro parte tribus Neptalim.

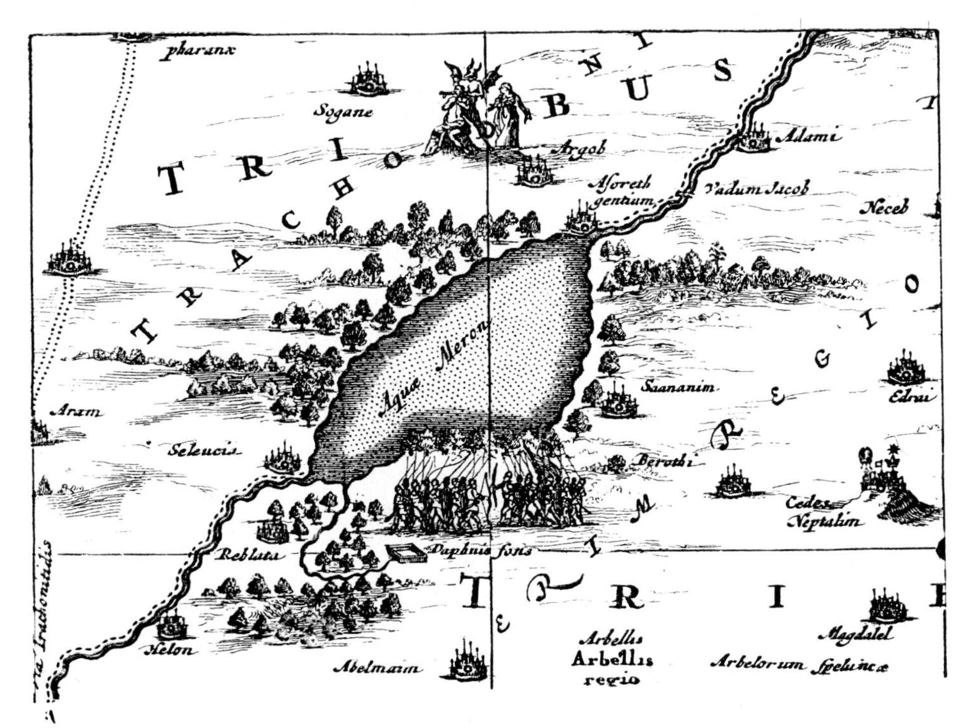

459. Map of the Lake of Hula 1681

A section of the map attached to the book of Olf Dapper, 'Asia, oder genaue und gründliche Beschreibung des gantzen Syriens und Palestinas', 1681.

The Lake carries its biblical name: Aquae Meron—Waters of Merom. The battle of Merom fought by the Israelites under Joshua against the Canaanites is depicted on the shore.

The River Jordan falls into the Lake and comes out of it. The Lake is further fed by a rivulet originating in the small spring of Daphne—Daphnis fons, as related by Josephus Flavius: 'Its marshes reach as far as the place Daphne... and hath such fountains as supply water to what is called Little Jordan'.[1]

At the bottom of the map appear the ancient cities of Abelmein and Arbel—Arbellis, the Caves of Arbel – Arbelorum Speluncae,[2] the town of Kadesh-Naphtali – Cedes Neptalim, on top of a mountain, and a few towns of the Tribe of Naphtali: Adrai—Edrai, Saananim, Adami and Nekeb—Neceb.[3] On the Jordan is seen the bridge with the name Vadum Jacob, Ford of Jacob.

East of the Lake, the region of Trachonitis is indicated, and also the biblical town of Argob and the towns of Seleucia and Sogane mentioned by Josephus Flavius.[4]

1) Wars IV, 1, 1. 2) Wars I, 16, 2. 3) Joshua 19, 33—36. 4) Wars II, 20, 6.

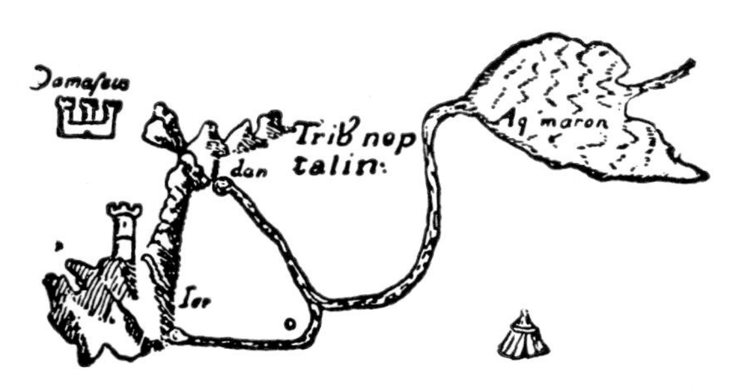

460. Lake Hula and the sources of the Jordan
About 1310

Section of a map drawn by the Italian pilgrim, Marino Sanuto, who was in the Holy Land in 1310.

Lake Hula, indicated by its biblical name: Waters of Meron – Aq(uae) maron, is fed by the Jordan, which flows from two sources: Ior and Dan, which combine to form the name of the river according to an ancient legend.

Another explanation derives the name Jordan, in Hebrew Yarden, from the Hebrew Yarod, meaning to descend, since the River Jordan runs down to the Dead Sea, at a depth of about 400 metres below sea-level. The region of Hula lies within the territory of the Tribe of Naphtali – Trib(us) neptalin. In the east is Damascus, in Syria.

461. Beduin attack an English traveller in the Hula swamps 1868

The Beduin and their black slaves carry him bodily in his canoe over the bank.

462. First encounter In the waters of Hula 1868

463. A Beduin hamlet in the Valley of Hula 1868

A typical scene of the Hula at the time. A poor Arab settlement, partly of tents and partly of huts made of the stalks of the papyrus collected in the swamps, and a buffalo standing in the mud.

All the illustrations on this page are taken from John MacGregor's, 'Rob Roy on the Jordan', 1869.

464. Beduin types in the Hula Valley 1868

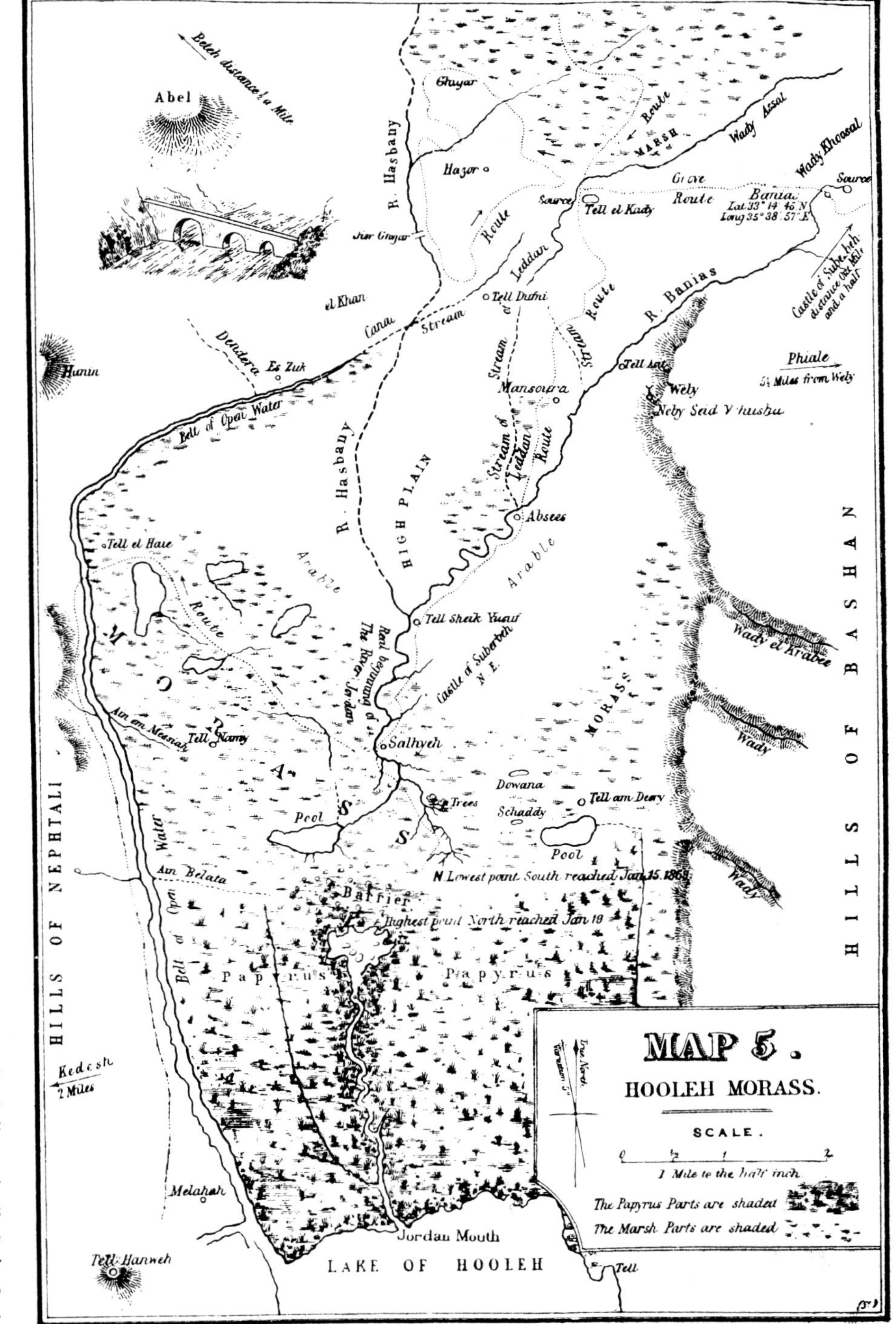

465. Map of the Valley of Hula (Hooleh Morass) 1868

John Mac-Gregor, 'Rob Roy on the Jordan', 1869,

The Valley stretches north of the Hula lake, ensconced between the 'Hills of Naphtali' rising in the west and the 'Hills of Bashan', to the east. At the south-western tip of the marshes, the name 'Melahah' is marked at the spot where the springs known today by the name of Einan emerge. Further north, the direction to biblical 'Kedesh' is indicated (figure 455), and further up, 'Hunin', the site of a Crusader fortress (figure 456). In the top left-hand corner stands the hill of biblical Abel (Beth-Maacha), today a forlorn height. Encompassing the marshes is a 'Belt of Open Water' further nourished by two small streams: 'Ain Belata' and 'Ain em-Messiah'. Next to 'el-Khan', once a caravanserai, a triple-arched bridge, 'Jisr Gujar' (sketched on the side), spans the 'R(iver) Hasbany', which runs down to join the 'R(iver) Banias', thus forming the 'Real beginning of The River Jordan'. Further south the Jordan spreads into a vast 'Morass' overgrown with papyrus plants and other 'Trees'. Some of the water is collected in 'Pools', from the largest of which the Jordan eventually gathers enough momentum to reach the 'Lake of Hooleh'.

Today the Hula swamps have been entirely reclaimed for agriculture and support several new villages. Only a small section has been preserved, as a Nature Reserve where the luxuriant indigenous flora and colourful fauna are protected.

466. A bridge on the lower Jordan About 1830

Comte L. de Laborde, 'Voyage de l'Arabie Pétrée', 1830.

The bridge, called in Arabic Jisr el-Majamé, is a short distance south of the Sea of Galilee.

467. A bridge on the upper Jordan 1882

J. J. S. Taylor, 'La Syrie, l'Egypte, la Palestine et la Judée', 1839.

The bridge is called in Arabic Jisr Benat Ya'acub, after the daughters of Jacob the Patriarch.

468. Fakher ed-Din 1631

The Druze leader of Galilee.
E. Roger, 'Terre Saincte', 1646.

469. A Galilean Arab 1547

P. Belon, 'Les observations de plusieurs singularitez'... 1553.

470. The conquest of the town Ashtarot by the Assyrians About 732 B.C.

In the time of Tiglath-Pileser, King of Assyria.

Ashtarot, in the Land of Bashan, was an important town in biblical times, when its full name was Ashtarot-Karnaim. Today, it is named in Arabic: Ashtara, a mound south of Damascus.

This relief was found in the excavations carried out in the ruins of Nineveh, once the capital of Assyria. Preserved in the British Museum, London (no. 118806).

Four inhabitants of the defeated town, carrying bundles on their backs, are taken into captivity by an Assyrian soldier.

471. The ruins of Jerash – ancient Roman Gerasa About 1830

J. Carne, 'Syria, the Holy Land', 1845.

The most extensive and striking Roman ruins to be seen in Transjordan. A city of the League of the Decapolis, Gerasa was at its zenith in the second-third centuries.

472. The Roman gate – in the ruins of Gerasa 1816

J. S. Buckingham, 'Travels in Palestine', 1821.

473. Gerasa – the Roman temple 1830

J. J. S. Taylor, 'La Syrie, l'Egypte, la Palestine et la Judée', 1839.

474. Philadelphia (Rabath-Ammon) – the Roman amphitheatre 1830

From the above mentioned book.

475. Ruins of the town Rabath-Ammon, the Roman Philadelphia 1864

H. B. Tristram, 'The Land of Israel', 1865.

This site is today occupied by Amman, the capital of Jordan.

476. A caravan of Moslem pilgrims encamp at the fortress of Aqaba 1828

Comte L. de Laborde, 'Voyage de l'Arabie Pétrée', 1830.

The pilgrims are on their way to Mecca and Medina, the holy cities of Islam. On the right, behind the palm-trees, the Red Sea gleams in the sunlight.

477. Petra 1828

Comte L. de Laborde, 'Voyage de l'Arabie Pétrée', 1830.

To the left the majestic remains of the Roman amphitheatre carved out of the side of the mountain.

478. Petra 1928

From the book mentioned above.

The facade of the ruined monument named by the Arabs: ed-Deir – the Monastery. In true Petra style, this monument was carved on the rock-face and served as a front to sepulchral caves.

479. The ruin named in Arabic – el-Khazne 1828

From the book of the Comte de Laborde mentioned above.

A facade similarly carved in the rock and serving as a front to burial caves. The Arab legend held that it was the treasury of an Egyptian Pharaoh.

480. Petra 1828

From the same book.

Front view of the above facade.

481. The Tomb of Aaron the Priest 1838

Jules de Bertou, 'Le mont Hor, le tombeau d'Aron', 1860.

482. The Tomb of Aaron – interior view 1838

From the above mentioned book.

483. The Military expedition of the Egyptian king in the Desert of Sinai About 1300 B. C.

After a study by A. H. Gardiner: 'Journal of the Egyptian Archaeology', VI, 1920.

The relief pictures the return of Seti I, Pharaoh of Egypt, from a military expedition in Palestine. It is carved in the large 'Hypostyle Hall' of the ruined Temple of Karnak, Upper Egypt.

Triumphant Pharaoh rides in a splendid chariot drawn by a pair of white steeds. In front of him walk rows of bound prisoners, whom the hieroglyphic inscription identifies as 'chasu', Beduin inhabitants of the Desert of Sinai. On the right, a vertical water channel, where fish and crocodiles swim, represents the most eastern branch of the Nile, which ran along the border of Egypt and Sinai, in the zone of today's Suez Canal. At the bottom of the picture, the channel joins the sea, where only fish are to be found. Here and there, above the horses' backs, between their legs and under the chariots, the towns and stations standing along the ancient 'Way of the Sea', from Egypt to Palestine, are indicated, each described by its name in hieroglyphic characters. The first part of the highway leading out of Egypt was known by the Egyptian name of 'Highway of Horus' after one of Egypt's main gods, Horus the rising sun and son of Osiris.

This is the oldest known representation of towns and settlements in Palestine and Sinai.

For a separate reproduction of the towns and stations appearing on this relief see next figure.

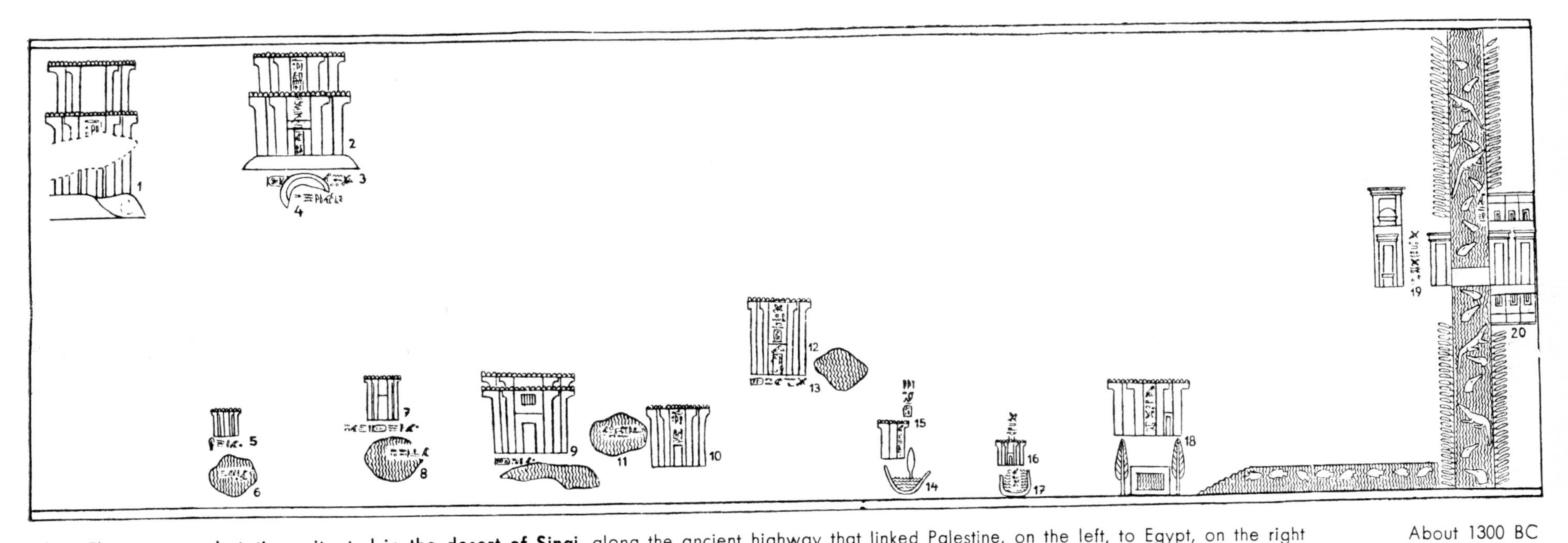

484. The towns and stations situated in the desert of Sinai, along the ancient highway that linked Palestine, on the left, to Egypt, on the right About 1300 BC

From the ancient Egyptian relief appearing on the previous page. 1) Fortified town built on a height, its name obliterated; possibly Raphiah, that stood in Southern Palestine, at the start of the track to Egypt. The ancient name is retained in the Arab town of Rafah near the same site, now at the southern end of the Gaza Strip. 2) 'The town that was built anew by His Majesty, next to The Well Men-mat-re (is) Great in Victories'. 3) 'The Stronghold of Men-mat-re, the heir of Re'. 4) Name obliterated... '-b-r-b-t'. 5) 'The Stronghold Men-mat-re'. 6) 'N-h-s of the Prince'. 7) 'The well Men-mat-re (is) Great in Vicotries'. 8) 'The well (called) Sweet'. 9) 'The Well of Seti Meneptah'. 10) 'Town which (His) Majesty (built) newly'. 11) 'The well of Ib-s-k-b'. 12) 'The castle of Men-mat-re (called) the... his Protaction'. 13) 'The Stronghold of Seti Meneptah'. 14) 'The well tract of...' 15) 'Buto-of-Seti-Meneptah'. 16) 'The Migdol of Men-mat-re'. 17) 'The well of H-p-n'. 18) 'The Dwelling of the Lion'. 19) 'The fortress of Thel'; it was situated in the vicinity of the Egyptian station of Kantara of today. 20) 'The Dividing Waters'. This is the name of the eastern branch of the Nile that flowed in the zone of the modern Suez Canal. Possibly it is the same as the River of Egypt mentioned in ancient texts, describing the borders of the Land of Israel.

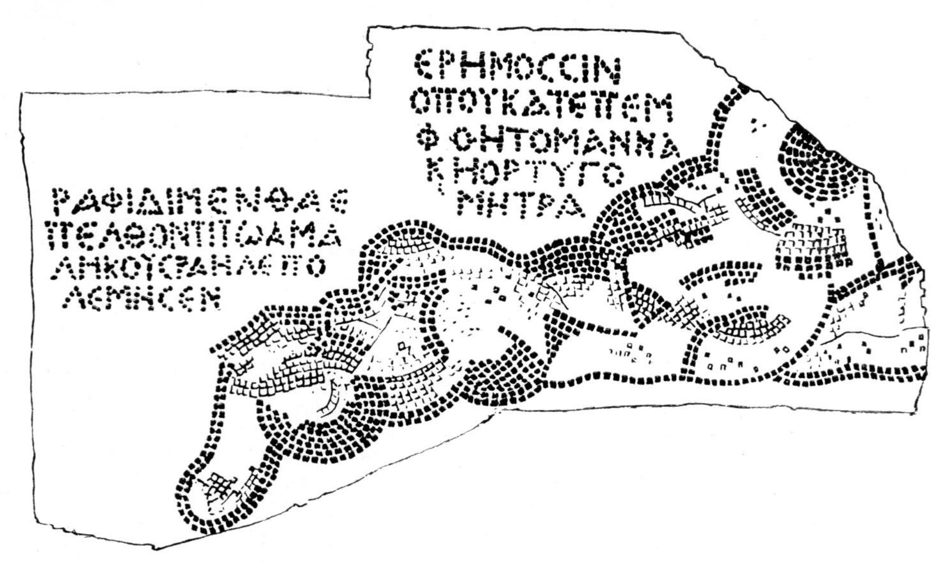

485. The Mountains of Sinai Sixth Century

The Greek inscription on the top reads, 'The Desert of Sin, where the manna and the quails were sent down'. On the left, 'Raphidim, where Amalek came and fought Israel'.

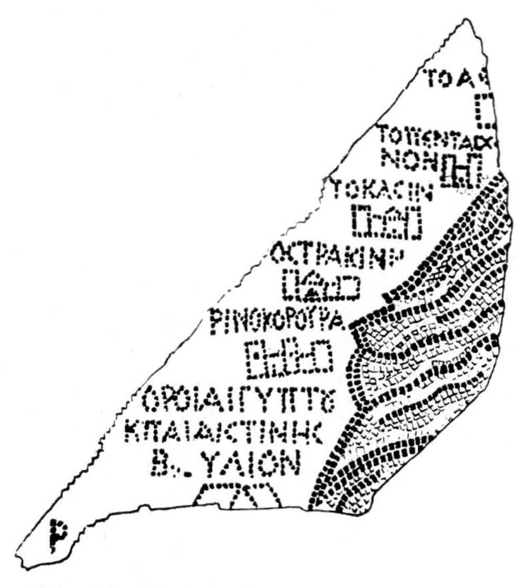

486. The Coast of Sinai Sixth Century

Apparently the Greek letter P at the bottom is the first letter of the name 'Raphiah', today the Arab village of Rafah. Above it appears the name 'B(eth)ulion', with the following legend in red characters: 'Border of Egypt and Palestine'. Further up, a building is marked 'Rinocoroura', the name of a Greek settlement which has been succeeded today by the Arab townlet of el-Arish, the capital of Sinai. Southwards along the coast is 'Ostracine', a well-known settlement in ancient times, then 'Casius', 'Pentasch(oi)non' and 'Aph(taion)', now all ruins buried in the desert sand.

487. A branch of the Nile Sixth Century

The eastern branch of the Nile, 'the Pelusiac (Arm)', which flowed in the zone of the modern Suez Canal. It was named after the settlement pictured at the bottom of this fragment, the city 'Pelusium', now a ruin named in Arabic Farma, near the ancient highway linking Egypt and the Holy Land.

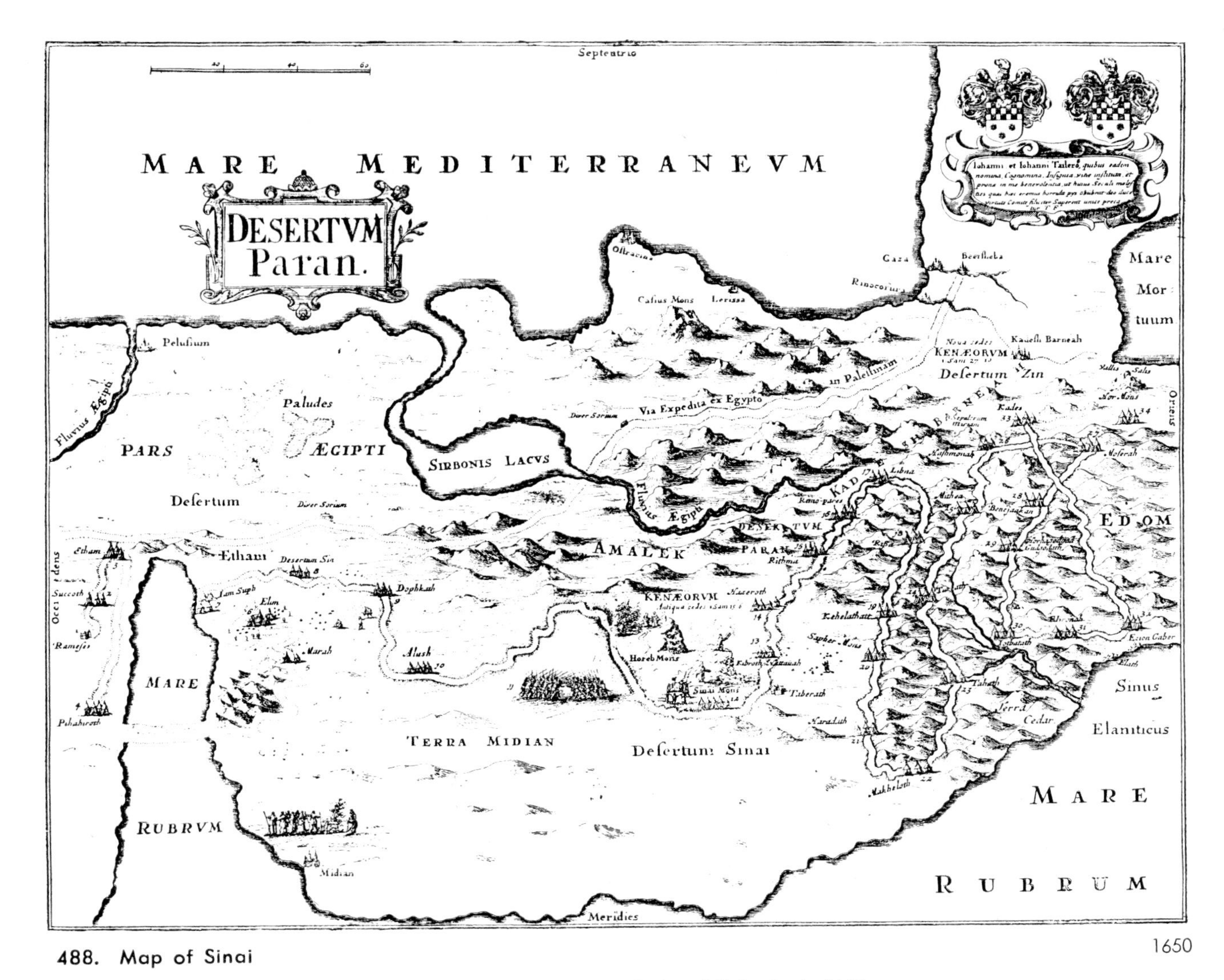

488. Map of Sinai 1650

Thomas Fuller, 'A Pisgah - Sight of Palestine', 1650.

It shows the Desert of Wanderings, the Desert of Paran – Desertum Paran, stretching along the Mediterranean – Mare Mediteranneum. To the left lies Egypt with the important sites of the biblical story: Rameses, Etham and its desert, Pihahiroth, and the passage of the Red Sea – Mare Rubrum.

Beyond the Red sea, the winding route followed by the Israelites continues through the lands and stations mentioned in the sacred texts. The Land of Midian and the town of the same name are placed within the Desert of Sinai, while their correct site is more to the east, outside the boundaries of the desert.

On the route followed by the Israelites in the desert stands Mount Sinai and next to it Mount Horeb – Horeb Mons. The Israelites also reached Eilat and Etzion-Geber, in the Gulf of Eilat – Sinus Elaniticus, on the eastern branch of the Red Sea. On the extreme right, near the top, the southern end of the Dead Dea – Mare Mortuum, appears.

On the left, the eastern branch of the Nile, designated in ancient texts as the River of Egypt – Fluvius Aegipti, enters the sea next to the town of Pelusium.

Lake Sirbon – Sirbonis Lacus, the recipient of another branch of the Nile, here adopts a strange shape. Along the coast of the Mediterranean, on the Palestinian side, appear Ostracina, also mentioned in talmudic literature, Casius Mons, and Lerissa – a distorted form of the Arabic name el-Arish, today the main town of Sinai. At a long distance from this last, up the sea-shore, appears Rinocorura, which is none other then the Greek name of the townlet that occupied the site of the self-same el-Arish.

The track leading from Egypt to Palestine – Via Expedita ex Egypto in Palestinam, passes by the staging post Diversorium, crosses the southern end of Lake Sirbon, and finally comes to Beersheba, the southernmost town of the Holy Land.

489. Canaanites going from Canaan to Egypt About 2200 B.C.
A fresco on the wall of the ancient burial cave of Beni-Hassan, Upper Egypt.

490. Caravan of pilgrims making its way from Egypt to the Holy Land 1675

Otto Friedrich von der Gröben, 'Orientalische Reise-Beschreibung', 1694.

491. A caravan of pilgrims crossing the Desert of Sinai to Palestine 1838
H. von Mayr, 'Malerische Ansichten aus dem Orient', 1839.
Some of the travellers carry parasols against the fierce desert sun.

492. French soldiers of Napoleon in Sinai 1799

On their way to Palestine, to fight the Turks.

493. English tourist in Sinai, on the way to the Holy Land. 1847

John Cadsby, 'Wanderings', 1855.

494. The border of Sinai and Palestine 1838

H. von Mayr, 'Malerische Ansichten aus dem Orient', 1839.

On the coastal track leading from Egypt to Gaza, two ancient columns mark the border between Palestine on the left and Sinai on the right.

495. El-Arish, now the capital of Sinai 1842

From the report of the British Military Expedition (Royal Engineers), printed in 1843.

The stronghold flies the Turkish flag.

496. The Springs of Moses, in Arabic – Ayun Musa 1845

V. H. Bartlett, 'Forty days in the desert on the track of the Israelites', 1848.

This oasis is situated on the way from Suez to Mount Sinai.

497. The valley named in Arabic – Wadi Gharandal About 1880

Charles W. Wilson, 'Picturesque Palestine, Sinai and Egypt', 1880.

It is generally agreed that Elim, one of the stations of the Israelites in the desert, was situated in Wadi Gharandal. The Torah relates about their wanderings: 'And they came to Elim, where were twelve springs of water, and three score and ten palm-trees: and they encamped there by the waters'.[1]

1) Exodus 15, 27.

498. The oasis named in Arabic – Firan About 1880

Charles W. Wilson, 'Picturesque Palestine, Sinai and Egypt', 1880.

One of the largest and most luxuriant oases in Sinai with the typical palm-trees which provide the staple food of desert dwellers. It is held by some to be the place of Rephidim, a famous station of the wandering tribes: 'And all the congregation of the children of Israel... encamped in Rephidim; and there was no water for the people to drink... Then came Amalek and fought with Israel in Rephidim '.[1]

1) Exodus 17, 1—8.

499. The Red Sea opens in front of the Israelite tribes Third Century

A fresco on the wall of the ancient synagogue of Dura-Europos, on the bank of the River Euphrates.

Right: the Egyptians drowning in the Red Sea and Moses pointing his staff against them.

Left: the tribes of Israel carrying shields and banners march boldly, in serried ranks, on the dry bed of the Sea. Fish and shells lie under their feet.

Over Moses and the Israelites are outstretched the hands of Divine Providence.

500. The Israelites and the Egyptians in the Red Sea 1695

From a Passover Haggada printed in Amsterdam.

In Hebrew, under each section of the picture, the corresponding verse of the Holy Scriptures. On the left: 'But the children of Israel walked upon dry land in the midst of the sea'.[1] On the right: 'And the Lord overthrew the Egyptians in the midst of the sea'.[2]

1) Exodus 14, 29. 2) Exodus 14, 27.

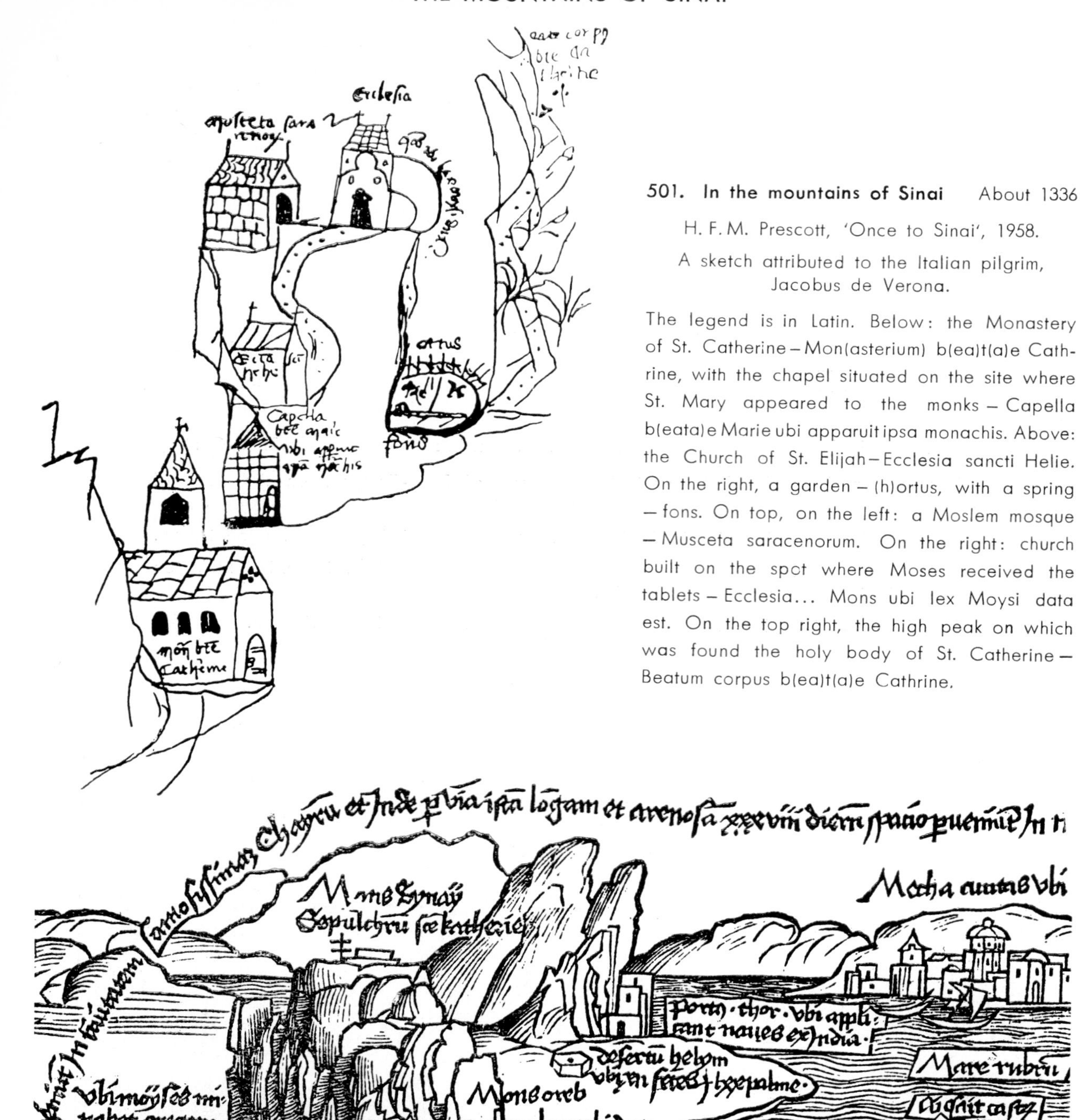

501. In the mountains of Sinai About 1336

H. F. M. Prescott, 'Once to Sinai', 1958.

A sketch attributed to the Italian pilgrim, Jacobus de Verona.

The legend is in Latin. Below: the Monastery of St. Catherine – Mon(asterium) b(ea)t(a)e Cathrine, with the chapel situated on the site where St. Mary appeared to the monks – Capella b(eata)e Marie ubi apparuit ipsa monachis. Above: the Church of St. Elijah – Ecclesia sancti Helie. On the right, a garden – (h)ortus, with a spring – fons. On top, on the left: a Moslem mosque – Musceta saracenorum. On the right: church built on the spot where Moses received the tablets – Ecclesia... Mons ubi lex Moysi data est. On the top right, the high peak on which was found the holy body of St. Catherine – Beatum corpus b(ea)t(a)e Cathrine.

502. Mount Sinai – Mons Synaÿ 1483

Section of a pictorial map of Palestine attached to the book 'Peregrinationes', by B. von Breidenbach, 1486.

(See explanation at bottom of next page).

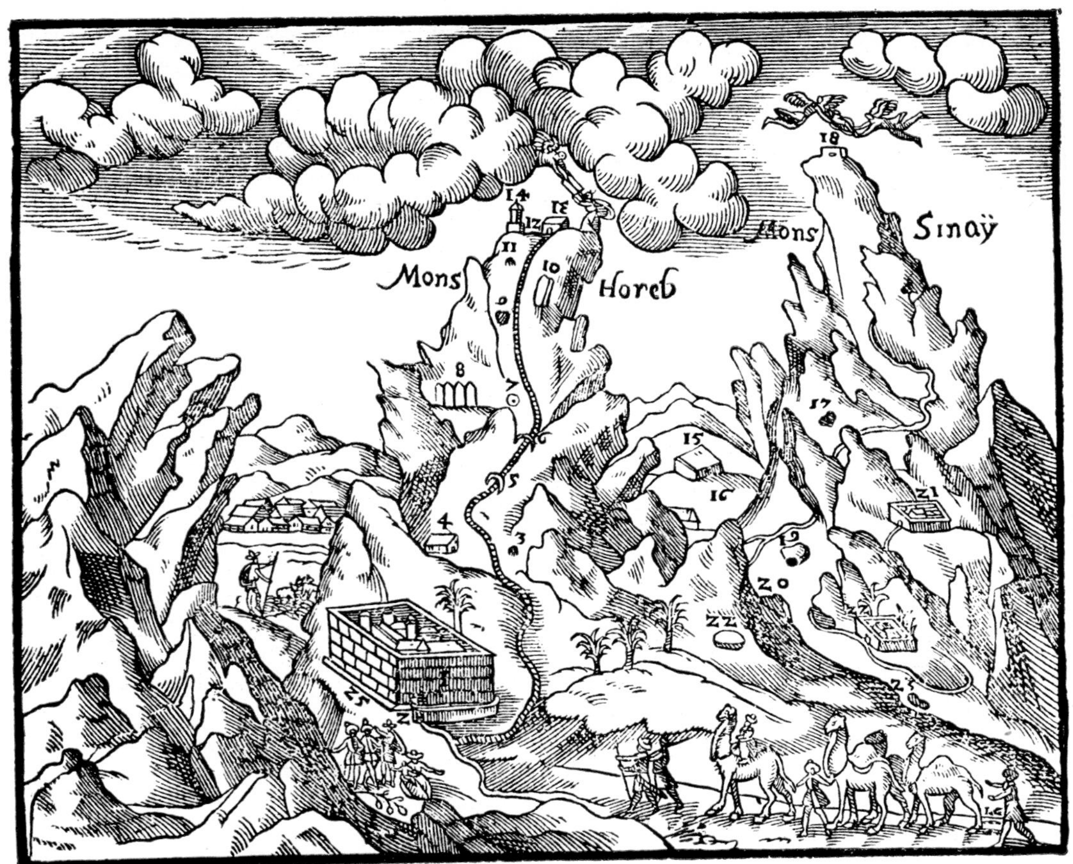

503. Mount Sinai, Mount Horeb and the Monastery of St. Catherine 1587

B. W. von Waltersweil, 'Einer Reisz... in das gelobte Land Palestina... auch auff den Berg Synai', 1609.

The monastery lies in a valley amidst high mountains. Two peaks hang over it, Mount Sinai and Mount Horeb. Steps cut in the mountainside lead from the monastery to the top of Horeb. 1) The monastery of St. Catherine. 2) Entrance to the monastery. 3) Monks' cavern. 4) Church of St. Mary. 5—6) Arches built on the path leading up Mount Horeb. 7) Well of St. Elijah. 8) Church of St. Elijah. 9) Imprint of the hoof of Mohammed's camel. 10) Rock of the Prophet Elijah. 11) Cavern of Moses. 12) The cavern where Moses dwelt for forty days and nights. 13) Church of St. Salvador. 14) Moslem mosque. 15) Monastery of the forty martyrs. 16) Place named for St. Onophrius. 17) Well of cold water. 18) Church of St. Catherine. 19) Rock named for St. Catherine with the imprint of her form. 20) The rock that Moses struck with his staff. 21) Church named after Saints Cosmos and Damianus. 22) Place named after the Twelve Apostles. 23) The site where Moses melted the golden calf. 24) The site where the (brass) serpent was set up. 25) The place where the Arabs receive food from the monks.

Explanation to figure 502

On the left, the Sinai Range, and on the right, the Red Sea, its shores and part of Egypt. Among the mountains of Sinai lies the monastery of St. Catherine — Monasterium S(ancte) K(atheri)ne, and above it rises Mount Horeb — Mons Oreb, with the legend: 'The place where the Ten Commandments were given' — Locus ubi datus fuit decalogus. At its foot a small house indicates: 'The place where St. Onophrius did penance' — Ubi Sanctus Onuffrius egit penitenciam. On top of Mount Sinai is the Tomb of St. Catherine — Sepulchrum Sancte Katherine, and on the left slope of the mount an inscription: 'The place where Moses led the flock into the desert' — Ubi Moyses minabat gregem ad interiora deserti. On the right is the Red Sea — Mare Rubrum, with the small townlet of Tor which still exists: 'The port of Tor to which boats come from India' — Portus Thor ubi applicant naues ex India. Near it is a well with the indication: 'Desert of Elim', a well-known station of the tribes, and a quotation from the Bible: Desertum Helym ubi XII fontes et LXX palme — 'And they came to Elim where were twelve springs of water and three score and ten palm-trees...'. The passage of the Israelites through the Red Sea indicated by a double line across the waters, carries the legend: 'The way along which the sons of Israel crossed the Red Sea on foot' — Via per quam filii Israel sicco pede transierunt mare rubrum. On the right, the land of Egypt, and on the opposite shore of the Red Sea the town of 'Mecca' — Mecha, is represented as a powerful city rising on the coast. The legend written around the map reads: 'The Arabs (Saracens) come from far-away regions by foot to Mecca. First they come to the town Cairo, the most famous of all, and from there along a long route covered with sand, they arrive in thirty eight days at Mecca and to their false prophet'.

504. The Monastery of St. Catherine on Mount Sinai 1565

J. Helfferich, 'Kurtzer und warhafftiger Bericht... Reise... nach Hierusalem... auff den Berg Sinai...', 1577.

Within the fortified monastery stands out the Church of the Burning Bush, next to the minaret of the mosque that the monks built for the use of their Beduin servants.

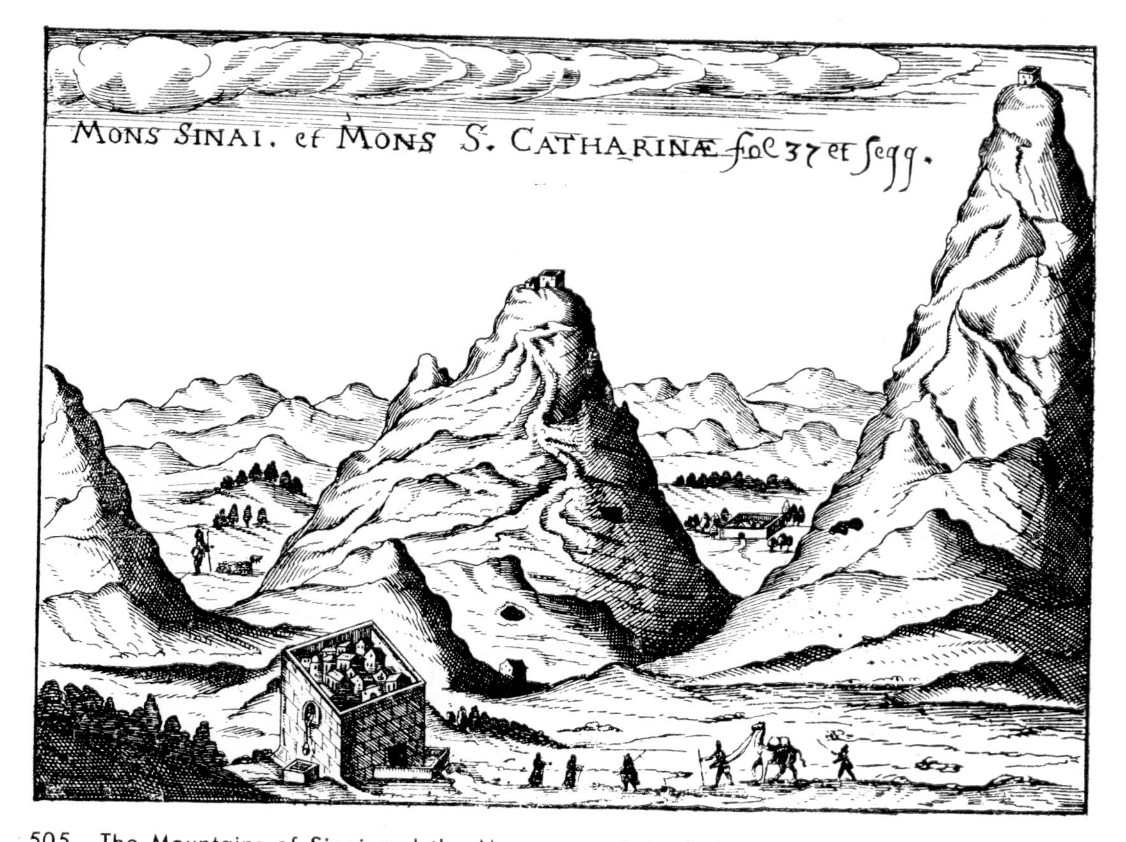

505. The Mountains of Sinai and the Monastery of St. Catherine 1566

C. von Haimendorf, 'Itinerarium Aegypti, Arabiae, Palaestinae...', 1570.

506. The Mountains of Sinai and the Monastery of St. Catherine 1675

Otto Friedrich von der Gröben, 'Orientalische Reise-Beschreibung', 1694.

507. The Mountains of Sinai 1668

Jacques F. Goujon, 'Histoire et Voyage de la Terre Sainte', 1670.

Two heights are pictured: the Mount of Moses and to its left, rising higher still, Mount Horeb. At the foot of the Mount of Moses, on the right, are the monastery of St. Catherine and her church known as 'The Burning Bush'. On the path leading to the top of the mount, half-way up, stand the Church of St. Mary and the cavern named after the Prophet Elijah. At the peak, a church, and next to it, a mosque. At the bottom of Mount Horeb, another monastery, and a third farther to the left.

At the foot of the Moses Range, on the left, still another monastery, next to the site of the 'Golden Calf' and the 'Tombs of the Israelites'. Beyond Mount Horeb, on the left, appear the village Tor (35) and the shore of the Red Sea (36).

508. Mountains of Sinai 1722

From the French translation of the book of travels of the Englishman Thomas Shaw, printed in 1743.

View of the Mountains from the west, from the coast of the Red Sea, in French – La Mer Rouge. On the shore, in a small semi-circular bay, stands the townlet of Tor. East of it is Elim, a station in the wanderings of the Israelites in the Wilderness of Sin – Le Desert de Sin. Mount Sinai rises to the east.

509. The Rock of Moses 1565

J. Helfferich, 'Kurtzer und warhafftiger Bericht von der Reise... nach Hierusalem... Berg Sinai', 1577.

To this day, this rock is sacred to the Beduin nomads of Sinai, who call it the Rock of the Prophet Moses – Hajjar en-Nabi Musa. From this rock, tradition has it, Moses brought forth water for the tribes of Israel, and it still carries the marks of the twelve blows that he struck with his staff to provide a spring for each tribe.

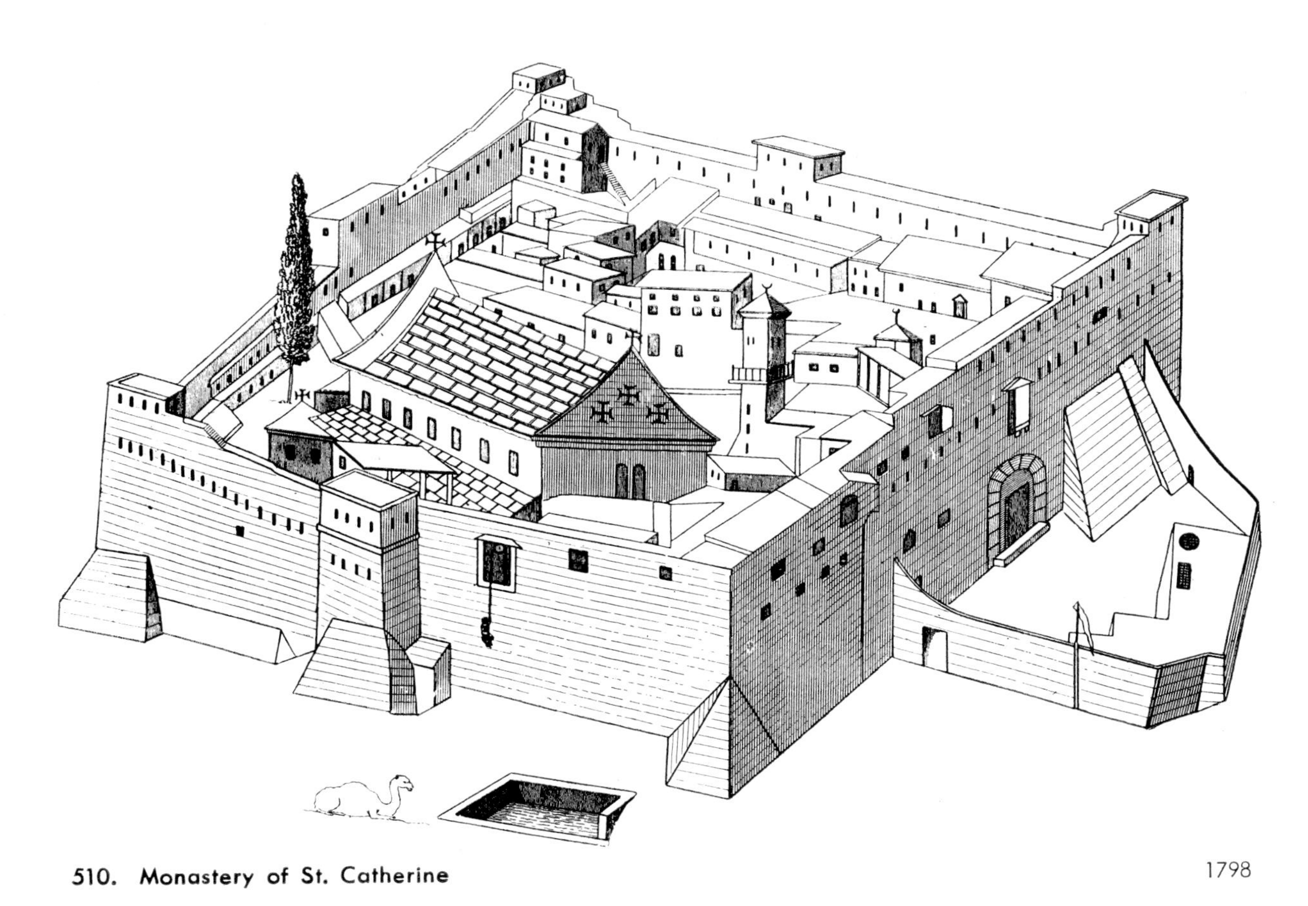

510. Monastery of St. Catherine 1798

'Description de l'Egypte', II, 1817, fol. 103. no. 3.

A drawing made by a member of Napoleon's expedition in the Sinai Desert.

511. Monastery of St. Catherine – interior view About 1830

J. J. S. Taylor, 'La Syrie, l'Egypte, la Palestine et la Judée', 1839.

512. Monastery of St. Catherine 1834

E. Ch. Döbel, 'Wanderungen', 1843.

The monastery was built in the sixth century, when Byzantium ruled the Holy Land.

513. Monastery of St. Catherine About 1851

J. J. Bourassé, 'La Terre Sainte', 1860.

514. Monastery of St. Catherine About 1830

An illustration by the French artist, Adrien Dauzats.

For long centuries, from fear of their isolation in the lawlessness of the desert, the monks kept the gate of the monastery blocked up and devised an ingenious way of entrance which ensured their security. From an aperture pierced near the top of the fortified wall, they lowered a large basket attached to the end of a rope. The person allowed to enter the monastery settled in the basket, and was then hauled up from within by the casement pulley. In the figure a man is seen half-way up the wall.

515. Amidst the Mountains of Sinai About 1880

Charles W. Wilson, 'Picturesque Palestine, Sinai and Egypt', 1880.

516. Mount Sinai About 1880

From Charles W. Wilson's book mentioned above.

At the foot of the mountain spreads the Valley named in Arabic er-Raha—the Rest, where, according to local tradition, the Israelites encamped and rested. On the left, in a rocky vale, is the monastery of St. Catherine.

517. Moses receiving the Torah
Fourteenth Century

An illustration from the Passover Haggadah of Sarajevo, Yugoslavia.

518. Moses receiving the Torah 1723

From 'Sefer Haminhagim' – the Book of Customs, printed in Amsterdam.

519. Moses receiving the Torah 1766

An illustration from the book 'Tsena u'Rena' (Go forth and see), the popular translation into Yiddish of the Pentateuch, printed in Amsterdam.

520. Moses receiving the Torah on Mount Sinai 1826

A copper engraving made by Joseph Hertz.

Moses stands on the peak ot Sinai, in a cloud, holding the Tablets of the Law, while thunder and lightnings shake the mountain[1]. Pickets set around the base of the mountain are the artist's naive illustration of the Lord's injunction to Moses: 'And thou shalt set bounds unto the people round about, saying: Take heed to yourselves, that ye go not up into the mount, or touch the border of it; whosoever toucheth the mount shall be surely put to death...'[2]

In the foreground, the agonized face of an Israelite holding his head expresses the awe which struck the heart of the people who were present at this scene.[3]

1) Exodus 19, 16. 2) Exodus 19, 12. 3) Exodus 20, 15.

521. The Israelites in front of Mount Sinai 1854

From a Mahzor (prayer-book) for the Feast of Shevuot (Pentecost), printed in 1854, Prague.

INDEX OF PLACE-NAMES

(the number indicates the page)